PLATE 1: White bean well-dressed soup (recipe on page 11).

PLATE 2: Summer vegetable broth (recipe on page 27)

PLATE 3: Chickpea and tomato ten-minute soup; Notepaper bread (recipes on pages 37 and 294)

PLATE 4: Spiced butter and yellow split peas; Instant soft flatbreads (recipes on pages 52 and 295)

PLATE 5: Macaroni cheese with sweet cooked tomato (recipes on pages 64 and 400)

PLATE 6: Braised chicken rice, steamed with allspice (recipe on page 68)

PLATE 7: Apple tart – quick (recipe on page 117)

PLATE 8: Birthday cake (recipe on page 119)

PLATE 9: Warm tomatoes, oregano and feta cheese with fridge dough breads (recipes on pages 127 and 409)

PLATE 10: Top rump steak with tender herbs and warm olive oil sauce; Potato, garlic and cream gratin (recipes on pages 137 and 255)

PLATE 11: Léa's leaves and fried bread, with a smoked-herring dressing; Jacqueline's tomato and olive oil (recipes on pages 142 and 146)

PLATE 12: Crisp smoked bacon, polenta cubes, bittersweet chicory (recipe on page 171)

PLATE 13: Pan-fried plaice with lettuce hearts and lemon (recipe on page 173)

PLATE 14: Monkfish and bacon cakes; Caper and tarragon mayonnaise (recipes on pages 178 and 417)

PLATE 15: Eighty degrees beef (recipe on page 199)

PLATE 16: Oxtail stew (recipe on page 209)

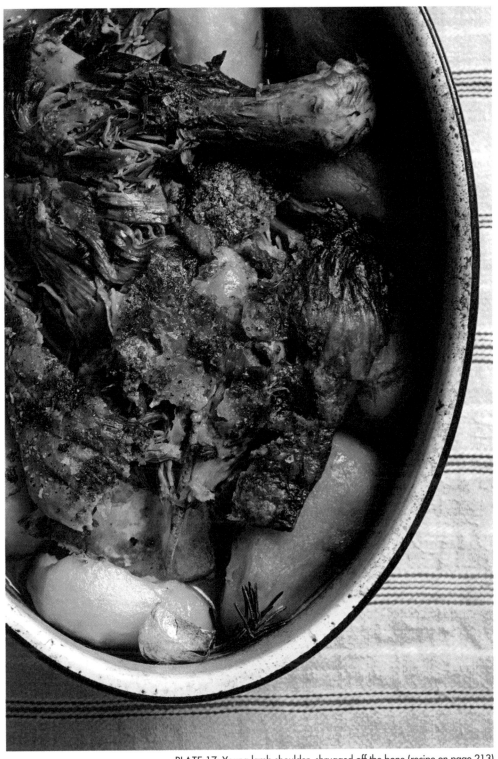

PLATE 17: Young lamb shoulder, shrugged off the bone (recipe on page 213)

PLATE 18: Pot-cooked spring chicken with young veg (recipe on page 226)

PLATE 19: Argiano pork with herbs and garlic (recipe on page 250)

PLATE 20: Mother's aubergines (recipe on page 259)

PLATE 21: Picnic pie (recipe on page 274)

PLATE 22: Banana and almond cake (recipe on page 298)

PLATE 23: Crepe-wrapped asparagus with grated cheese (recipe on page 312)

PLATE 24: Raspberry clotted-cream fool, with honeycomb (recipe on page 315)

PLATE 25: Wild garlic omelette, with chilli, cheese and ham (recipe on page 319)

PLATE 26: Roast rabbit saddle, stuffed with liver and kidneys; Slow-cooked rabbit (recipes on pages 334 and 336)

PLATE 27: Potato, beef and parsley hash (recipe on page 362)

PLATE 28: Toffee bread pudding (recipe on page 381)

PLATE 29: Courgette, basil and egg soup (recipe on page 393)

PLATE 30: Risotto (recipe on page 395)

PLATE 31: Aunts' pasta, with sweet cooked tomato and anchovy (recipe on page 403)

PLATE 32: Onion tart (recipe on page 410)

Kitchenella

Rose Prince is a freelance food journalist and writer; she has a weekly column in the *Daily Telegraph* and her work appears regularly in the *Telegraph* magazine, as well as other national publications. Passionate about buying food wisely and eating well, Rose is the author of the highly acclaimed *The New English Kitchen*, *The Savvy Shopper* and *The New English Table*. Rose has also contributed regularly to BBC Radio 4 on food issues. She lives in London with her husband, journalist Dominic Prince, and their two children.

ROSE PRINCE

Photographs by LAURA HYND

Kitchenella

THE SECRETS OF WOMEN: HEROIC, SIMPLE, NURTURING COOKERY – FOR EVERYONE

FOURTH ESTATE · *London*

First published in Great Britain in 2010
Fourth Estate
A imprint of HarperCollins*Publishers*
77–85 Fulham Palace Road
London W6 8JB
www.4thestate.co.uk

www.roseprince.co.uk

9 8 7 6 5 4 3 2 1

A catalogue record for this book is available from the British Library

ISBN 978-0-00-732887-1

The author is grateful for permission from Grub Street to reproduce
the recipe for pain perdu from *The Constance Spry Cookery Book*
on p380 and for permission from Mabecron Books to reproduce
the recipe for pasties on p101 from *Pasties* by Lindsey Bareham.

Typeset by Birdy Book Design

Printed in Italy by L.E.G.O. SpA – Vicenza

 For my children

Contents

Acknowledgements

Many of those who plant good ideas in my head will find their names in these pages, and my thanks go both to them and others I have met, overheard, watched, or whose wise words were quoted to me second-hand. I want especially to thank Louise Haines, my editor at Fourth Estate who so carefully guided me through writing this book. She is also a contributor, being someone with whom I have had many long and fascinating conversations about food and cooking. A very big thank you, to Julian Humphries of Fourth Estate, for his dazzling design; Laura Hynd for the most elegant, delicious photography; copyeditor Mari Roberts; Elizabeth Woabank and Patrick Hargadon, who both championed the idea from the start; Georgia Mason and Chris Gurney. Thank you, too, to Isobel Widdowson and Eva Salkova for their very hard work with me in the kitchen.

I must also make a special mention of my editors at the *Telegraph* who have given me such great support while I work on both jobs. My gratitude to Tony Gallagher, Casilda Grigg, Jon Stock and especially Michele Lavery, whose passion for food and stories is an inspiration. Thanks are also due to many on these editors' teams, especially for their patience. Several books were an inspiration for this book, and I must credit in particular *Simple French Cooking* (Cassel, 2001) by George Blanc and Coco Jobard, for the valuable insight into the lives of the famous French mother cooks. Nor could I have managed without the works of a number of brilliant authors, including Anna Del Conte, Margaret Visser, Joanna Blythman, Nigel Slater – and the late Alan Davidson, Lesley Blanch and Jane Grigson.

Finally all my love and thanks to my family, most of all to Dominic, to my children Jack and Lara, my amazing sisters, aunts and cousins, and of course my mother, whose eye for beauty sparked my own interest in good things.

Introduction

My earliest memories are full of the voices of women, telling you things. Their kitchen secrets, handed down, were at the heart of good suppers. Whispered advice or stern warnings, they are still there in my head, impossible to rub out, simply because they are useful. I collect these morsels now. I can't let something good pass by without asking 'how?' In all honesty, I cannot cook unless I tune in to that busy frequency of influence.

This is a book about feminine cookery, at its best heroic: generous, practical and nurturing. It is more than a bag of worthy survival tools (though it has a proven track record in that respect). Feminine cookery is creative. Nurture is a deal, an agreement that can be a real struggle to sustain. The heroic feminine cook, Kitchenella, transforms it into a gentle art.

For most, stepping into the kitchen raises one dilemma or another. It is rarely the leisurely activity unrealistically promoted in the media. Often the need to cook is just a matter of answering hunger with little time and limited ingredients: dinners made with whatever can be bought in a late-night shop on the way home from work. But the idea of a pan filled with a hot, bubbling lava of melting salty cheese and tomatoes, ready within minutes to eat with bread, dissolves the problem, leaving behind a work of beauty.

We eye our children and plan to please them, but how? On the one hand they are difficult customers who run up a lot of credit, on the other they are much loved people we spend far too little time with. We aim to choose food that avoids arguments, but encourages adventure: sweet cooked tomato, whizzed into a non-bitty sauce, to use in at least seven dishes, has become a fridge standby to bless. Gently-spiced rice with chicken is an everyday staple, the crispest roast potatoes or pancakes a treat. This is family food with a long history of clean plates.

Balancing the extravagance of a special roasting joint by making good use of every scrap; planning the week's meals ahead or creating dishes that are filling, cheap, yet still gorgeous to behold – these are typical tasks faced by home cooks, and need a practical, unselfish approach. It is work that is often done – astonishingly – for little thanks.

This is not to suggest bringing back the martyred, Fifties kitchen deity, whisking up unmatchable sponges each day at teatime. Recipes for modern life need to be realistic, and flexible enough to fit into very busy lives, yet the answers still lie in the feminine approach to cookery. Only it is not there. Trends show a decline in cooking fresh ingredients from scratch, while the consumption of convenience food continues to rise. Since women remain the main carers of others, their voices are silent and secrets are not passed on. The result is a generation of kitchen orphans growing up without any sort of good food ancestry.

Meanwhile, our chief food influence comes from men. Chefs dominate television cookery shows yet their efforts do not appear to convert more viewers to take up cooking – in spite of the hype to the contrary. We witness them telling mothers how to feed their children then weeping when their pleading is ignored. Viewers admit that while they are entertained, ultimately they are put off, even frightened to cook.

Traits in male cookery, while often inspirational and – thanks to some extreme competitiveness – technically astounding, are not the ones best suited to the everyday job of feeding others in the home. The customary man enjoys being a general in the kitchen, running a brigade of assistants, hence their success in professional kitchens. There is a tendency to cook for show, often extravagantly, and with an expectation of applause for doing so (something a regular home cook learns never to anticipate).

Such characteristics are admittedly stereotypical, though still very recognisable. It is difficult to pin the gender argument on clichés, however. There is a marginal new wave of young men who cook keenly at home, and fathers that approach family food in ways that emulate great women cooks. Women are also perfectly capable of rejecting their nurturing instinct and instead borrow traditional, tough-talking male traits. With the genders impersonating each other, the picture gets very blurred.

The highly potent influence of food television fails to sort the problem out because broadcasters determinedly characterise women in cookery programmes either as pouting goddess or dependable headmistress, expecting obedience. Where are the real mothers, facing genuine predicaments and solving problems? Nurturing cookery is absent in television. It is a reality show too far, perhaps.

But the fate of home cooking was sealed long before many of our TV chefs were born. Feminism made cooking a symbol of a woman's drudge, successfully and rightly, bringing to an end girls-only cookery classes in schools and empowering women to seek the same jobs and pay awarded to men. You couldn't, they reasoned, do both. In truth, for the 70 per cent of women in work who have dependent children, having it all still means having to put supper on the table at the end of the day.

Not surprisingly then, an eager and efficient food industry has galloped to the aid of liberated women. The industry that grew up after feminism rode on cheap and convenient food, cooked by someone else. It once seemed a great model, the answer to the busy person's prayers, until the environmental and health costs of fast food and ready meals was judged unsustainable.

But feminism does not mean having to drop femininity. When prominent feminist voice Germaine Greer made chicken stock one night for her fellow inmates in the Big Brother house, her practical, generous act said it all. Similarly, there is evidence that young women are rediscovering and celebrating unique feminine skills, learning to sew, knit and cook.

More and more people, men and women, now say they wish they could cook and want good food to be part of their life. It is a question of finding that ingredient that switches aspiration into reality and the most effective food education has always been the unwritten, hand-me-down knowledge given to children by their mothers.

If this knowledge is not already there, Kitchenella, the heroic, modest feminine cook is a workable surrogate. Useful good ideas can become easily lost. Unless passed on they float in the ether, the verbal tradition looking for a receptive ear. The pity is that ideas can disappear forever, because they are typically the notions of people who would never have thought to write them down.

By the time I left school, I knew what I was bad at, but I was aware that information about cooking, especially when it linked to something good, would always stick in my mind. I am not even sure how much of it got there, or when it began to fill my head. Food was important in my family, discussed often. Snippets, thoughts, exclamations of pleasure – clocked. A mistake: a burned pan, an overdone roast – registered.

This is a recipe book but it is also a book of answers and ideas, a conversation between people who share an interest in solving problems. Much of what is inside its covers has been learnt from others: people I love, writers I read and individuals I meet every day. Good food should naturally lead to a moment of chat, a chance to ask, 'How did you do that?' The opposite is silence. Listen carefully for Kitchenella's voice, though. It is not the loudest. She won't show off, but nor will she bully you. She just wants to leave her mark: indelible, delicious influence.

White bean well-dressed soup
Tomato and mascarpone cream
Garden 'essences'
Lettuce and courgette 'butter' soup
Toasted garlic bread and squash soup
Golden broth with parsley and pearl barley
Bean and pasta broth
Summer vegetable broth
Autumn vegetable 'harvest' soup with grains
Winter vegetable stew-soup
Watercress butter dumplings
Mushroom broth with sausage, oats and parsley
Leek and potato soup with cream
Green cabbage and pickled duck garbure
Chickpea and tomato ten-minute soup
Clam, cider and potato chowder
Coconut spiced soup with chicken
Flawless mashed potato
Boiled floury potatoes
Roughly mashed haddock and potato with spring onion
Mashed sweet potato with green chilli and coriander relish
Spiced butter and yellow split peas
Everyday mountain lentils
Instant polenta and grilled polenta, with variations

QUICK, CHEAP AND FILLING

Is that the time? Time to cook – again? Keeping up a supply of food, among everything that needs doing every day, is a lot to ask anyone new to cooking. When you decide that good food matters, you enter a conflicting world. Loving food is bittersweet. A passion that is painful without guidance from someone who really knows how hard it can be. You need someone to say, 'I know. I know what to do – it won't be showy or hard to make. It is not the kind of supper that costs a lot or needs a trip to a special shop. It will not mean you have to grow your own, rear pigs or catch a mackerel on a line. But everyone will be full, and remember how good it was.'

These are the secrets of women for you to use every day when it is time to cook. Big, good dishes in one pot to get ready quickly: modest, nurturing, heroic food that solves a daily dilemma.

Reality, pitched against aspiration. That is the sum of my daily life. Of course I would like to bake cupcakes or cure hams all day, but the truth is that under the roof of my home, the daily summit of my cooking ambition is simply to provide enough good food for us to continue to exist. It is not that I do not make forays into more extreme areas of cookery – it is my job to do that – but the recipes I want are very different from those I need. My dilemma, shared by millions, is that I am short of time, I do not have unlimited funds to spend on food yet I – and everyone in my home – need real nourishment.

What can I make that is fast, economical and filling? This is the trinity of subsistence for most people in full-time employment, those who turn the key in the front door in the early evening aware that their day's work is a long way from done. Not everyone feels this way. That is why ready meals were invented. Yes! Those things that taste good while watching a cookery show on telly!

Knowing how to make soups with delicate white beans, an ingredient that is rather wholesome yet seems so glamorous, so well dressed, when eaten with transparent splinters of crisp smoked bacon. Understanding how to cook a pan of faultless, smooth mashed potato, or make a dish of spiced pulses that tickles with interest. A lot of us want to do the right thing but not all of us have the tools to do it. There are many lost domestic skills, but while life will go on without darning the children's socks every night, it is threatened by the loss of home cooking that uses fresh ingredients.

More bizarrely, this is not the result of there not being enough to eat. In the West, the loss of cooking skills does not cause starvation – but it is the root of serious ill-health epidemics. A few clever ways to feed ourselves, our families and friends with food that is cheap to buy, quick to make and fills the tummy with goodness would do much to change lives – and that is what this chapter is about.

The verbal tradition

I am a self-taught cook and I, too, have my disasters, some of them highly embarrassing. But I love to pick up secrets from others. There are people to meet in every part of this book whose knowledge I want to pass on to you. Some were women who have been very much part of my life, like my mother, a perfectionist with a great creative mind. Others are people I know, some well, some not, or those whose lives I have studied, like les mères, the working mother cooks of France who understood completely how to fit good food into a busy day.

Never be afraid, when someone serves you something good, to ask them how they did it. This is the verbal tradition: the passing on of information and secrets, so easily lost when the talking stops. It is the single most vital tool in retaining traditions of cookery and needs to be there with each jotted recipe, every cookery book, any time there is a pan on the cooker.

My mother

Being full is something I knew before anything else. As a small child, I remember our round tea table and its wicker chairs, the piles of sandwiches and toasted, buttered currant buns. I was my mother's fourth child – she would eventually have six. Tall and blonde, my mother had her hair done weekly in the hairdressers at the end of the street: backcombed on top and curling down to her shoulders. I noticed her long nails were pale pink as she made our supper after school. She claimed not to have been able to cook a thing when she married, aged only 18, but she became a very good cook.

Her mother had lived in France since 1950, and with every visit the French commonsense way of eating must have bled into my mother's attitude. She made creamy soups, melting gratins and beat her mustard-yellow mayonnaise by hand. She always peeled tomatoes by plunging them in hot water, then dressed them in real vinaigrette made with genuine Dijon mustard which sank deep into their flesh – and she made heavenly dauphinoise potatoes. She never cheated, but like a French housewife she saw nothing wrong in buying in a terrine or a tart when she did not want to cook. As children we probably smelled more garlicky than our school mates.

My mother was not one of those to make fairy cakes with. We never had hilarious squirting sessions with piping bags and hundreds-and-thousands. She did not 'play at cooking', but taught us to cook – and she could be a terrifying perfectionist. It was she who drove me to make sweet pastry so thin it was possible to shine a light through it. She was the person who came up behind me when I was peeling potatoes at the sink for the roast, and said, 'I never cut them up that way, myself,' with chilling authority. When we were teenagers, visiting friends would gasp at the achievements of my mother and her brigade of cooking daughters. I loved to cook but already, before I was grown up, I knew it was hard work. I think my home tuition went a little far and was overly obsessive – though useful for my career. For me, cooking has always been an exhausting passion, though I have now learned how to enjoy it and not be worn down by it.

At primary school age we had our fair share of fish fingers, baked beans and Heinz tomato soup, but more and more, as we got older, we ate 'grown-up' food at weekends. On one occasion my mother came back from shopping carrying a tray of soft raw bread dough, covered lightly with greaseproof paper. 'What is that?' I asked. 'I am going to make a pizza,' she answered, unwrapping a pack of Danish 'mozzarella'. It was the early 1970s. She was a long way ahead of her time.

Running out

As a family we were unusually preoccupied with food and there was at one point a definite fear of 'running out'. Not due to poverty; financially we were privileged, though my mother knew how to be frugal, often cooking oxtail and tongue, and giving us an early introduction to dumplings, lentils and beans. At the time I hated the meals with pulses. Lentils especially, which tasted floury – I longed for potatoes. I adore lentils now.

My parents had divorced when I was three. We lived with my mother but spent half of our school holidays with my father. My mother remarried when I was six and we moved from London to north Buckinghamshire, about two hours' drive from my father's house.

My stepfather, Teddy, was a commodity broker who commuted daily to London by train, flamboyant 'kipper' tie around his neck. In the mid-1970s, just prior to the power cuts and three-day week, he predicted a food shortage. For several weeks we spent each Saturday at the cash and carry, picking up dry food supplies that would be taken down to the cellar of our house for storage. He bought whole butchered lambs from Wales and filled a chest freezer with them. I remember my mother making meat pies and stewing apple for crumbles and filling a second freezer. We installed a generator and bought a lot of candles, sacks of sugar and flour, Marmite, ketchup, even jars of sweets.

There was no food emergency after all. We ate from that cellar for years, even moving house later on with some of the ketchup and Marmite. But we had experienced something unusual and it has stayed with me. Witnessing my mother caught up in survival mode for those few months, however ultimately unnecessary, left its mark. What I saw (and my siblings are bound to accuse me of melodrama) would for a short period have been similar to that of a child observing their mother during food rationing in World War II, or even a degree of the desperation felt by the women just ahead of the French Revolution who could not feed their children. My stepfather had provided the means for obtaining food; my mother had set about cooking her way out of trouble.

Stuffed

After that we were always full – if anything, I was rather overfed. 'Being stuffed,' answered one of my sisters when I asked her for her earliest memory. And I became interested in cooking, imitating my mother, learning from her, helping her and eventually leaving home a reasonably competent cook. Being in a large family meant I learned to make heaps of food from very little. Filling food on a budget – and always, as my husband remarked with horror when we met – far, far too much of it.

None of this mattered for years. I did eventually learn to temper the size of my helpings and to waste less, though I admit to a deep-seated fear of an empty fridge or store cupboard. I hate the idea of running out. It seems vaguely paranoid, but now I am in a new phase of this. Here it is again: the sense that the food supply is once again threatened, this time not only because of politics but also global warming. The added dissatisfaction with the food industry has narrowed my choices with food and as a consequence our food bills are rising. Once again there is the need to use cooking, combined with good economics, to deal with a crisis. The battle has begun.

Money

Two strong arguments are always put forward by women who do not cook: time poverty and money – poverty itself, in fact. They feel these are powerful reasons why cooking has more or less stopped in their home and every meal is eaten out or is bought ready made. But time is a commodity that cooking does not eat up unless you want it to.

Most of the recipes in this chapter take between 20 and 40 minutes to prepare, an acceptable period of time for a hungry person to wait and not much longer than reheating a ready meal. It is true that skill helps save time – obviously the quicker you can crush and peel a garlic clove or chop an onion, the sooner the food will be on plates. Cooking regularly hones those skills – and the process becomes faster all round.

The actual will to cook is quite another thing, but that is a slow process of persuasion that has much to do with building a series of good memories: experiences where things have gone well and left nice thoughts in the part of the brain that keeps a record of smell and flavour.

But money. That's a good one. Discussing the cost of food is like talking about religion. Someone is going to become upset. People who have money are traditionally not permitted to tell people who have little how to spend it. So that rules out most of our TV chefs –

both they and the broadcasters become rather indecisive. They either broach the subject with supreme clumsiness and drive the bad eaters underground, or they are just plain unconvincing. It is hard to get inside the skin of those for whom budgeting is a daily concern, unless it is an experience you genuinely face. Anxiety about money also overwhelms creativity, experiment and adventure. This is the reason why so many on low incomes rely on trusted, branded ready-made foods that may not be as nourishing as other low-cost meals but which every mum knows she can serve and every plate will be emptied. The thought that anything bought on limited means will be rejected is nothing short of disastrous. This is why it is so necessary, when giving up convenience food and embarking on becoming a home cook, to know the secret of how to do it well each time.

SOUPS

Knowing how to make just a few soups is the secret of survival. Most take only 20 minutes to make, the ingredients are cheap and, after a bowl of soup, you feel full to the ears. We don't want much more than that, do we? The food industry has a long tradition of making our soup for us, and selling it in cans, packets or 'fresh' in cartons. But in terms of goodness, it always falls short of the real thing.

Soups are to most Europeans what dal is to India and Pakistan – a vital, nourishing food that is affordable. But the British and Americans are a little soup-shy. The wealthy traditionally view soups as a starter, or diet food, and there is an educated margin of bowl-food enthusiasts – but on the whole we typically avoid all but the best-known canned varieties. A pity all round, not least because a bigger love for soup would instantly solve the catering problems of schools and hospitals.

Italian mothers rear their children on minestrone and pasta e fagioli, the delicious garlic-scented white bean and pasta soup capable of supplying a slow stream of energy for the rest of the day. The soup-devoted French have their Niçoise pistou, similar to minestrone yet greener and with more garlic; they also have their famous fish stew-soups and a delicious heartening cabbage and pork broth from the hilly Auvergne. In central Europe buttery dumplings float in rich and gamey meaty soups, while potatoes dominate the soups of colder Nordic countries. That is not to say we do not have some great broths in Britain, such as mutton and pearl barley, likely based on the lost medieval pottages, soups made with peas, grains and herbs.

Velvet soups

These are the smooth, creamy-textured soups that are sometimes just the essence of one vegetable, sometimes two, but never too many. The good news, for those still not persuaded to make meat or vegetable stock, is that you do not need to use it in these soups. There is another, time-saving and effective way, using additional butter, which is typically found in French home cooking but less in chefs' books (chefs tend to be slavish to bouillon). When making a soup in which one ingredient stars, like lettuce or watercress, the butter method is especially successful. In the meantime, soups should begin in their humblest form.

White bean well-dressed soup

see PLATE 1

A big energising soup, its creaminess comes from the beans and adding wholemilk or Greek yoghurt at the end of cooking, which also gives the soup a refreshing, citrus taste. Onion, garlic and one of a number of green vegetables are added to lighten the floury texture of the beans. 'Well dressed' means it has a number of guises and can be many different soups, depending on what you add from the list of embellishments.

The secret value of beans

The trick of balancing the food budget yet feeling happy with what you eat lies in some of the humblest foods. Bean soups like the one below are something I turn to often – but with great enthusiasm. All types of bean are now fairly easy to find. Even the otherwise unimaginatively stocked late-night grocery across the road from where I live sells a range. I will sometimes buy dried beans, reconstitute and boil them, but it is a longer process (see page 230) and this section is about time poverty. Beans, like all pulses (lentils, chickpeas, peas), are in many ways the perfect food. They contain a vast range of nutrients and are high in fibre, growing them is great for the environment and though they are not grown in the UK (some ought to be) they are never air-freighted. Canned beans and pulses, incidentally, are not an inferior food to dried. With one can costing under £1 yet containing enough to serve 2–3 people, learning to use them in soups should be an essential part of every home cook's abilities.

SERVES 4

4 tablespoons olive oil

2 medium white-fleshed onions, roughly chopped

4 garlic cloves, crushed with the back of a knife and peeled

1 fennel bulb, roughly chopped, or choose from: 2 celery sticks, sliced; 2 leeks, sliced; half a cucumber, seeds removed and thickly sliced; 3–4 medium-sized turnips, including green tops, sliced

2 x 400g/14oz can white haricot beans or cannellini beans

900ml/1½ pints water or stock

salt and white pepper

400ml/14fl oz Greek-style, wholemilk strained yoghurt

EMBELLISHMENTS

Add one or more of the following (you can also eat this soup plain):

＊ Slices of ciabatta, baguette or other open-textured bread, fried until golden in olive oil

* Melted butter, with chopped garlic
* Red chilli, the seeds removed, then sliced
* Crisp sautéed bacon or pancetta, chopped
* Basil pesto sauce
* Black olive tapenade sauce
* Roasted red peppers
* Flakes of raw, undyed smoked haddock (they will cook in the hot soup)

Put the oil in a large pan and heat over a medium flame. Add the onions, garlic and fennel or other green vegetable and cook until transparent and fragrant, but not coloured. Add the beans with their liquid, then the water or stock. Bring to the boil and then cook for about 10 minutes until the beans and vegetables are soft. Transfer all to a food processor or liquidiser and blend until smooth. Taste and add salt if necessary. Add a good pinch of white pepper.

To serve, reheat until almost boiling. Add the yoghurt and heat until nearly boiling, then remove from the heat. Ladle into bowls and add one or two of the extra 'outfits' from the list.

Tomato and mascarpone cream

My father also remarried, when I was five. My stepmother Annie Lou, who at the time had no children, was suddenly faced with four children to feed for half of every holidays and little sympathy from her instant family. There was a kind of competence and reliability about her cooking, learned from Cordon Bleu recipe cards, Arabella Boxer's *First*

Slice Your Cookbook, and *The Joy of Cooking*, which we displaced children found reassuring. I am not sure how much joy Annie Lou found in cooking itself, but she saw it as a duty and shopped enthusiastically with the village butcher, and even grew vegetables. She did not make all the many different dishes my mother made, nor share my mother's love of southern European food, but she had a few great staples that became 'old friends'. You knew where you were in the week by what was on the table. If it was fish pie, it was Friday; cottage or shepherd's pie was usually there on a Monday, the day after a magnificent roast, the joint bought from Mr Vigor in Woodborough. I have no complaints. On winter picnics at horsy events (not my favourite days as I did not share the family's devotion to all things equine) she always filled flasks with very hot, Heinz tomato soup 'let down' with milk. I loved that stuff. Later, when making my own tomato soup with milk, I laughed to find its eventual flavour not unlike the one from the can. Adding fresh mascarpone cheese, however, takes the flavour of tomato soup to a new, richer level.

SERVES 4
4 tablespoons olive oil
2 garlic cloves, crushed with the back of a knife and peeled
1 x 400g/14oz can plum tomatoes, chopped
225g/8oz fresh cherry or other ripe tomatoes, roughly chopped
2 sprigs basil
1 dessertspoon sugar
200ml/7fl oz water or stock
250g/9oz mascarpone cheese
salt and black pepper
To serve: extra olive oil, extra basil leaves, bread such as baguette or
    ciabatta

Put the oil, garlic, canned tomatoes, fresh tomatoes and basil into a large pan and heat. When the mixture boils, cook for 10 minutes, then add the sugar and water or stock. Simmer for 20–30 minutes until sweet. Cool for a few minutes, then transfer to a liquidiser or food processor. Process until smooth and return to the pan. Stir in the mascarpone thoroughly and reheat. Do not allow to boil. Taste and add salt if necessary, then add pepper. Ladle into bowls, pour over a little more olive oil in a thin stream, then scatter over some extra basil leaves. Eat with slices of baguette or ciabatta (or other open-textured bread) fried until golden in olive oil.

The soups of French mothers
The French mother cooks, les mères, understood better than anyone the beauty of seasonal soups. These nineteenth- and twentieth-century cooks, who cooked in their famous restaurants as they would in their homes, were both experimental with their ideas and yet always down to earth, understanding the limits of their small kitchens and low budget. They made soup every day, with whatever produce had come into its glut season and had lowered in price. Soups were made quickly, preserving the green freshness of the vegetables. No one was given only a bowl of soup, the whole tureen would be brought to the table and ladled into diners' bowls, often over something to make the dish more substantial: a piece of toasted bread and cheese, a poached egg, some steamed shellfish or braised bone marrow. When the bowl was clean, more would be offered. Imagine that in a restaurant today.

Garden 'essences'

These soups are made only with a single dominant vegetable, preferably without anything else other than water and butter, with maybe a few drops of cream at the end. They are very typical of the lunchtime soups offered by les mères in their restaurants. They have a light, quite thin texture, so put plenty of toast or fresh bread on the table. Or put another ingredient in the bowl, such as a poached egg, some grilled shards of bacon or some fresh goat's cheese, spread on toasted bread. This method is ideal for the delicate sugary flavours of freshly picked seasonal vegetables. These soups must be eaten as soon as they have been liquidised, before they discolour or become starchy. The following soup is made with young broccoli, but there are various different vegetables this method is friendly to.

SERVES 4

6 walnut-sized lumps of butter

1 onion, chopped

450g/1lb fresh broccoli (in peak condition, no yellow flowers), chopped

1 litre/1¾ pints water, at boiling point

salt and white pepper

To serve: cream or crème fraiche (optional); a few cress leaves or 'micro leaf' herbs, pea shoots or even just tender parsley leaves; you can also serve over a poached egg or toast spread with fresh goat's curd

Melt the butter and add the onion. Cook over a low heat for 2 minutes then add the water. Wait until you are on the point of sitting down to eat then add the broccoli. Cook for a further 4 minutes until the broccoli is just tender, then transfer to a food processor and liquidise until smooth. Taste and add salt if necessary, then add pepper.

Serve immediately, with a few blobs of crème fraiche, if you like, and some little leaves scattered over the top.

THE SAME ESSENCE SOUP – WITH ALTERNATIVE VEGETABLES
Replace the broccoli with:
* Watercress – use the upper leafy part of 3 bunches.
* Celery leaves – look for celery that has not been trimmed, and use about 4 handfuls of leaves, cooking them for about 5 minutes.
* Spinach – use 150ml/¼ pint less water with 450g/1lb spinach; if it is large-leaf spinach, this must be without the stalks.
* Fresh shelled peas, 450g/1lb. You can also make this with frozen petits pois but only simmer for 1 minute after adding the boiling water.
* Mange tout, 450g/1lb.
* Wild garlic, available in March/April – use 2 large handfuls, chopped, stringy stems removed.
* Sorrel – the lemon flavour of this leaf is beautiful, but be prepared for the leaves to quickly turn brown when cooked.
* Asparagus sprue or 'kitchen asparagus' – these are the thin stems; buy in mid-season when the glut brings prices down.
* Young nettles – available in March/April; you can pick them yourself using rubber gloves.

Lettuce and courgette 'butter' soup

The British-based French chef Raymond Blanc talks often about the influence of his mother. I have always liked his book *Cooking for Friends*, which I have owned for 18 years and which is filled with practical recipes. It exemplifies the well-organised cooking of France and reflects Blanc's upbringing, including this classic recipe for a vegetable 'crème'. 'This simple soup,' says Blanc, 'reminds me of the plain wholesome cooking of my childhood.' I love it not only for its lovely colour and delicate flavour – the lettuce adds a sharpness that sits beautifully with the soup's buttery richness – but because I can buy the ingredients anywhere, at any time of year. Make this soup with water; the secret is in adding a larger amount of butter than usual.

SERVES 4

1 litre/1¾ pints water or stock
4 onions, roughly chopped
1 garlic clove, crushed with the back of a knife and peeled
1 floury potato, peeled and cut into dice, then rinsed under water
3 walnut-sized lumps of butter
3 courgettes, sliced
1 large green lettuce (romaine or cos is ideal) or two butterhead
    lettuce (the soft-leaved English type), roughly chopped
salt and white pepper
90ml/6 tablespoons whipping cream

Put the water or stock in a pan and heat to simmering point. Pour into a jug and put the onions, garlic, potato and butter into the same pan and cook over a medium heat for about 10 minutes. Stir from time to time, and, if the potato sticks to the bottom of the pan, add about half a mug of water.

Add the courgettes and lettuce leaves and cook for another 2 minutes, then add the hot water or stock. Cook for 5 minutes, transfer to a liquidiser or food processor and process until very smooth. A perfectionist French cook would sieve the soup to remove any leaf fibres, but this will not make any real difference to the enjoyment. If you want to do this – put the soup through a hand-operated food mill, or mouli legumes.

Return the soup to the pan and reheat to just below boiling point. Taste and add salt if necessary, then add pepper. Add the cream, stir, and serve immediately.

ADAPTING THE SOUP TO OTHER INGREDIENTS

* Carrot – use 8 medium-sized young carrots, ideally from a leafy bunch to be sure they are fresh, sliced thinly on a mandolin. Add at the onion and potato stage, substituting them for the courgettes and lettuce); add lemon juice or (in January) Seville orange juice to counteract the sweetness.
* Jerusalem artichoke – add 10 peeled and thinly sliced Jerusalem artichokes at the onion and potato stage, substituting them for the courgettes and lettuce.
* Potato and onion with peppery leaves – add 5 extra potatoes, cut into small dice, at the onion stage. Substitute them for the courgettes and lettuce. Serve with a 'pesto' made from peppery leaves like chopped rocket, mustard leaves (easy to find at farmers' markets) or exceptionally fresh radish leaves – mixed with chopped walnuts and olive or walnut oil.

* Green garlic – in spring and summer you will see fresh or 'green garlic' in markets and some supermarkets. They are soft and can be used whole. Substitute the garlic clove and lettuce with 2 heads of green garlic, sliced and added with the onion and potato, to make an aromatic and heady soup – only for garlic devotees.

Mind and stomach

My sister Laura is an artist and a talented self-taught cook. It must be her fascination with texture and colour but she has a built-in sense of what is the right and wrong thing to do to any ingredient. She rarely makes anything that needs more than one pan and a gas hob, but everything she makes is fragrant and pretty. She is the mother of my nephew Tom, now at primary school age, who has cerebral palsy and great difficulty eating. While she cooks beautifully when we visit, every day she makes Tom dishes especially designed to tempt him and boost his appetite – and to nourish him. Laura understands completely the link between mind and stomach. When we are miserable or shocked, we always feel it in our gut, while, equally, delicious things can restore contentment. She often approaches food like a scientist, recording what works and what does not.

Toasted garlic bread and squash soup

Years ago Laura pointed out to me that sweet vegetables like squash and pumpkin make slimy, cloying soups unless other textures are added. This recipe uses toasted garlic-rubbed bread, which also dilutes the sweetness to just the right degree.

SERVES 4
3 walnut-sized lumps of butter
450g/1lb – 1 whole butternut – squash, peeled and diced
2 garlic cloves, pounded to a paste with salt
2 slices of ciabatta or white sourdough bread, toasted until golden
1 litre/1¾ pints water, at boiling point
salt and black pepper
90ml/6 tablespoons whipping cream

Melt the butter in a large pan, add the squash and cook for 3 minutes. Meanwhile, rub the garlic paste onto the bread and allow it to sink in. Add the water to the pan and bring to the boil. Cook for about 10 minutes until the squash is tender. Add the bread and allow to soften in the soup. Transfer all to a food processor and liquidise until very smooth. Clean the pan and put back the soup. Taste and add salt if necessary, then add pepper. Add the cream and reheat. Serve hot – this soup stores well.

THE SAME SOUP – WITH ALTERNATIVE VEGETABLES
Replace the squash with the equivalent weight of pumpkin (with 2 extra garlic cloves because it is so sweet), sweet potato, turnip, celeriac or golden beetroot.

BROTHS

My mother always shopped at a butcher's, even when supermarket shopping was at the height of its new-found popularity. True, she had no full-time job (though up to six children to look after, depending who was at home) and could find time to drive to a shop within its 9–5 opening hours in order to buy the best meat. Yet it was remarkable that she dedicated herself to buying meat this way. At that time in the 1970s there was no especial reported concern about animal welfare or hygiene in mass-produced meat. She may as well have trotted off to Safeway with everyone else. She had a keen instinct about what was right, however, and there we would be, at least once a week, standing in a queue.

Bored as I was, I must have learned much while hanging about in that line; overheard snippets that taught, in some kind of gradual osmotic sense, how to buy meat. I watched boning and rolling, found out how many sausages there are in a pound and which were the prime cuts. Occasionally I heard my mother and other customers complain that a Sunday roasting joint had been a little disappointing, or the butcher explain how long a leg of lamb needed in the oven. Thanks to this, I emerged from my childhood partly food-educated. Aged 18 I could walk into a butcher's and make an informed decision about what to buy.

Today mothers often leave their children behind when shopping, mainly because they shop at supermarkets who sell thousands of 'lines' of food. With so many of these designed to appeal to the pestering, articulate three-year-old in the trolley seat, a traipse around a superstore can be very wearing. No wonder we give in and buy the packet of crisps or whatever they are whining on about. Worse than this is the fact that there is rarely anyone to talk to in supermarkets who has a professional knowledge about ingredients, so a child misses out on those overheard tidbits that form part of their food education.

In the 1980s thousands of these small shops, butchers in particular, closed, thanks to the advent of the superstore. Supermarket chillers tend only to sell unchallenging cuts. Where are the kidneys, the liver, the trotters and tongues? And where are the bones? Without a supply of bones I cannot make my kitchen work. Making stock from bones underpins so much of what I cook because the small effort it takes produces an ingredient that will bring others to life in minutes, notably soups and rice dishes.

I do not know how many times I have been rescued by a supply of broth or stock in the fridge. Knowing it is there reduces the panic I feel if dinner is not planned and needs to be made within the next 45 minutes. The flavours it adds to soups and anything braised, including risotto, give these dishes resonance they cannot have with water. There are many examples of ways to use stock in Halfway to a Meal.

When meat stock is the star of an epic, big-meal soup, its flavour echoes for hours in the mouth and for much longer in the memory. The following recipes are much better for it. Few take longer than 20 minutes to prepare – as long as you have a meat stock supply (see page 390). You can buy fresh meat stock ready made – but read the label to check the ingredients are natural. You may want to take a look at the salt content per 100ml. Keeping in mind that 6g is the maximum recommended for an adult each day, a salty shop-bought stock can do more harm than good.

Here are two extremely simple, everyday broths . . .

Golden broth with parsley and pearl barley

A soup I eat often for lunch. I make a pot of it earlier in the week and heat it when needed. It costs little, and with a supply of stock to hand, it takes only 20 minutes to make. Its golden colour not only comes from browning the poultry bones when making stock (see page 390), but also from adding ground coriander seed, a subtle spice with the ability to 'join up' the flavours of the various ingredients as they simmer in the pan.

SERVES 4
2 tablespoons olive oil or butter
1 onion, finely chopped
1 teaspoon ground coriander seed
200g/7oz pearl barley
1.2 litres/2 pints chicken or vegetable stock
salt and black pepper
flat-leaf parsley, chopped, to serve

Heat the fat in a pan and add the onion, coriander and pearl barley. Stir over the heat for a minute or two until the onion softens, then add the stock. Bring to the boil and cook for 15–20 minutes until the pearl barley is just tender. Do not boil too vigorously or the liquid will evaporate. Season to taste, then add chopped parsley to each bowlful just before you eat.

Bean and pasta broth

Usually served so thick you could eat it with a fork, this Italian-inspired pasta e fagioli soup can be made with store-cupboard ingredients within minutes – providing there is stock to hand. A little more broth in the ratio is nice – it is good to stick to the basic idea that you sip or drink soup, not load it into your mouth.

SERVES 4
1.2 litres/2 pints meat stock
4 tablespoons olive oil
2 garlic cloves, chopped
pinch of dried rosemary leaves
pinch of dried thyme
1 x 400g/14oz can cannellini, borlotti or white haricot beans, drained
100g/3½oz dried soup pasta
salt and white pepper
To serve: grated mature hard cheese (Grana Padano or Parmesan, mature Cheddar), a little extra olive oil or chilli oil

Heat the stock in a large pan until it boils, then pour into a jug. Warm the oil in the same pan over a low heat and add the garlic.

Cook until fragrant, but not coloured, then add the herbs, beans and pasta, and cover with the stock. Bring to the boil and simmer for 5 minutes. Add a little boiling water if the soup is too thick. Season, ladle into bowls and pour a little more olive oil (or chilli oil) over each in a thin stream. Serve the grated cheese separately.

Kitchen note

To use dried beans instead of canned, take half the quantity (200g/7oz), soak in cold water overnight then boil in fresh water for about 1–1 ½ hours until tender.

THREE SEASONAL SOUPS

A lesson in being instinctive, choosing ingredients yourself from what is in season and making a simple soup thickened with either potatoes, grains or beans. Remember, buying seasonal vegetables when they are in their glut and abundant is always cheaper. An understanding of the seasons is a valuable secret weapon for a cook. Each of these recipes serves 4.

Summer vegetable broth

see PLATE 2

I sometimes add ready-made fresh potato gnocchi (easy to buy in the fresh pasta section of supermarkets or in Italian delis) to this soup, having cooked them first for a few minutes in boiling salted water until they float.

BASE SOUP:
4 tablespoons olive oil
2 rashers smoked streaky bacon, cut into small pieces
2 spring onions, chopped
2 waxy potatoes, washed and cut into small dice
2 large ripe tomatoes, nicked with a knife, put in boiling water for
    1 minute then peeled, deseeded and chopped
1 garlic clove, chopped
leaves from 2 sprigs basil or marjoram, torn or chopped
1.2 litres/2 pints chicken or other meat stock
salt and black pepper
fresh pesto sauce, to serve

Plus any 3 or more of the following vegetables:
2 medium courgettes, chopped; handful of French beans, chopped;
   handful of podded garden peas; handful of mange tout, chopped;
   small fennel bulb, chopped; 1 kohlrabi, chopped; a few asparagus
   spears, chopped; butterhead (soft English) lettuce, shredded; 2 kale
   leaves, shredded

Heat the oil in a large pan over a low heat, then cook the bacon
for 2 minutes. Add the onions and potatoes and cook for another
5 minutes. If the potatoes stick to the pan, add half a mug of water.
Stir from time to time. Add the tomatoes with the garlic and herbs.
Cook for a further 2 minutes; pour in the stock and bring to the boil.
When the potatoes are just tender, add the green vegetables. Cook
for 3–4 minutes, then taste and add salt if necessary, then add
pepper. Serve with fresh pesto sauce.

Kitchen note

You can buy pesto ready made, or simply blend together
ground pine nuts, basil leaves, olive oil and grated Parmesan to
make your own.

Autumn vegetable 'harvest' soup with grains

BASE SOUP:

4 tablespoons olive oil

2 rashers smoked streaky bacon, cut into small pieces

1 onion, chopped

3 tablespoons whole rye, wheat or spelt groats

2 large ripe tomatoes, nicked with a knife, put in boiling water for
    1 minute then peeled, deseeded and chopped

1 garlic clove, chopped

2 sprigs thyme

1 teaspoon ground coriander seed

1.2 litres/2 pints chicken or other meat stock

salt and black pepper

To serve: olive oil, Greek-style yoghurt, paprika, black onion seed

Plus any 3 or more of the following vegetables, cut into small pieces:
butternut or other squash, marrow, courgette, eating apple, turnip,
    carrot, kohlrabi, sweet potato, pumpkin, runner beans or green
    cabbage

Heat the oil in a large pan over a low heat, then cook the bacon
for 2 minutes. Add the onion and grains and cook for another
5 minutes. Stir from time to time then add half a mug of water. Add
the tomatoes with the garlic, thyme and coriander, followed by any
of the other vegetables. Cook for a further 2 minutes; pour in the
stock and bring to the boil. Simmer for about 10–15 minutes until

the grains and vegetables are tender. Taste and add salt if necessary, then add pepper. Pour over a little olive oil to serve. This soup is also good with the addition of a little Greek yoghurt and a pinch of paprika or black onion seed.

Winter vegetable stew-soup

BASE SOUP:
4 walnut-sized lumps of butter or 4 heaped teaspoons dripping
1 gammon steak or thick piece of cooked ham, cut into large dice
2 onions, chopped
2 large ripe tomatoes, nicked with a knife, put in boiling water for
   1 minute then peeled, deseeded and chopped
1 garlic clove, crushed with the back of a knife and peeled
leaves from 2 sprigs rosemary and thyme
1 teaspoon ground coriander seed
1.2 litres/2 pints chicken or other meat stock
salt and black pepper
To serve: dry toasted ciabatta or sourdough bread, chilli oil, chopped
   parsley

Plus about 2 handfuls of any 3 or more of the following vegetables,
   cut into pieces: potatoes, carrots, swede, parsnips, celeriac,
   marrow, squash, fennel, endives, chicory, radicchio, Savoy
   cabbage, Brussels sprouts, black cabbage (cavalo nero)

Heat the butter or dripping in a large pan over a low heat and cook the gammon for 2 minutes. Add the onions and cook for another

5 minutes. Stir from time to time. Add the tomatoes with the garlic, herbs and spice. Cook for a further 2 minutes; add the other chosen vegetables, pour in the stock and bring to the boil. Simmer for 20 minutes until everything is tender. Taste and add salt if necessary, then add pepper. Serve over toasted bread, with chilli oil and parsley, if you like.

Watercress butter dumplings

Add these rich, peppery dumplings to any of the seasonal broths above. Make sure not to make them too large.

MAKES 10 – ENOUGH FOR 4 HELPINGS
125g/4½oz plain flour
1 teaspoon baking powder
pinch of salt
70g/2½oz salted butter, very cold, straight from the fridge
leaves from 1 bunch of watercress, chopped (see Kitchen note, below)
ice-cold water

Sieve the flour into a bowl with the baking powder and add the salt. Grate the butter (on the coarse section of the grater) and lightly but thoroughly stir into the flour with the watercress. Add just enough water – about 3 tablespoons – to form the mixture into a loose-textured, slightly sticky dough. With floured hands, make 10 small balls. To cook the dumplings, drop them in the simmering broth about 5 minutes before the end of cooking. They will swell and become firm.

Kitchen note
You can leave out the watercress to make plain dumplings. Or add grated horseradish to plain or watercress dumplings and drop them into a wintry broth.

Remedies

Nourishment has become a somewhat wacky science. Fed a constant diet of either shock headlines or news about the latest superfoods, confusion reigns. All fresh foods are essentially super, but eat too much of any and there is bound to be an unpleasant side effect. Lettuce, for example, is from the same family as valerian. Eaten in vast quantities it could potentially send you to sleep. Some foods, however, we really should eat more of. Our mothers always said eat your greens, but did they ever say eat up your mushrooms? Perhaps they would have, had our parents known how highly valued fungi are in every other country in the world where forests were not decimated to make way for cultivated land, as they have been in Britain. In all Asian and mainland European countries, wild and cultivated mushrooms are revered for their medicinal qualities. On a visit to a mushroom farm in Hampshire, I was told by farmer Jane Dick that, even with woodland covering only 4 per cent of the UK, we still need to eat fungi and learn to cultivate a wider variety. She grows and sources an interesting and wide range of delicious mushrooms, species both from Asia and Europe. Together we looked at some scientific studies into the health benefits of fungi. It is well documented, for example, that the protein-bound polysaccharides in shiitake mushrooms protect the immune system from a number of diseases, even cancer. 'Don't forget antibiotics are derived from fungi,' Jane reminded me, motherly in her campaign for a more nutritious diet.

Mushroom broth with sausage, oats and parsley

This soup, dedicated to the revival of mushroom eating, needs lean sausages like Cumberland – very bready, smooth-textured bangers will turn to mush. If you live near an Italian deli, their meaty sausages are ideal. Otherwise a few chunks of a smoked German-style sausage would be good.

SERVES 4
4 tablespoons olive oil or 2 walnut-sized lumps of butter
1 onion, finely chopped
2 garlic cloves, chopped
4 tablespoons whole oat groats or pearled grain (barley, spelt, durum wheat, etc, from wholefood shops)
4 lean sausages or smoked sausages, cut into bite-size pieces
450g/1lb shiitake mushrooms, chopped (or another type of cultivated mushroom, if you like)
1 litre/1¾ pints fresh stock
salt and black pepper
chopped flat-leaf parsley, to serve

Heat the oil or butter in a large pan and add the onion and garlic. Cook over a medium heat until soft but not coloured, then add the grains and sausage. Fry for 1 minute longer, stirring, then add the mushrooms. Cook for 2 minutes, stirring, then add the stock. Cook for 20 minutes, until the grains are just tender. Taste and add salt if necessary, then add pepper. Serve with chopped parsley.

Leek and potato soup with cream

The difference between a good and a bad soup can be all about texture.
Smooth soups are what they are but when making a 'stew-soup' it
matters that the vegetables are cut in a way that makes them nicer to
eat. I love the grassy allium flavour of leeks, but have a hatred of leeks
cut into rings or, worse, left whole to become limp, soaked and slimy
once cooked. Cut into small squares, however, their layered flesh sits
neatly in a broth with squares of potato, further transformed by a swirl
of rich tarragon-scented cream.

SERVES 4
4 walnut-sized lumps of butter
4 medium leeks, quartered lengthways, then sliced to make small
    pieces – and washed
approximately 20 new potatoes, washed and cut into small dice
1 litre/1¾ pints fresh stock
salt and white pepper

FOR THE CREAM:
150ml/¼ pint whipping cream
2 egg yolks
leaves from 3 sprigs tarragon, chopped

Melt the butter and add the leeks. Cook over a medium heat for
1–2 minutes, then add the potatoes. Cook, stirring occasionally, for
another 2 minutes, then add the stock. Bring to the boil and simmer
for about 10 minutes until the potato is tender. Taste and add salt if

necessary, then add pepper. Meanwhile, combine the 'cream' ingredients thoroughly in a separate bowl. Serve the soup hot, stirring in some of the cream mixture at the last minute.

Those dying leaves

In the bottom drawer of the fridge lies many a dirty secret. I have a habit of buying too many vegetables and not using them. They hide there, in their bags or loose, composting shamefully away. This infuriates my husband, so I have to throw out their rotting corpses when he is not looking. For this reason I find vegetable box schemes hard to sign up to, no matter how much I admire them. I suffer from a condition I call aspirational greed. I buy things not because we need them but because I think we as a family should be eating them. There are vegetables I find incredibly beautiful on the shelf – big bluey-green cabbages, for example. But two weeks later they are still unused and, worse, losing their initial goodness. The children are lukewarm about boiled cabbage, even beside a roast. Then I discover cabbage soup. In a soup, everything everyone loathes about cabbage disappears. It becomes tender and yielding; it benefits from the amalgamated flavours of the other ingredients and, amazingly, it looks pretty – especially the dark-coloured varieties.

Green cabbage and pickled duck garbure

You must look overseas for interesting cabbage soup. Nigel Slater loves the purity of the Portuguese caldo verde, a humble, rough-textured pot of potato and cabbage, seasoned with garlic and chorizo sausage. Thanks to cookery writer Jane Grigson, I have discovered the earthy peasant soups of the Auvergne, and another particularly delicious one, the 'garbure' from Gascony, a nearly perfect stew-soup made with confit (preserved) duck legs. You can buy confit duck legs in tins, or make them (see page 417). Duck legs are an economical ingredient; the costly part of a duck is the breast meat. If you cannot get confit duck, you can use salt pork, ham or garlic (Toulouse) sausage in this recipe. Ultimately, what really makes it taste so nice is the duck fat.

SERVES 4
3 tablespoons duck fat
4 rashers unsmoked 'green' streaky bacon, cut into small dice
2 onions, finely chopped
4 potatoes, cut into small dice
half a green cabbage, thinly shredded
4 confit duck legs, any extra fat and skin removed (see page 417)
1.4 litres/2½ pints fresh stock
To serve: 4 thin slices toasted rye or sourdough bread, 4 tablespoons
    grated Gruyère cheese

Melt the duck fat in a large pan, then fry the bacon until it begins to crisp. Add the onions and cook until they begin to turn pale gold; put in the potatoes, stir-fry for 1 minute over a medium heat, then add the cabbage. Cook for another 2 minutes, put in the confit duck legs and pour in the stock. Bring to the boil and simmer for 30 minutes. Serve the soup hot, with the toasted bread on top and cheese scattered over.

Chickpea and tomato ten-minute soup

see PLATE 3

Lunch is at home for me because that is my workplace. It is a much-anticipated break in the middle of a long day's work and I find it matters enormously that I have something good made from good ingredients, which suits my mood and is also nutritionally balanced. I rarely eat sandwiches, though the occasional egg and cress roll is irresistible, because they make me sleepy. So if we have had something with pulses or rice the night before, I warm it, cheer it up with some fresh vegetables and may eat it with some yoghurt sauce or herbs.

I like to make fresh soups at lunchtime, taking no more than about 15 minutes. But it is time I enjoy. It can be meditative and, being my own boss, I am always looking for something to do that is not work. Alan Bennett admits to cleaning shoes and cleaning out the dust filter in the tumble-drier when he is meant to be writing scripts. Cookery writers make soup, and particularly this one, which seems to hit all the right places as a middle-of-the-day meal. The secret is in adding the sugar, so you do not have to wait so long for the tomatoes to sweeten.

SERVES 4

4 tablespoons olive oil

2 garlic cloves, chopped

300ml/½ pint passata

1 x 400g/14oz can chickpeas

1 teaspoon ground coriander seed

½ teaspoon paprika

1 teaspoon sugar

300ml/½ pint stock

salt and black pepper

juice of half a lemon

To serve: extra olive oil, wholemilk yoghurt, parsley or other fresh
  herbs

Heat the oil in a large pan and add the garlic, passata, chickpeas,
spices and sugar. Cook over a medium heat for a few minutes,
stirring occasionally, then add the stock. Bring to the boil, then
simmer for 5 minutes. Taste and add salt if necessary, then add
pepper. Stir in the lemon juice. Either eat this soup with the
chickpeas left whole, or mash them a little with a potato-mashing
tool. You can also transfer the soup to a liquidiser or food processor
and process to something smoother. Serve with a little olive oil
poured over, a spoonful of yoghurt and some fresh herbs.

Clam, cider and potato chowder

My mother used to trawl through recipe books, looking for ideas that were practical and contained ingredients she could buy in our local market town (incidentally a very narrow remit, yet still a familiar one to many, all these years later). She was always good at spotting not only a decent, do-able recipe in the depths of some book or other, she also had a talent for picking out ideas that would look pretty. She used to cook a lovely white fish chowder, made with monkfish, prawns and waxy potatoes. With a few spikes of spring onion here and there, it was a lovely palette of pink, green and white. Monkfish was cheap then. No one appreciated it as they do now. It is now popular, expensive and over-fished in places. Clams, on the other hand, have all the sweetness this stew-soup needs, yet are easy to buy, quite economical – and ecologically sound.

SERVES 4
3 walnut-sized lumps of butter
1 celery stick, with its leaves if possible, finely sliced
1 large leek
1kg/2lb 4oz new or young waxy potatoes (yellow fleshed are best),
    washed and quartered
600ml/1 pint fish, vegetable or chicken stock
600ml/1 pint dry cider
1kg/2lb 4oz venus or other small clams, washed under running water
300ml/½ pint whipping cream or crème fraiche
fried white bread, to serve

Melt the butter in a pan and add the celery and the white part of the leek, sliced and washed beforehand (finely chop the tender green part of the leek to add later). Sauté the vegetables over a gentle heat, then add the potatoes. Cook for another 2 minutes, adding a ladleful of stock to prevent the potatoes sticking.

Add the remaining stock and the cider, and bring to the boil. Cook until the potatoes are just tender, then add the cream and all the clams. Add the remaining green part of the leek, put a lid on the pan, bring it to the boil and cook for about 3–5 minutes. The clams should open fully – discard any that do not. If you can, remove some – or even all – of the clam shells, leaving the meat in the soup. Eat with hot fried bread.

Kitchen note
Cockles, mussels or queen scallops can also be used,
even mixed. I sometimes make this soup with raw
organic tiger prawns.

Coconut tea

As much as I love the clever, inspired cooking of southern Europe, at least once a week we eat something at home made with coconut, lemongrass and warming spices like cumin and cinnamon. I cannot pretend to be an expert on this kind of cooking. I am not well travelled enough to have seen much of it in situ and I have relied on books to give me the basics of authentic South-east Asian cooking. But then it does not really matter. When you do travel to the places where these dishes come from, you find they are not made the same way in any one place, and you can adapt, providing the raw materials you use are genuine – or appropriate.

Coconut is under-used in the West yet processed the right way it is a highly nourishing ingredient. I avoid canned coconut milk, which often contains starch and emulsifiers to give it a creamy texture, and prefer to make a 'tea' from the flesh. Travelling in Sri Lanka this year I had breakfast with Champika Sajeewani, mother of two-year-old Sewwandi. Champika's family are part of an organic farming producer group. They grow tea and spices and their products have Fairtrade certification.

Coconut spiced soup with chicken

Champika is known for her delicate cooking, and she showed me how to brew fresh coconut flesh to make a stock to add to curries. I cannot buy fresh coconut in the UK but I have used unsweetened desiccated coconut to very decent effect. The bonus is that you have a byproduct of soaked coconut to use in biscuits, or to make the raw pickle that is added to this gently spicy soup.

SERVES 4

4 chicken thighs, deboned, skinned and sliced

1 tablespoon raw coconut oil or olive oil

4 garlic cloves, chopped

1 stalk lemongrass, crushed with a rolling pin but left whole

1 medium onion, finely chopped

4cm/1½in piece fresh ginger, grated

2–3 teaspoons mild curry powder

¼–½ teaspoon ground cayenne pepper

200g/7oz desiccated coconut or fresh coconut flesh if available –
    soaked in 1.2 litres/2 pints boiling water for 5 minutes to make
    a 'tea'

salt (optional)

FOR THE RELISH:

4 tablespoons soaked coconut flesh

1 handful of mint leaves

1–2 shredded, deseeded red or green chillies

1 chopped shallot

Cut the chicken into small pieces and put in a pan with the oil, garlic, lemongrass, onion, ginger and spices. Warm it all through until the onion softens, then add the strained coconut 'tea'. Bring to the boil and simmer the broth for about 10 minutes until the chicken is cooked. Meanwhile, combine the ingredients for the relish.

Taste the broth and add salt if necessary. Serve hot with a spoonful of the dry coconut relish, removing the stick of lemongrass from the soup beforehand.

Kitchen note

It is fine to substitute the desiccated coconut with 1 block
of coconut cream melted in 1 litre/1 ¾ pints boiling water.
Blocks of coconut cream are easy to find in ethnic shops and
supermarkets and are the most natural form of processed
coconut, better than canned coconut milk. One-third of the
block is fat, the rest flesh and you can choose how much
of each you want to include. Adding the fat will make
this soup richer.

A sub for 'cuisine grandmère'

Just thinking about Jacqueline makes me hungry. I have to come
clean and admit that the grandmother's table I talk of so
nostalgically in this book was not heaving with food she cooked
herself. My grandmother could barely make toast. She ran a business
with her husband in France and they employed a live-in
housekeeper who cooked. Jacqueline was Belgian, and in kitchen
matters she was my grandmother's body-double and collaborator for
every meal. Only she did all the work. She was married but had no
children, and my grandmother was convinced she was better at
French food than the French themselves. 'Except she can't make
omelettes,' she complained. Jacqueline shopped each morning,
stopping for a tall glass of blond beer in the bar next to the épicerie.
She was like a mother to all of the grandchildren. She dished out
advice, some of it remarkably unscientific. 'Les cornichons,' she
whispered to me, watching me take the eighth handful of baby
pickled gherkins from the jar, 'make you infertile.'

On other matters she was spot on. When my grandmother sold up and moved back to Britain, after 40 years in France, Jacqueline was gloomy. 'England is a horrible place,' she warned (she had never been there). 'Madame will die if she lives there.' She did, within two years. Jacqueline came to the funeral in London, her first sad visit. 'I told her she would die,' she said, crying furiously. Going into the kitchen of my grandmother's London flat after her death, I noticed there was still a sticker seal across the door of the microwave, bought for her new kitchen. It had never been used.

Jacqueline's great dishes were many. Her roast chicken with its dark juices, her skinless tomato and fine bean salad, her pommes frites which she cooked in small crisp batches, her violently red raspberry ice and her airy circle of choux pastry that she filled with tiny mushrooms cooked in cream. Everything she made I have cooked again and again throughout my life, but without her direct instructions. I have tried to recreate that twist in her method that made the particular thing so good: the extra tang of Dijon mustard in her salad dressing and the generous quantity she would use, for example; there was always a pool of it in the bottom of the olive-wood salad bowl, with delicious skinned tomato segments and leaves of butterhead lettuce – floppy English-style not crisp curly types – literally drowning in it. She always served chicken with its natural cooking juices, none of that last-minute gravy-making nonsense. Looking back, I think her talent lay in tasting her food, seasoning it properly and using herbs. She also adhered to a fairly classical road – tarragon went with chicken and nothing else, for example. There was a lot of safety and comfort in this approach for us.

I tried to get her mashed potato right on many occasions and could make a passable potful, but it was not 100 per cent. It did not have that slightly baked taste that made hers so good, or the sloppy, almost pourable texture. Then one day I rediscovered it, thanks to my son Jack.

Flawless mashed potato

Jack's mashed potato is puréed, strictly speaking. He watched it being made in Anthony Demetre's modern bistrot, Arbutus in London's Soho, where he did a few days' training, and came home and made it. It had that unmistakable Jacqueline-ness. It is almost more dairy than it is tuber, rich and slightly runny with the creaminess cut with the hint of lemon that the right potatoes will give. Always try to buy the red-skinned types for mash if you can; they have perfect texture and acidity. Here are the secrets of Jacqueline's mash, excavated by Jack.

SERVES 8
2kg/4lb 8oz red-skinned potatoes, such as Desiree or Romano
1 litre/1 ¾ pints wholemilk
250g/9oz butter
sea salt

Peel the potatoes and boil in salted water until tender. Some people cook them with skins on and peel them afterwards, but this is more time-consuming; as long as you let the potatoes steam-dry after boiling, peeling before cooking will make as good a purée.
Allow the potatoes to sit in the colander for 10 minutes. They do not

have to be kept warm. Clean out the pan and add the milk and butter. Heat until the butter is melted. Turn off the heat. Place a food mill (sometimes called a mouli) over the pan and grate the potato into the milk.

Place back over a medium heat and whip the potato slowly with a spatula. It will begin to heat up and eventually to cook a little, puffing out great bubbles and leaving the sides of the pan. Continue like this – it can be an achy few minutes. Be careful not to overheat the pan and actually burn the potatoes – you want the mash to become only hot enough to erupt with pockets of steam. This is a dish you need to stand over, but not for long.

You can add more butter and even cream if you want, for even richer potatoes, but make sure any addition is well heated through. Season with salt to taste. Keep hot in the pan, with a teacloth placed over the top, and the lid on top of that.

Eat with anything from cheese to hot ham, grilled gammon or bacon, sausages, frankfurters, faggots, haggis, grilled chops and roasts.

MORE MASH

You can use the above method to make mash from other roots. In most cases it is always politic to add a peeled potato or two, to help the texture become velvety and smooth. Each quantity serves 4 generously:

* Parsnips with clotted cream – peel, dice and add 2 peeled potatoes for texture. For 1kg/2lb 4oz parsnips, use 200ml/7fl oz clotted cream.
* Swede and butter – this is my favourite alternative mash. Just add about 175g/6oz butter to 1kg/2lb 4oz mashed swede. Peel and dice the swede before boiling.
* Carrot and crème fraiche – peel and slice 1 kg/2lb 4oz carrots; boil with 2 peeled, diced potatoes until soft and add 100g/3½oz butter and 150ml/¼ pint crème fraiche.
* Beetroot and sour cream – bake 1kg/2lb 4oz whole beetroot until tender (oven set to about 200°C/400°F/Gas 6). Put through the food mill and reheat with 150ml/¼ pint sour cream.

BOILED FLOURY POTATOES

The purée route can be for purists. Roughly crushed, boiled floury potatoes, with an invading force of melted butter penetrating some but not all of their flesh, is as satisfying as the most refined gratin dauphinoise.

Look out for the traditional varieties, now in supermarkets as well as sold by specialist growers at farmers' markets. Arran Victory are one of the best, with bluish skins, or Red Duke of York.

Roughly mashed haddock and potato with spring onion

A sort of lazy fish pie, which all happens in one pan.

SERVES 4

1kg/2 lb 4oz floury potatoes
150g/5½oz butter
2 tablespoons double cream or crème fraiche
600g/1lb 6oz smoked undyed haddock
2 spring onions, chopped into small rings
sea salt and black pepper

Peel the potatoes, then boil in salted water until soft. Drain them and while they sit in the colander, steaming, melt the butter in the same pan. Add the cream, haddock and spring onions. Cook over a low heat until the haddock flakes, then add the potatoes. Roughly stir, then season with some salt – watch the amount because the haddock will be salty – and plenty of black pepper.

Mashed sweet potato with green chilli and coriander relish

Bravely growing in our cold climate, the sweet potatoes I pick up in weekend markets deserve to be eaten for supper. I like their slightly sticky, floury flesh, even their alarming colour. When I was at school I knitted a fiery sweater with unflattering raglan sleeves in my needlework class. At the time I was unable to place the colour, chosen by my mother to 'match my green eyes' – it was darker than orange, lighter than terracotta. Now I realise it was definitely sweet potato.

SERVES 4
4 sweet potatoes
200g/7oz butter, melted
sea salt and black pepper
2.5cm/1in piece fresh ginger, grated
2 spring onions, chopped into small rings
2 red chillies, deseeded and chopped
6 sprigs coriander, plus roots if possible, chopped

Boil the sweet potatoes whole in salted water for about 15 minutes or until tender, then drain, cool a little and cut in half. Place on plates and mash the flesh while it is still in the skin, just roughly – it really does not matter if it loses its shape. Pour over some melted butter, add a few pinches of the other ingredients and eat while hot.

More pulses and grains

Solutions to the problem of feeding nourishing meals to many mouths are found all over the world, and often come in the form of pulses and grains. The British are always surprised at the quantity of rice, dal, noodles or pasta consumed by individuals in Asia or southern Europe. In Asia the average annual consumption of rice per person is 80 kilos, for example, while in the West it is less than 5 kilos. While we generally seek protein from meat and dairy foods, no family in India goes without a daily dish of dal, made either with lentils, yellow split peas or chickpeas. These are the most valuable foods in terms of survival but the least expensive to buy.

The best of the kill

I admit having some trouble persuading my children to eat dal, although they enjoy the chickpea and tomato soup on page 37. I find that in our house we spend more on ingredients for the children's suppers than on our own. It can sometimes feel as if Dominic and I, and anyone visiting, exist on pulses so that Jack and Lara can have their roast chicken and breaded white fish. I view this as one of my many failures as a mother who cooks – but it is also second nature to give your child the best of the kill, as it were. My mother used to put lentils on the table, to a horrified response from all her six children, but we gradually came round, one by one, and if you visited any of my siblings now you'd find pulses on the table at least once a week. Influence can be a very slow process.

BRAISED PULSES WITH SPICES, ONION AND BUTTER – DAL

There are dishes I often describe with the fondness I feel for a favourite piece of warm clothing. Tarka dal, a dish of lentils or peas, braised with buttery onions, a gentle mix of spices and herbs, is a caressing bowl of food. It is not just the low cost that makes it immaculate; dal takes little time to cook. It packs into one meal so much of the nourishment a person needs in a day and releases a slow trickle of energy, going a long way to prevent a 'picker' like me from raiding the bread bin in the middle of the afternoon. But it is also, and most essentially, just unutterably delicious to eat. I love recipes that build with colour and fragrance as they are made: the scent of the cumin as it simmers in foaming butter; the excitement and zing of ginger; the fruity heat of garlic which, when added, must not brown, and the transforming technicolor drama of turmeric.

I cook the dal separately, and keep a store in the fridge so I can make small quantities of freshly prepared dal when needed. (See page 383 – Halfway to a Meal.) There are various pulses and peas to choose from and some, like chickpeas, are best bought in cans simply because they take a long time to cook. As long as the pulse is hulled (the skin removed), it can be made into dal. The most economical are red and green lentils, which can be cooked quickly from scratch. Yellow split peas, which are also very cheap to buy, have a delicious flavour of peas but with none of the floury texture that I find makes other slow-cooked peas taste stodgy and unpleasant. Chickpeas, bought in the can, are a good beginner's dal, being sweet-tasting and easy and cheap to buy. In India, Bengal gram, a type of small chickpea, is a very popular dal.

Spiced butter and yellow split peas

see PLATE 4

This is my version of tarka dal, inspired by a North Indian recipe. Use yellow split peas or choose another hulled dal or gram, or drained canned chickpeas. Tarka roughly translates as 'spiced butter', patiently cooked with the aromatic ingredients and onion for about 10 minutes without burning to allow all the flavours to bind together. Indian cooks view this as a very important part of perfecting the flavour of their food.

SERVES 4

250g/9oz yellow split peas
3 tablespoons butter
2 teaspoons black mustard seed
1 tablespoon cumin seed
1 onion, finely chopped or grated
1–4 whole green chillies, deseeded and chopped
4cm/1 ½in piece fresh ginger, peeled and cut into matchsticks
3 garlic cloves, chopped
¼ teaspoon salt
1 teaspoon ground turmeric
2 teaspoons garam masala
2 teaspoons ground coriander seed
5 large tomatoes, chopped
100ml/3 ½fl oz water
leaves from 4 sprigs fresh coriander, plus chopped stalks and roots
extra melted butter, to serve

Put the yellow split peas in a pan and cover with approximately 1 litre/1¾ pints water. Boil for 40 minutes, skimming away the foam that rises to the top, adding more water if necessary. Drain in a colander and mash a little with a fork to break up the dal slightly. Set aside.

Melt the butter in the same pan and add the mustard seed and the cumin. Cook over a low heat – cumin burns quite easily – and then add the onion, chilli and ginger. Cook for about 3 minutes before adding the garlic, salt and spices, followed by the tomato. Add the water and cook for about 10 minutes. The contents of the pan should look glossy and be very fragrant. Stir in the dal (cooked yellow split peas), cook for another 10 minutes (add a splash more water if the dal seems a little dry), then add the fresh coriander and about 1–2 tablespoons extra melted butter at the end. Eat with rice or flatbreads. Sometimes I add a little chicken stock to make a soup.

Everyday mountain lentils

This is a dish we eat all the time at home for lunch, with some Greek-style yoghurt or fresh goat's curd, and usually with a few leaves of parsley scattered on top. It is not unlike the lentils my mother bravely put on the table when we were children, where they were received with the same enthusiasm as algebra homework. I am devoted to these lentils now, eating them often with roast meat, grilled fish – almost anything in fact. Ground coriander seed is my favourite spice. I love the way it binds the flavours of the braise, releasing a restrained earthiness.

SERVES 4
4 tablespoons olive oil
1 onion, finely chopped
2 garlic cloves, finely chopped
2 celery sticks with leaves, finely chopped
3 teaspoons ground coriander seed
250g/9oz Puy or other small lentils with blue-green speckled skins
salt and black pepper

Heat the oil in a saucepan and add the onion, garlic, celery and coriander. Cook over a low heat for about 3 minutes, then add the lentils. Cook for another 2 minutes, cover well with water and simmer for about 25–35 minutes until the lentils are just tender. Add more water if necessary, but be careful not to overcook the lentils. When they are done, tip the contents of the pan into a bowl and add a dash of olive oil to stop the cooking process. Season with salt and pepper. Eat hot or cold. These lentils will keep in the fridge for about 3 days.

Rice rescue

Rarely a week passes without my reaching for short-grain arborio rice to make a risotto. It is a dish that epitomises economy and eating for comfort. I made my first risotto in 1989. I had watched my mother make it, using Elizabeth David's recipe from *Italian Food*. I bought a copy and followed the recipe to the letter, and it worked beautifully. David's recipe, simple and true to the northern Italian original, yielded a pan of buttery rice, each grain having absorbed wine and chicken stock but without losing something to bite on. Risotto should never become like porridge. I added saffron to that first pan, and still love the way the exotic scent of the roasted crocus stamens combines with the Parmesan and butter. David issued the Italian rule that no more than two extra ingredients should be added, but that still leaves a vast risotto menu to explore. Two methods for making risotto can be found on pages 383–421, along with suggestions for added ingredients.

Polenta

I admit I did not join the ranks of those who raved about polenta when the craze for River Café-style food hit the UK. I think I had an unfortunate experience, and my mind was poisoned by a bland batch. I did not touch the stuff for years and ignored all encouragement to try it. I did not discover until much later that good polenta has real character in its flavour. When, only two years ago, I tried it out on the children in an attempt to cook something cheap and different for them, it got the thumbs-up from one child (typical) – but I was smitten.

Instant polenta

Traditional polenta takes up to an hour to cook, slowly bubbling like volcanic lava in a pan (see page 109). It is, admittedly, the most delicious, but good-quality instant polenta takes 5–8 minutes to cook and has a firm place in this chapter. After cooking, you can eat the 'wet' polenta immediately with Parmesan or sweet cooked tomato (see page 400) or with fresh cheese, meat stews, sausages, grilled fish, stir-fried greens – the list of things that match polenta is infinite. Alternatively, pour the 'wet' polenta onto a board and allow it to cool.

It will form a firm loaf and can be sliced and grilled. I buy the popular Italian brand Polenta Valsugana from supermarkets.

1.5 litres/2½ pints water
375g/13oz polenta
2 teaspoons salt
To serve: Parmesan, and extra virgin olive oil or melted butter

Bring the water to the boil, then, while stirring with a wooden spoon, slowly add the polenta and salt, pouring into the water in a thin stream. The mixture will immediately begin to thicken to a paste-like consistency. Continue to stir over a medium heat for 5–8 minutes or until the polenta begins to come away from the side of the pan. Serve immediately, with Parmesan and extra virgin olive oil or melted butter.

GRILLED POLENTA
As soon as the wet polenta is cooked and coming away from the side of the pan, pour it onto a clean (preferably wooden) board, large enough to accommodate the amount. Leave to cool. It will set firm when cold. Cut it into slices and grill on both sides in an oiled grill pan. Cooked polenta will keep for up to 4 days, wrapped in greaseproof paper in the fridge. It tends to sweat a little water in storage, so pat it dry before grilling to prevent hot spitting fat.

GOOD TO EAT WITH POLENTA
With wet polenta – braised meat, sausages, grilled kidneys or pork liver, grilled fish, sautéed spring greens with sausage, finished with a little wine (see page 172), mushrooms cooked with red wine and butter, sweet cooked tomato (page 400). Put a little fresh grated

Parmesan on the table, too. Add fresh parsley if you are not using Parmesan.

With grilled polenta – sweet cooked tomato (page 400), sautéed chicory with garlic, parsley and grated cheese, sautéed mushrooms, grilled courgettes and aubergines, sautéed tomatoes with garlic, butter and basil, crisp bacon or pancetta and Parmesan, rocket and Parmesan salad, fresh tomato salad (page 146), chickpeas and rocket (page 149).

Seven plates of sweet cooked
    tomato
Braised chicken rice, steamed with
    allspice
Mince with hidden roots
Pheasant curry
Pork shoulder chops with apple
    sauce
Three ways with cheese
Fresh cheese gnocchi
Egg pots
Hot sugared ham
Red braised pork
Clay-pot rice with rice crackling
Special fried rice
Lahmacun
Steamed clams with linguine
Moules, frites
Crumbs
Pasties

Potato omelette
Roast potatoes
Caramelised carrots
Bacon sandwiches
Buttered sweetcorn and grilled
    polenta
Sticks and wings
Baked beans
Beefsteak burgers and all the
    trimmings
Rich pancakes
Rich pancakes, stacked with a
    pear and fudge sauce
Buttermilk 'snow' with caramelised
    apples
Simmered apples, baked in rice
    pudding
Apple tart – quick
Plain, soggy chocolate brownies
Birthday cake

THINGS
THAT
PLEASE
CHILDREN

Unpredictable, fussy, unceasingly critical – if you ran a restaurant, at least you could throw customers like these out. But when they are in your home, needing nourishment until adulthood, you can feel like the head chef who got the rubbish job: unpaid double shifts with no staff, no union and often no gratitude. Amid all this, somehow you have to command some respect. Rescue comes with just a few good recipes, the good advice of real mothers, tearing a few pages out of the rule book and having a little sympathy.

Until I had children, I had one formula in my head with regard to feeding others: that good raw materials combined with good cooking equalled empty plates. But six-month-old baby on knee, I found those first few, soft rubber spoons of baby rice and apple purée were not exactly welcome. Put it this way, no one had ever spat something back in my face before.

Feeding children is an art or at least a very inexact science. Children have a remote control of your emotional core and quickly learn that these powers are especially potent at mealtimes. The ever changing preferences, varying between siblings and age group; the fussiness ('It's not cooked like you did it last time'), the utter waste of time and money – I have been quite undone by feeding children. They can make cooking a horrible job, removing any chance of adventure or attempt at creativity because they hate mixtures or the sight of a green herb leaf in their supper. You are never hailed, like a chef, and rarely rewarded. After two decades of this, many parents want to give up cooking altogether. The adult children, on the other hand, are often out there in the big wide world banging on to others about how brilliant your food is.

Often I have been driven to distraction by my children's demands. I cannot have that time again, but what I can do is pass on some experience. This chapter is all about what succeeds in my family kitchen, and it also draws on the wisdom and knowledge of others.

I have learned much, mostly by word-of-mouth, from cooks who are familiar with the daily grind of cooking for the family. The authorities seem overly obsessed with nutrition rather than cookery. Good cooking is about balancing diet. Better to teach parents food psychology: for example, how to understand the foibles of young children and the pressure they feel from their peers. Getting inside the mind of a child is far harder than boiling a pan of pasta. Learning a few management skills would be useful, too, such as handling and budgeting for the mountainous hunger of a 14-year-old boy (and all his friends).

I worked it out the hard way. Begin from the standpoint – which I did not – that you will probably not get it perfectly right. This is real, normal and expected of someone who cares about food yet is busy and not necessarily able simply to throw money at the situation. You will be proud of some weeks, ashamed at those where you gave in. But aim to balance good and bad experiences and look for an overall average in the good zone.

Many of the recipes in this chapter are adaptable, because busy people juggling work and children thrive on flexibility. The days are over when a dedicated housewife could afford a protracted row, sometimes lasting the whole afternoon, over an unfinished lunchtime plate of spinach. Instead I will often put the 'building blocks' of a meal onto the table, then offer things to go with it that the less fussy might consider.

A large pan of rice cooked with strips of chicken and flavoured with the hidden earthy scent of coriander seed and allspice could be served alone, but little dishes of herbs, a yoghurt sauce, toasted pine nuts, even hot green chilli is there for those who want it. Building blocks can also be cooked things that serve as a base for more than one recipe. For example, I make large quantities of a smooth tomato, olive oil and basil purée, which can be transformed into seven dishes for children and several more that will please adults, too.

Sympathy is important. Some children, school age in particular, seem genuinely scared of certain foods when confronted for the first time. Textures seem to be the greatest challenge. Often their noses will lift with interest at the aroma of sizzling onions, rosemary, thyme and garlic – but they do not want to find 'bits' in their food. Reward is also vital for good behaviour at mealtimes – gooey puddings in return for clean plates. Well, nearly clean anyway.

Ask yourself what you want to achieve, and set the bar a little lower. In the end, your efforts will pay off. It is a big claim, but when there is intermittent peace in the home kitchen, good things on offer and a sense of where it all came from, the adults who emerge from that home have a little more than an education, they have the tools to survive.

Busy
I imagined, with some smugness, that I would be very good at family food. A typical new mother, I privately believed others had it wrong (you only had to meet their children!) and that the realm of

nurturing had been waiting for me to come along and show them all how to do it. I wonder now if this rather familiar thought pattern is activated by a hormonal switch when pregnant, in order to fog the actuality of the work ahead.

But why think otherwise? My mother set a great example and even trained me to cook. But the difference between my mother and my life now is that she was a housewife in the classic sense. Managing a healthy kitchen for children takes concentration. My children make toast and rampage through the biscuit supply as soon as they are sure I am in my office, working – and spoil their supper appetite. As a child I was not allowed to pick between meals. Like jewellery shop staff, we were kept pretty much under surveillance. When the meals came, though, they were generous and delicious.

You can set out a blueprint, which I did, then watch as various forces unravel it. As any parent in full-time employment knows, it is very hard to stick to plans, and it is no surprise, yet so sad, that cooking is killed by a reliance on ready-made food.

The children of busy parents soon discover that you are too tired to argue, give in easily and get very tetchy if, having spent precious time preparing food, they do not eat it. This can become a sport. What would I do in retrospect? Ban sugar and TV, probably, or consorting with friends who hold birthday parties in McDonald's and are allowed to eat Oreos while doing their homework. But of course you can't do this. Just say why you are different, and occasionally give in to show you are human. My son Jack says don't try to be a good mother. But I do – the skill is not letting it show.

Seven plates of sweet cooked tomato

Asked to nominate a recipe that makes a difference to how my week goes, something with integrity that is economical and essentially useful, and I look no further than my store of sweet cooked tomato.

This tomato sauce or 'compote' imitates the best Italian in that it tastes full of fruit, sunshine and herbs, yet it can easily be made in a British kitchen. I make a large quantity of this sauce routinely and use it in many ways – seven of them regularly for the children, saving a lot of preparation time. It is at once a sauce for pasta, polenta (see page 55) and gnocchi, and needs only a warm through before using. It can be the base of a soup, a curry, a risotto (see page 395) and is also good with mozzarella cheese, toasted between two slices of flatbread or ciabatta. The recipe for the base sauce can be found in Halfway to a Meal (see page 400), with a number of ways to use it, but the ones listed here are ideal family food.

USING SWEET COOKED TOMATO IN CHILDREN'S MEALS

* Pasta and gnocchi – warm the sauce and dress the boiled pasta or gnocchi (3 tablespoons of sauce per person). To make a quick baked pasta dish, cook some tubular pasta (penne/rigatoni) and dress with a mix of ricotta and mascarpone with added grated Parmesan. Pour over tomato sauce, add more grated cheese and bake until bubbling.
* Macaroni – a more traditional macaroni can be made by stirring béchamel (see page 413), grated Parmesan and a little mascarpone into a gratin dish full of cooked macaroni, pouring over some tomato sauce, scattering over a little more grated cheese

then baking at a high temperature for 25–30 minutes. See plate 5.

* Polenta – serve the sauce over wet polenta (the freshly cooked, sloppy type) or with sticks of grilled polenta (see page 56).

* Tomato risotto – for 4 people, sauté 1 grated onion in 30g/1oz butter, add 200g/7oz arborio or carnaroli rice and 300ml/½ pint sauce. Bring to boiling point then slowly add chicken stock or water (use extra butter if you use water), a ladleful at a time, until the simmering rice is tender; takes about 25 minutes. Serve with cheese.

* Tomato and spelt or oat groat soup – for 4 people, sauté 1 grated or finely chopped onion in 2 tablespoons olive oil; add the chopped leaves from a sprig of rosemary, 4 heaped tablespoons grains and 300ml/½ pint sauce with 450ml/¾ pint stock (or water combined with 1 more tablespoon olive oil). Simmer for about 15 minutes until the grains are just tender. Season and serve with olive oil. (Spelt and groats are available from wholefood shops.)

* Curry – for 4 servings of a good, not-too-hot curry flavoured with ginger that many children will like, gently sauté 1 teaspoon each of ground cumin seed, ground coriander, garam masala and (if desired) a pinch or more of cayenne pepper in 4 tablespoons oil. Add ½ teaspoon fine sea salt, 2.5cm/1in piece of fresh ginger, grated, and ½ teaspoon cinnamon, followed by 60g/2oz butter, 4 finely chopped garlic cloves and about 450–600g/1lb–1lb 6oz raw chicken thigh meat, diced. Cook for 1 minute then add 350ml/12fl oz tomato sauce and 4 tablespoons water. Cook for about 10 minutes and eat with rice.

* Toasted flatbreads – for very easy emergency meals, place slices of mozzarella cheese and a spoonful or two of the tomato sauce between 2 pieces of focaccia or ciabatta (or any open-textured bread roll – or inside a pitta) and toast in a dry pan, on both sides, until the cheese melts. Use a panini grill if you have one.

GETTING WHAT YOU ARE GIVEN

My mother was a housewife. 'You are all so lucky,' she said not long ago, 'in the way you can do jobs.' She had six children in total; when the last was born, her eldest was sixteen. For more than twenty-six years she was caring for school-age children. We were not always all together at home but there was a period when the brood was young and looking after us all must have been hard emotionally and physically. The argument against women with young children taking other employment is strong. But for many of us there is no option. I am not a full-time mother, to coin a horrible phrase used by non-working mothers, so I have to concentrate the duties into a shorter time when I am not working.

In contrast, my mother devoted herself to home-making. She was a perfectionist. She decorated her house cleverly and collected pretty, original things; she gardened with extraordinary knowledge, tending a vegetable garden, and out of her kitchen came wonderful food. Due to the sheer number of children around the table, pleas were not heard if we did not like something. We got what we were given. I hear many people say that it is absurd the way today's children get away with refusing food. 'If we did not eat it, we had nothing else,' they recall.

Giving in
If my kitchen was a third world country I would be described as a failing nation. The infrastructure would need rebuilding and new law established. But if you visited, I bet you'd find there was charm in the chaos. My mother's excellent example of a firm but fair regime is not often repeated in my kitchen. Surveying the supper table, I know

all has gone wrong when everyone seems to be eating something different. One child is eating an omelette because shepherd's pie is the dish they hate more than anything. Another is heading for the toaster complaining that the shepherd's pie is not like the one we had last time, and my husband has refused the courgettes. ('You know I hate courgettes.')

And, yes, I agreed to cook the omelette, because I like to see a teenager eat. I should have stopped the other one making toast. Like many, I avoid rows, and older, literate children have the ability to argue until midnight. After a day's work and feeling frayed, I am not sure I want to spend the evening with angry young people.

What matters is finding a pot to please children. Food they like, and which you like, too.

Helping themselves
I have found an answer in dishes that can be shared; taken in the amounts each person wants. It makes for a much more peaceful meal and is similar to the Asian style of eating. The various components of a meal are put on the table – for example, meat, bread, salad, sauces – and everyone eats communally. Plating food is the antithesis and bound to raise conflict. The most obvious example of a help-yourself meal is a roast. There are no fights over roasts (except for extra potatoes) because the child with a huge problem with cabbage or bread sauce can avoid it. This may sound like giving in, and if a child refuses to eat a diet with any balance then help is needed, but in my experience children will come round to foods if they are not pressurised. It is a matter of timing.

But what of everyday food – the more economical things we can prepare quickly after school?

* Pasta can be served with either smooth tomato sauce, or just with olive oil and grated cheese, with pesto or with fresh ricotta.

* A simple stew can sit ungarnished in a casserole, while baked potatoes, sour cream, herbs, vegetables, sautéed mushrooms are there too, if anyone wants them.

* Mildly spiced meat curries go on the table, but adults can pep up theirs with hot chillies and sambals. Children can try yoghurt sauces and dal – and I have found they become more adventurous with this unpressured style of serving food.

* I serve sausages with mashed potato, for the comfort-food addicts, but also make a pot of homemade white haricot beans, garlic and tomatoes, which can be stored in the fridge for other meals if it is not eaten.

Braised chicken rice, steamed with allspice

see PLATE 6

There is a recipe I have cooked consistently since the children were tiny. It takes only 20 minutes to make and can be made both with fresh or cooked chicken. You can also vary the other ingredients – there is a list below the recipe. It is a dish of modern compromise that makes peace in a battle of wills. An easy pilaff that would be plain without the addition of the earthy scent of ground allspice and the mellowing flavours of ground coriander seed. Once cooked, put it on the table, surrounded with bowls containing the yoghurt sauce, herbs and nuts.

Boneless free-range chicken thighs are easy to find and cheap to buy, but I have also made this with leftover leg meat from a roast – there always seems to be some over because everyone eats the white breast meat.

SERVES 4

2 tablespoons pinenuts
2 tablespoons dripping or butter
1 onion, finely chopped (see Kitchen note, below)
5 allspice pods, crushed in a pestle and mortar, or 1 teaspoon ground allspice
1 teaspoon ground coriander seed
4 boneless chicken thighs, cut into children's bite-sized pieces (or equivalent of leftover roast chicken)
200g/7oz basmati rice, rinsed in a sieve under the cold tap
water or chicken stock to cover – about 1.2 litres/2 pints
salt and black pepper
To serve (optional): Greek yoghurt, chilli sauce, coriander leaves

Use a large heavy-based frying pan to cook this dish. Cut out a circle of greaseproof paper or baking parchment that is 1cm/½in larger in diameter than the pan. Place the pan over a medium heat and add the pinenuts. Toast for about 3 minutes, shaking the pan from time to time until they are golden. Transfer them to a separate plate.

Put the fat into the pan. When it melts, add the onion and cook over a low heat for about 5 minutes or more, stirring, until it is pale golden. Add the spices and the meat and cook for another 2 minutes, stirring slowly. Add the rice, stir over the heat for 1 minute, then add enough water or stock to cover to a depth of about 1.5cm/¾in. Bring to the boil, turn down so it slowly simmers, then cover with the paper, pressing the paper down on to the surface of the pan's contents. Leave to cook for about 12–15 minutes, then lift the paper and test a grain of rice to see if it is tender. Give it a few more minutes if not, paper lid on. Add about 100ml/3½ fl oz more water or stock if it seems dry. When the rice is tender, lift off the lid, season with salt and pepper and stir. Put on the table with a bowl of Greek yoghurt to eat it with, plus the pine nuts, chilli sauce and coriander leaves in separate dishes.

OTHER WAYS

* Herbs – fresh mint, parsley, chives, dill leaves.
* Nuts or seeds – unsalted shelled pistachios, toasted flaked almonds, sunflower seeds, nigella seeds.
* Sauce – sour cream, crème fraiche.
* Also – sliced mild red or green chillies for the brave, shallots sautéed in oil until crisp and sweet, sautéed or grilled tomatoes, roast pepper.

Kitchen note

Much of the time, children do not like home cooking because the basics are not right. You have to prepare and cook the fundamentals, such as onions, properly, or they are disgusting to children. Cooking them slowly – about 5–10 minutes in simmering, not smoking, oil – will make onions sweet. It makes all the difference. The texture needs to be right, too. Children do not want to encounter great greasy squares of roughly chopped onions in their food – nor do I, for that matter. The sympathetic Spanish and Greek mothers have a clever technique and often grate them, so they 'disappear' into the dish. Gently drawing children into eating difficult food will not spoil them. Once they love the flavours that ingredients like onions give food, they will worry less about the textures. But always give chopped onions a proper amount of time to cook.

Foibles

Sarah Husband knows all about the foibles of children's appetites. She should do, because as a school cook she prepares food for over 260 of them a day between the ages of 8 and 18, and is in charge of menus. She also has school-age children of her own. She cooks adventurously at the school and at home, and keeps choice to a minimum. Conversations with her have changed everything for me.

'Where am I going wrong?' I asked her, during a period when my son refused to eat the smooth tomato sauce in the recipe on page 400, claiming that it was not 'real Italian like on pizzas'. He was ten years old at the time.

'You went wrong because you caved in to him,' she said. 'Instead of being firm, you let him dictate. You should be saying: "Don't give me all of that twaddle about tomatoes," and win the argument. Children are not born with eating problems, they are put upon them by outside influences, often the parents. Only a child with anorexia nervosa will try and starve, and there is a point when a healthy child's hunger becomes bigger than its will to mess you around.'

I agreed with all this, yet admitted not feeling up to a fight when the six o'clock swill is in full swing.

'You have to know when to get angry, and show it. When a child who can understand reason is consistently not eating you have to show you are upset. If you keep smiling, they'll think you are too easy-going.'

At the school she offers the 260 children a one-pot dish with a vegetable for lunch. She makes braises, risottos, curries, pilaffs, pasta and noodle dishes. The obligatory salads offered are substantial. 'The girls are not going to get away with eating a lump of cucumber,' she says. Husband's sons, George, Alfie and Joe, are good eaters. 'I am tough with them about food but despite this my children hug me and say they love me. Being weak can be so cruel,' she adds.

Her advice turned the tomato argument in my favour. The next time I served both my children pasta with tomato sauce, the response was predictable. 'I'm not eating that,' said Jack. I stuck to my guns (large gulp of white wine), took the food away and ended his meal. The ensuing row was painful but at the end of the awful evening, I detected a whisper of mutual understanding. It was Sarah's word 'twaddle' that inspired me. Children are often not reasonable – they talk twaddle all the time and we fall for it.

SECRETS OF SUCCESSFUL CHILDREN'S MEALS

* In the early stages, do not give up and try another food if a very young child spits something out. Give the same ingredient, prepared another way. If they really don't like it, however, don't force it.
* If a child likes something you give them, don't bombard them with it or they will go off it.
* Once a child is old enough to reason, be brave enough to take a refused dish away and tell them the meal is over.
* Do not give puddings as a matter of course but only once or twice a week. Encourage healthier puddings that include fruit and yoghurt instead.
* A child is not a restaurant critic; never ask him or her if they liked a new recipe. If they have something to say, they will tell you.
* Once the meal is on the table, sit down with the child even if you are not eating. Keep distraction to a minimum – no TV and not too much talking.
* Last – and this is important and will take up all your steely will – if you spend the whole afternoon cooking something and they taste it and say 'ugh', turn your back so they cannot see the hurt and disappointment on your face. Try not to let a child know they have the power to do this.

Mince with hidden roots

I have published this recipe of Sarah's before – but many have said how good it is and it has a place here, too. You can make it with fresh mince (beef or lamb) or minced leftover beef or lamb. The genius of it is that all the goodness and delicious flavour of vegetables are there, but they are invisible. Eat with mash or Yorkshire puddings.

SERVES 6–8

2 tablespoons olive oil

1 large onion, finely chopped or grated

900g/2lb fresh minced beef or lamb (or minced leftover meat)

20 button mushrooms, grated

2 carrots, grated

about 4 heaped tablespoons grated root vegetables – parsnip, turnip, swede, celeriac (mix them, if you wish)

1 heaped teaspoon English mustard powder

1 litre/1 ¾ pints beef stock

sea salt and black pepper

3 tablespoons Worcestershire sauce (optional)

Heat the oil in a large casserole, add the onion and cook for at least 5 minutes over a low heat until lightly browned. Add the minced meat, the mushrooms and all the vegetables and cook, stirring, over a medium heat for 1 minute. Add the mustard, stir a few times and pour in the stock. Bring to the boil, then reduce the heat to very low and simmer for about 40 minutes to 1 hour, until the beef is tender. Add more stock or water if the braise is becoming dry. Season to taste with salt and pepper, then add the Worcestershire sauce, if using.

The beginning - pheasant curry

'Mine eats pheasant curry.' I am showing off to other mothers of three-year-olds who have not got past the baby pasta stars phase. It was true. We used to buy cheap pheasants, then make a mild curry, mix it with rice and yoghurt and watch it go down by the bowlful. Pride is dangerous. On arrival in primary school he soon clicked that this was not normal among his peers and had the famous pheasant curry dropped from the menu. Back to pasta, though it was possible by now to feed penne, not stars. Tastes evolve in unpredictable ways. From being force-fed eclectic dishes as an unquestioning weaner, to the monolithic predilections of pre-teens – pizza, pasta and nothing else – to a sudden liking for searingly hot and sour tom yum soup at fourteen. It is like running a restaurant and keeping an eccentric, long-term regular happy. Nothing surprises me any more. In the meantime, try the weaners' curry. I used to love finishing up the leftovers in the bowl.

SERVES 4–8, DEPENDING ON APPETITE
2 tablespoons butter
1 small onion, grated
1 garlic clove, finely chopped
1 dessertspoon mild curry powder
2 pheasant breasts, sliced into children's bite-sized pieces
4 tablespoons smooth tomato sauce (see page 400) or passata
4 tablespoons water
1 tablespoon smooth mild mango chutney (sieve or process the usual type)
To serve: boiled rice, wholemilk yoghurt

Melt the butter in a pan over a low heat and add the onion and garlic. Cook for a nice long time, about 10 minutes, until the onion is transparent but not coloured. Add the curry powder and sizzle for half a minute, then put in the pheasant and stir until the meat turns opaque. Add the tomato with the water and cook until the pheasant is tender. Remove from the heat. For very young children with no molars, give the curry a little whiz in a food processor. Older ones should manage the textures. Stir in the mango chutney. To serve, mix the heated curry with freshly cooked rice and a little wholemilk yoghurt.

Shall I be mother? Whose job is it anyway?
I do not believe that the libbers of the 1960s, who unchained women from household tasks, are happy with the outcome as it is. Women can now – in theory – succeed in the same jobs as men on identical pay, but they are still the ones taking care of most domestic tasks. On top of a 40-hour week, a European woman in full-time employment is doing an additional 30 hours in the home, while an employed man does only eight hours of domestic tasks. In the UK women are doing most of the childcare, shopping and housework but little cooking. Suspicious that cooking is a laborious chore involving no pleasure, many will not even attempt to learn. And it is a skill, about that there is no doubt at all. Not only does the aspirational cook need to learn how to make food taste good for others, so they will eat it and not waste it, he or she must learn how to shop in a savvy way, buying better quality food that is good value for money. It is all frighteningly daunting for beginners and there is an industry of fast food and ready meals there for the millions who are timid in the kitchen.

Diet trends show that in the UK we are eating out more and more. This immediately sounds like good news. At last, Britain has become a brasserie society, unafraid to eat out for the sake of it rather than for occasion. But, sadly, not a bit of it. On average we spend only 25 minutes a day eating – just 175 minutes per week. Calorie intake, including starchy, sugary foods, has increased dramatically in the last ten years. We buy three times more ready meals than we did then, too. This brings to light the depressing image of a Fast Food Nation. Eating lots, quickly, never cooking – just like the portrait of America painted by Eric Schlosser in his 2001 exposé.

The awful truth is that the women have a responsibility. It is an inescapable fact that women remain the main carers of families. They accept this – or there would surely have been a real revolution – and yet they are being totally irresponsible about the food aspect of guardianship. There is no position to take about this except that from on top of a very high horse, because poor nutrition is now a cause of ill health and obesity in too many youngsters. If no one says 'it's the mothers, stupid', the situation will get worse.

Insisting that schools teach children to cook is not the answer unless the parents are also brought in and become involved. Attitude can only change at a pace to suit the one who needs persuasion – which is why I always detest government interference and bans. Other channels of influence are more subtle. Good food experiences are something to share between children and their parents. It is part of a child's education and preparation for survival in the outside world as an adult, but one that must be based at least to a degree at home.

Climbing down off my immense horse, can I say that it is really not that difficult. Like any art – try not to think of cooking as a chore – the quantum of the performance is flexible. You can do something well that takes a few minutes, or spend all day working at it. Knowing two good, quick-to-make dishes and how to buy the right ingredients will make a dramatic change at home. There is no need to be able to cook everything ever invented.

TV cookery should take the blame for some of the problem. It is obviously not doing something, because while the number of people who aspire to cook rises, and these must include those who watch cookery, few actually do it. The trend is moving in the opposite direction. But if you look at the stars cooking on TV, you can see why. None of the TV chefs can really relate to the home cook's many dilemmas. Few have to worry about a budget or a work-life balance. Few either have children or are the main carers of those they do have. Even the women are far removed from life's reality, with many expected to simper and be more tasty than the dishes they cook. Nevertheless, watching TV remains the favourite leisure activity of both women and men in the UK, which suggests that cookery is enjoyed as pure entertainment. It would not matter, if there were not a real need to encourage cooking in the homes where it is most needed.

Juggling

Born to a Somerset farming family in 1928, my mother-in-law, Joyce, might have followed a typical path: marriage after school to a countryman, then a life combining children, housework and possibly farm duties. But Joyce, one of three sisters, was extraordinarily bright and took up midwifery in order to get a degree (one of the few ways in which a girl could finance herself through higher education at the time). She went on, determined to have a profession, eventually becoming an eminent criminal psychologist and an author. She also worked for the Department of Health. She was an early libber, really, and the world is a better place because she followed this path. She wanted to have equality, to put her considerable talent to use and to escape domestic work. She and I have long debates. She is for cheap food and convenience, yet she does cook, and her sons, who tease her about her food, also have good memories of it. Pork chops and apple sauce, easy to buy and quick to cook, are among them.

Pork shoulder chops with apple sauce

I am not a fan of loin chops. The border of fat around the edge never crackles and the lean meat can be dry. Shoulder chops, aside from being cheaper, are much juicier and the little pockets of muscle are tender for small teeth.

SERVES 4
4 small shoulder chops (on or off the bone), 1–2cm/½–¾in thick
2 teaspoons chopped rosemary
2 tablespoons extra virgin olive oil
1 garlic clove, roughly chopped
juice of quarter of a lemon
black pepper
To make apple sauce: 4 dessert apples and 1 tablespoon butter

Put the pork, rosemary, oil, garlic and lemon juice in a bowl, add some black pepper and turn the meat over and over again with your hands so it gets a proper coating of everything in the bowl. Leave for about 20 minutes.

Peel and core the apples then cook in a pan with the butter until soft. Mash to a smooth purée, then store in a jar until needed. Trim the slices of shoulder meat if necessary, cutting off the fat.

Heat a sauté or grill pan and gently cook the pork over a low heat for about 5–7 minutes each side, turning once. You will see red droplets form on the surface of the meat after it has been turned. When these turn clear the pork is cooked. You can always cut a little off to test it. Remove the pan from the heat, cover with foil and leave for 5 minutes for the pork to rest and become really tender. Serve with the apple sauce, fried or mashed potatoes or buttered tagliatelle noodles, and something green.

Cheese

Lucky are those people whose children love cheese. I have one who does and one who does not (except cheese on pizza) and cannot count the times I lament this. I would love to be able to enter a kitchen at the end of the day and quickly make croque monsieur (toasted cheese sandwiches), or a dish of mashed potato with cheese, or a cheese omelette. At least I'd know they were getting their protein and calcium, and at a lower cost than buying free-range meat. What is more, most cheese recipes are quick to cook.

Good cheese is easy to buy. You do not have to enter a cheese boutique to buy cheese for cooking. The generic Cheddar, Cheshire, mozzarella, Gruyère, ricotta, Parmesan and fresh goat's cheese are more than adequate. At least, unlike other cheaper staples like bread, it does not contain additives. Even basic organic Cheddars are good value for money. I do not agree with the red health warning on cheese packaging issued by the Food Standards Agency. A little goes a long way and – especially for children who 'go off' milk or cannot drink it – it provides essential nutrition. It is worth finding a green vegetable or salad they like to serve with cheese dishes for balance, however, or offer walnuts afterwards, which the French (famous cheese eaters with low rates of heart disease) believe reduce inflammation in the arteries.

Three ways with cheese

I could write a hundred pages on cooking with cheese, and you will find cheese recipes in other areas of this book, but these ideas please children.

* Pan-cooked cheese sandwiches – a slice of Gruyère, and a slice of ham if liked, put between two pieces of bread, then fried gently in olive oil on both sides. The French tie these bundles up with thin string like a postage parcel – a sweet idea to tempt a reluctant child, perhaps.

* Cheese omelette – see the recipe for omelette on page 104, and add cheese halfway through cooking, choosing from various suitable types. I prefer the gentle nut flavour of Gruyère, but Cheddar, Cheshire, fresh goat's curd and feta are also good. Basil

is a flavour children seem to like with eggs; add it with the fresh cheeses.

* Soufflé – with a supply of white sauce (béchamel) in the fridge (see page 413), it is easy to make small soufflés within a few minutes. To make 2 supper-sized soufflés, butter 2 average-sized ramekins or individual ovenproof dishes. Add 2 egg yolks to 200ml/7fl oz béchamel and 100g/3½oz grated Gruyère. Mix well, then, using a table knife, lightly fold in the 2 egg whites, whipped until stiff. Fill the ramekins almost to the top, and bake for 15 minutes at 200°C/400°F/Gas 6.

Fresh cheese gnocchi

Little dumplings, made with fresh ricotta, not potato, to serve with sweet cooked tomato (page 400) or a little melted butter and Grana Padano. Handling the soft dough takes a little practice but they are surprisingly sturdy in the pan. The sage in the butter may not be to all tastes but most children taste it and think it is 'sausagey'.

SERVES 4

500g/1lb 2oz fresh ricotta, drained on a cloth for about 15 minutes
100g/3½oz Grana Padano (similar to Parmesan, but less mature), grated
pinch of grated nutmeg
1 egg
2 tablespoons flour
about 200g/7oz semolina flour, for dusting (available from Italian food shops)
salt
100g/3½oz unsalted butter
2 sage leaves (optional)
extra grated Grana Padano, to serve

Mix together the ricotta, Grana Padano, nutmeg, egg and flour until you have a thick paste. Scatter semolina flour on the work surface and more on a dish. Take two dessertspoons and scoop up a spoonful of 'dough' with one, then transfer to the other spoon, cupping one spoon inside the other. Repeat to make a neat lozenge shape. Drop gently onto the work surface and lightly roll in the semolina. Lift and place on the plate with the semolina. Repeat until you have used all the dough. You can store the gnocchi in the fridge for up to a day before using.

To cook the gnocchi, fill a large pan with water and add a little salt. While it comes to the boil, melt the butter in a second pan and add the sage leaves if using – then keep warm. When the water boils, drop in half the gnocchi, one by one (you are unlikely to be able to fit them all into the pan at once). They are cooked when they float to the surface. Place them on a plate, spoon some melted butter over, scatter with some cheese and serve.

Kitchen note
You can also serve gnocchi with sweet cooked tomato (see page 400) and grated cheese. Alternatively, put the cooked gnocchi into an ovenproof dish, cover with sweet cooked tomato, add a few halved cherry tomatoes and bake until lightly browned.

Eggs

As with cheese, there are dozens of ways in which eggs can be cooked to please children. Providing they like eggs. It is easy, perhaps in retrospect, to see how many children develop a hatred of eggs, however. If not cooked properly, gelatinous stringy raw bits in fried or boiled eggs can do it for life, with some. Be sensitive to squeamishness, which is absent until a child is three, then suddenly hits. Again, like cheese, fortunate are families with children who eat eggs, because quick, cheap, healthy meals are yours.

Egg pots

Go as far as you dare with these, in terms of adding other ingredients. Preheat the oven to 200°C/400°F/Gas 6. Butter a ramekin and place a slice of ham in the bottom. Crack in an egg. If it is for me, and I have some, I add 3 or 4 tarragon leaves. Cover with single cream and bake for 12 minutes until a little prod with a teaspoon indicates the whites are done. Eat with toast.

You can add many things to egg pots, choosing from these or combining: roast pepper, sweet cooked tomato (see page 400), undyed smoked haddock, slices of black pudding or even haggis.

Hot sugared ham

This was a favourite of my childhood, and one my children always ask for. A gammon (raw leg of cured pork, which is a 'ham' when cooked) or even a half gammon is a treat, however. On ordinary days I use hock – the cured shin of pork that rarely costs more than £5 and has enough meat on it, on average, for three. My mother studded her hams with cloves, and I do this too, but I remember how I hated to bite on a clove so I always make sure to remove them from this children's meal, in sympathy, before serving it.

SERVES 2–4, DEPENDING ON APPETITE
1 ham hock
1 star anise
1 bay leaf
4 juniper berries
To glaze: 1 tablespoon English mustard, 6 tablespoons Demerara
    sugar, 6 cloves

Put the hock in a good-sized casserole, cover with cold water, bring
to the boil then drain, discarding the water. (See Kitchen note for an
alternative method.) Cover with water once more. Add the spices and
bring to the boil. Simmer for 1½ hours until the meat becomes
tender but is not yet falling off the bone. Another way to tell if ham
is cooked is to insert a skewer and pull it out; if the skewer pulls out
smoothly, the meat is cooked. If the meat seems to hold onto the
skewer, it is still undercooked. This is always a good way to test
larger cuts like half gammons and whole ones.

Lift out of the casserole and throw away the water. Preheat the oven
to 220°C/425°F/Gas 7 and place a piece of foil in the base of the
casserole. Use a small sharp knife to cut off the rind, leaving behind
as much fat as possible. Spread the whole surface of the hock with
the mustard. Put the Demerara sugar on a plate and roll the hock in
the sugar so it is well coated. Stud with the 6 cloves. Put back into
the pan and bake until the surface of the hock is glazed with a layer
of bubbling sugar: 15–20 minutes. The foil is there to protect the pan
from drips that might burn. Take the hock out of the pan – remove
the cloves whatever you do or there will be strong protest. Carve it
from the bone and eat hot with mash.

Kitchen note
Instead of this quick method, you can soak the ham/hock
overnight. Discard the water after, then boil with the spices
and follow the recipe.

The Chinese paradox

Nothing surprises me any longer. The hours spent arguing over likes
and dislikes throw up some astonishing contradictions. The child
who is shy of 'mixtures' like stew, also loves Chinese food. Terrified
of finding a button mushroom or a herb leaf in a casserole, they are
quite content to put away bowlfuls of food made with fermented
beans, black cardamoms, star anise and spring onion. There is a
genius to the flavouring in all Chinese dishes that, while weird in
concept, is very sensual. Umami, the 'fifth taste', is a characteristic
of Chinese cooking. Umami foods contain natural glutamates (not to
be confused with the chemical MSG), flavours that have a way of
invading the whole mouth. It is found in a lot of fermented foods
(including cheese, Parma ham and wine) and it is very much present
in soy sauce, red bean curd and various other Chinese ingredients,
which explains why kids eat Chinese meals unquestioningly.

I cook Chinese food for the children often, seeking out authentic
recipes rather than simply imitating the salty, greasy stir-fries sold in
our local takeaway. There is a little more work in the preparation and
sourcing the ingredients. If I pass a Chinese supermarket I stock up
on store-cupboard items, but the fresh ingredients are relatively easy
to buy. Making this food at home also means the ability to use
naturally reared pork, duck and chicken – not usually at the top of
the list of concerns in Chinese restaurants and takeaways.

A meeting with Annie Leong, a cookery writer from Shanghai, opened my eyes to real Chinese home cooking and its suitability for children. Leong is a writer ahead of her time in her own country. She attempted to start an organic pig farm in mainland China but found there is still no receptiveness to welfare-friendly, naturally reared meat, even after some of China's recent food scares. Her plans for the farm are on hold. 'They [Chinese cooks] still cannot see the beauty of slow growth and using better breeds for flavour and meat quality,' she told me, sadly.

Leong is a devoted family cook. I met her through her son, an orthopaedic surgeon working in a London hospital. When I went to collect one of his mother's books from his home, he was preparing her Red Braised Belly Pork. He gave me a tub of red fermented bean curd, an evil-looking paste oozing a thin red liquid that is essential for this dish. Adding it to the braised meat at the end of cooking changed everything. The children came into the kitchen, sniffing the aromas with fascination. Watching them fall upon the food was almost frightening and they still ask often for Annie's red pork. Her recipe, which can be found along with many other good ones in her book *At Home with Annie*, is quite detailed. This is a shorter version.

Red braised pork

Kids

The secret to the success of this dish is to buy pork with a good layer of fat and to fry it for a long time until the fat is mostly rendered away and the pork pieces turn crisp. I find the meat crisps better when I use free-range pork from slower-grown pigs.

SERVES 4

1kg/2lb 4oz fat pork belly, cut away from the ribs and strip of lean meat – use this to make spare ribs, for another meal
4 tablespoons sunflower or groundnut oil
4 tablespoons Demerara sugar or palm sugar
500ml/18fl oz water
10 spring onions, sliced
2cm/¾in piece fresh ginger, sliced
4 tablespoons soy sauce
pinch of salt
2 tablespoons Shaoxing wine (or pale dry sherry, such as fino)
1 star anise
1 teaspoon red fermented bean curd
1 black cardamom

Bring a pan of water to the boil, add the pork and simmer for 10 minutes. Drain and pat dry, then cut into bite-sized pieces. Put 2 tablespoons of the oil in the pan and fry the pork over a medium heat, browning it on all sides until golden and crisp – this will take about 10 minutes and the fat should render away. Remove from the pan with a slotted spoon. Discard the fat, or save in a bowl to use for roasting potatoes. Wipe the pan clean with a cloth. Put half the sugar into the pan with 1 further tablespoon of the oil. Place over the heat and allow the oil to bubble with the sugar and caramelise, turning golden brown. Remove from the heat and add the water – be careful, because it will sizzle. Bring to the boil – you should have a thin caramel-flavoured liquid – then pour into a jug or bowl and set aside. Wipe the pan clean again.

Put the final tablespoon of oil into the pan with the onions and ginger and fry gently until fragrant and soft. Add the soy sauce, salt and wine and then the pork. Cover with the sugar stock, add the star anise, fermented bean curd and black cardamom. Braise in an open pan for 1 ½ hours until the pork is tender. The sauce will reduce and you may need to add a few tablespoons of water. In the last 5 minutes, add the remaining 2 tablespoons sugar and boil faster so the sauce is syrupy. Remove the black cardamom and star anise (I sometimes tie these two spices up in a bundle of muslin, because children hate to find them in their food). Serve with plain boiled rice (see page 405) or clay-pot rice (see below).

Clay-pot rice with rice crackling

Another of Annie Leong's recipes, delicious on its own with some stir-fried broccoli or pak choi, or with the red pork above. Use a cast-iron casserole with a lid or a lidded ceramic dish that is hob-proof. Annie uses Thai fragrant rice for this recipe but Chinese long grain is also suitable.

SERVES 4
225g/8oz Thai fragrant rice
1 teaspoon sunflower or groundnut oil
1 teaspoon white rice vinegar
½ teaspoon salt
180–250ml/6–9fl oz water
To make rice crackling: 1–2 tablespoons sunflower or groundnut oil

Put the rice in a bowl, cover with cold water and rub it with your fingers to wash the excess starch away. Drain in a fine sieve then put back in the bowl with the oil, vinegar and salt. Stir and leave to stand for 20 minutes.

Put the rice in the casserole and pour in the water. Bring to the boil, cover with a lid and allow to bubble vigorously for 5 minutes. This is important as it helps the exterior of the rice grain form a protective layer around the interior so that the rice remains firm despite the longer cooking time. After 3 minutes, lift the lid and stir the rice with a metal spoon, scraping the bottom of the pot. Cover and simmer for another 5 minutes.

Remove from the heat, lift the lid once more (there should still be a few drops of water bubbling on the surface) and stir the rice for the last time. To make the crackling, carefully pour 1–2 tablespoons oil down the sides of the casserole – a little in each place. It should dribble down to the base of the pan. Cover the pot again and place over a low heat and cook for another 10 minutes. Remove from the heat and rest the rice, keeping the lid on, for 5 minutes.

Special fried rice

The real thing, borrowed from Fuchsia Dunlop, who found this recipe on her travels in Yangzhou, China. In her book, *Shark's Fin and Sichuan Pepper*, Dunlop, a British journalist, writes of the conflict between her love of Chinese cooking and concerns about the quality of the ingredients used in China itself. Finding the original special fried rice in its birthplace, Yangzhou, she also found tender shoots of change, with some of her companions talking about eating less but 'greener' ingredients – something to cheer Annie Leong (see page 88). Explaining that the hardships of China's revolutionary twentieth century had bred a greed for plenty (not unlike the bad food habits that came after World War II in Britain), Dunlop finishes her book with a note of optimism and this recipe, which is delightfully clean and delicate. Great mountains of this economical and satisfying dish have been served to my son and his hungry friends, getting rave reviews. It is a great dish for using up leftovers.

SERVES 6–8, DEPENDING ON APPETITE

8 tablespoons groundnut oil

1 raw pork neck fillet, cut into small pieces (or use pork mince)

2 tablespoons defrosted peeled prawns (squeeze out excess water), chopped

2 tablespoons chopped cooked ham

1 cooked chicken breast or leg, chopped

2 tablespoons sliced bamboo shoot (from a can, drained)

2 tablespoons Shaoxing wine (or pale dry sherry, such as fino)

400ml/14fl oz chicken stock

salt (optional)

2 eggs, beaten

1.3kg/3lb cold cooked Thai fragrant rice

2 tablespoons frozen petits pois or podded edamame (soya) beans, defrosted (optional)

6 spring onions, green part only, sliced

Heat half the oil in a large pan or wok and stir-fry the raw pork and prawns briefly, until the meat is pale. Add the ham, chicken and bamboo shoot and fry 1 minute longer. Add the wine and stock and bring to the boil, season with a little salt if necessary. (I don't, usually, because of the ham.) Set to one side in a bowl and clean the pan.

Heat the remaining oil in the pan and add the eggs. Swirl with a wooden spatula to scramble the eggs a little, then add the rice. Stir-fry over a medium heat until the rice is hot. Try not to brown it, however. Fold in the prepared ingredients, the peas and spring onions and cook, gently stirring, until all is warmed through. Eat immediately.

Adventure

My niece and nephew Luke and Eve Clark have grown up in a restaurant family. They are the exception to the rule that children reject certain foods once they discover that their friends find it strange to be served a grilled razor clam or spiced chickpeas. It is not just because their parents, Sam and Sam, cook brilliantly. Since they were babies they have been among people who work with and socialise around food. They simply know no other life than that where something different is being tried all the time. Ask Sam which recipe from the restaurant, Moro, that Luke and Eve love to eat, and each time she comes up with something completely different – of course.

 Lahmacun

It's best to describe Sam and Sam's lahmacun as a Turkish 'pizza' – healthier than the cheese-and-tomato type, yet full of the sweet flavours children love. I find this easy to make once you have a store of the stewed lamb ready to use. The lamb can be prepared the day before, along with the tomato sauce.

MAKES 4 PIZZAS

FOR THE STEWED LAMB:

300g/10½oz boneless shoulder or neck of lamb, cut into 1cm/½in cubes (or you can use lean minced lamb with the same seasonings, so no stewing)

½ small onion, grated

¼ teaspoon ground allspice

100–150ml/3½–5fl oz water

salt and black pepper

Put the lamb, onion and allspice into a medium saucepan and stir
well. Add enough water just to cover – add a pinch of salt and
pepper and place a piece of baking parchment on top. Simmer over
a low flame for about 1–1 ½ hours or until tender. Uncover the pot,
increase the heat and cook until the juices run thick. Remove from
the heat to cool and keep aside.

FOR THE DOUGH:

450g/1lb unbleached strong white bread flour, plus extra for kneading
5g/1 teaspoon fast action yeast
¾ teaspoon fine sea salt
300ml/½ pint warm water
2 tablespoons olive oil

Put the flour, yeast and salt into a large bowl and add the water.
Mix to a paste, then add the oil and continue to mix until it has
come together. Transfer to a floured surface and knead well for about
5 minutes until smooth and elastic, adding more flour if necessary.
Set aside to rise, covered with a cloth, for 1 hour.

FOR THE TOMATO SAUCE:

600g/1lb 6oz ripe tomatoes
4 tablespoons olive oil
3 garlic cloves, sliced
salt and black pepper
pinch of sugar (optional)

First peel the tomatoes: remove the stalks, then lower the tomatoes
into a saucepan of boiling water for half a minute. Lift them out and
put them into a bowl of cold water. When cool, peel, quarter and

seed them. If the quarters are large, cut them in half. Pour the oil into a frying pan and fry the garlic over a medium heat until golden brown. Now add the tomatoes and a pinch of salt and pepper. If you are not cooking this dish in late spring to late summer, the tomatoes may not be so sweet, in which case you might find it necessary to add the sugar. Simmer for 15 minutes or until the tomatoes are cooked but not totally broken up and the excess liquid has more or less evaporated.

Kitchen note
You can make this with the sweet cooked tomato sauce on page 400.

TO COOK AND SERVE:
2 tablespoons roughly chopped fresh flat-leaf parsley
2 tablespoons sliced red onion (optional)
½ tablespoon Turkish pepper flakes or pickled chillies (optional)

About 20 minutes before you are ready to bake the pizzas, preheat the oven to 220°C/425°F/Gas 7. Divide the dough into four and roll out each piece into roughly an oval shape no more than 3–4mm/⅛in thick. Flour everything well. Transfer to 2 large, lightly floured baking sheets or tins. Now spread on the tomato sauce, using a quarter of the sauce for each flatbread, hardly leaving a border of dough. Then add the lamb. Put in the oven immediately and bake for 10–15 minutes until the bread is cooked. Remove from the oven, transfer to a plate and sprinkle over the chopped parsley and, if you like, sliced red onion and Turkish pepper flakes or pickled chillies.

The seafood paradox

Next on the list of anomalies, and even more surprising than the wing-of-bat, leg-of-toad aspect of Chinese food, is the way many children fall for shellfish and squid. I put this down chiefly to the sweetness of seafood and laugh as my son wolfs down entire potfuls of mussels and clams. 'I see you are enjoying the flavour of their excurrent siphons,' I say. 'What's that?' 'Their bums.' He does not laugh, but he has no intention of giving up the bivalve habit, either.

Steamed clams with linguine

Clams (or vongole, venus or carpetshell clams) are quite expensive, so this dish is considered a treat that only comes around once in a while.

SERVES 2
1kg/2lb 4oz clams
200g/7oz dry linguine pasta
4 tablespoons extra virgin olive oil
1 garlic clove, chopped
1 wineglass white wine
½ wineglass water
black pepper
2 handfuls of flat-leaf parsley, chopped

Put the clams in a colander under cold running water for about 3 minutes. Boil the linguine in plenty of water for the time specified on the pack – usually about 8 minutes.

In the meantime, heat the oil in a large pan and add the garlic. Cook over a low heat for about 1 minute until soft but not coloured, then add the clams. Stir over the heat then add the wine and water. Bring to the boil, cover with a lid and steam for approximately 4 minutes until all the shells open wide (discard ones that do not open). Shake the pan from time to time, keeping the lid on. Drain the pasta and stir into the clam mixture. Cover and cook for another 2 minutes. Season with black pepper, scatter over the parsley and serve.

Suppers with cousins

Jacqueline Chevalier cooked many memorable meals for me when as a child I used to visit my grandmother in France, along with my siblings and cousins. She was originally from Belgium, and one of her triumphs would always be great dishes of mussels, steamed with wine and celery, served with equally generous helpings of slim, crisp chips that we all knew were called pommes frites long before we knew many French words. Jacqueline made both in small batches, so the mussels were fresh and the chips cooked in practical quantities – you cannot make chips for ten all at once unless you have a deep-fat fryer of restaurant proportions. I am not one for deep-frying and sometimes bake chips in the oven brushed with oil and dripping.

When I have more time, and am feeling especially loving, I make proper chips. I learned to make good chips from a Greek chef who explained that Greek mothers simmer their chips, rather than blast them in hot oil. 'My mother believes the oil keeps its goodness that way,' he explained. It is true. At below 200°C/400°F, olive oil will retain its nutrients. I buy good value Greek extra virgin olive oil in cans, via mail order, from Elanthy (www.elanthy.com), which makes this economically possible, too.

Moules, frites

SERVES 4
FOR THE FRITES:
1kg/2lb 4oz red-skinned or Maris Piper potatoes, peeled and cut into
   chips
extra virgin olive oil

Rinse the chips in cold water and pat thoroughly dry. If you do not do this there will be more starch, which will colour darker brown in the fat. Heat about 2cm/¾in of olive oil in a large iron casserole or frying pan so it sizzles when a sample chip is dropped in, but is nowhere near smoking. Fry the chips in batches; they will take longer, and seem a little soggier, but with patience they will turn a sunny golden brown and develop a shiny, crisp outer edge. Serve them as each batch is ready, adding more to the pan afterwards. You will find that the later batches of chips cook more slowly, because free-flowing fatty acids develop in the oil after the first use, cooling it. Add more oil and reheat, if you see this happening.

FOR THE MOULES:
Purists, the food writer Elizabeth David being one, recommend cooking mussels only with wine and adding parsley. But I like a little celery leaf and find the children appreciate this now familiar flavour.

2kg/4lb 8oz mussels
2 small celery sticks with leaves, finely chopped
1 wineglass white wine (or dry cider, or water)
leaves from 6 sprigs flat-leaf parsley, chopped

Run the mussels under the cold tap for about 2 minutes then clean them, pulling off the hairy beards and scraping off any large barnacles using a short knife with a strong blade. Discard any that are open.

Place a large casserole over a medium heat, add the mussels and celery with the wine and bring to the boil. Stir a few times. When the mussels begin to open, cover with a lid. Allow to steam, shaking the pan now and again, for about 3–5 minutes until the mussels open wide. Discard any that are unopened. Throw the parsley over and transfer the mussels to 4 warmed bowls. Quickly pass the cooking liquid through a sieve to remove any grit then divide it between the bowls. If you do not want to serve with chips, eat with warmed baguettes and put some butter on the table.

Crumbs

Italian mothers have dozens of secret wiles and ways to convince children to eat foods they find difficult. After weaning, 1–2-year-olds are often fed meat scallopini in fine dry breadcrumbs before confronting it nude, as it were. I have fed fillets of hake, haddock, plaice and even lamb cutlets to children, dipped first in flour, then beaten egg, then breadcrumbs. They love it. Always fry gently in olive or sunflower oil; you do not want the breadcrumbs to be too dark or you lose their toasty flavour. To make your own breadcrumbs, dry leftover white bread in the oven then either crush in a plastic bag using a rolling pin or empty bottle, or put them in a food processor.

THREE STEPS TO CRUMBED FOOD
Dip the item of food into each of these coatings, in the following order:
* Bowl 1 – seasoned plain white flour
* Bowl 2 – beaten egg
* Bowl 3 – fine dry breadcrumbs

Pasties

Pasties are also hiding places for things that might otherwise come under greater scrutiny if laid out on the plate. Yet what I most like about food writer, friend and mother Lindsey Bareham's authentic Cornish recipe from her book *Pasties* (Mabecron Books) is that these can be made and cooked in one go – none of the ingredients needs to be precooked. You can also use leftover beef, cut into cubes.

TO MAKE 4 PASTIES
FOR THE PASTRY:
450g/1lb plain flour
pinch of salt
250g/9oz lard, frozen
6 tablespoons ice-cold water
1 egg, beaten

FOR THE FILLING:
200g/7oz onions, finely chopped
200g/7oz swede, cut into small dice
400g/14oz skirt steak, cut into children's bite-sized pieces
600g/1lb 6oz floury potatoes, cut into small dice
sea salt and white or black pepper

Preheat the oven to 200°C/400°F/Gas 6.

Sift the flour into a bowl and add the salt. Grate the nearly frozen
lard into the dry ingredients then fold in until it resembles heavy
breadcrumbs. Stir in 1 tablespoon of ice-cold water at a time, stirring
until the dough forms, then put it in a bag and rest it for 30 minutes
in the fridge. Divide into 4 equal pieces and roll out each on a floured
surface into a 20–23cm/8–9in circle.

Sprinkle half the surface of each pastry round first with a quarter
of the onion and swede (leave a border all round of 2cm/¾in).
Season with salt and white pepper (black if you prefer), then add
one-quarter of the meat, season again then add one-eighth of the
potato. Season again and add another eighth of the potato. Paint the
border of the pasty with water, fold the pastry over and press firmly.

Paint the edge with water then crimp into pleats. Make the other 3, brush all with egg wash and prick the top to make steam holes. Place on a baking sheet lined with baking paper and cook for 15 minutes. Lower the heat to 150°C/300°F/Gas 2 and cook for a further 45 minutes, until golden.

Kitchen note
You can store the cooked pasties and reheat them when needed. They freeze well, too.

How to make peace
The most powerful argument for feeding children good food is not just about nourishment but in the link between good cooking and good behaviour. With older children, especially teenagers, who can erect walls of indifference to their parents, good cooking smells coming from the home kitchen can break down impenetrable barriers. The scent of potatoes roasting in olive oil with sage, the come-hither draw of bacon frying in a pan or the sight of a pancake zigzagged with maple syrup can change moods in a way no plea for reason succeeds in. When relations reach deadlock, sometimes there is nothing to do but cook. It is a reminder, when the hormones are bouncing off the walls, of one of a parent's most important jobs.

Experts have also found that if children are given the responsibility of finding, growing and preparing food as a reward for good behaviour, the good behaviour is likely to be sustained. The award-winning chef of Penair School in Truro, John Rankin, involved a number of children, who had been identified as not doing well or fitting in, in the building of a patio vegetable garden. When I met him and toured the school, the same children were still committed to the project and revealed that since being involved, they no longer got detentions for missed homework. Rankin is also a very good cook who encourages the children of this comprehensive school to try unusual foods like game. Nothing has been forced on them; they can choose something different or eat simple sandwiches and pasta, as they did before his arrival. He views them as his clients and they respect his skill. He encourages them to sign up to butchery classes, and – best of all – their parents to come in and learn with them. Where the new school dinner initiative failed in many schools, due to the heavy-handed banning of certain foods and insistence on 'five-a-day' rules, Penair School succeeds because the culture has evolved for the better, naturally. Children have gradually migrated towards not only a better diet but a better life.

No matter how furious you (or they) are, make their favourite thing and see what happens. Even the most stubborn are slaves to their olfactory nerve centre. If you enjoy cooking, it will also calm you after a row. The following recipes are favourites that can weaken a mood of hurricane strength.

Potato omelette

Either use the olive-oil-fried potato chips on page 99, or peel, thinly slice and sauté rounds of new potatoes for this win-them-over special. The good news is that eggs have been cleared of being a root cause of high cholesterol.

SERVES 2–4, DEPENDING ON APPETITE
450g/1lb new potatoes, scrubbed and sliced into thin 2mm/⅛in discs
2 tablespoons olive oil
1 teaspoon butter
6–8 eggs
sea salt
4 basil leaves, torn into shreds (optional)

Wash the potatoes and pat dry (as on page 99). Heat the oil in the same large frying pan you would use to make the omelette (preferably non-stick) and add the potatoes when it sizzles but there is no smoke or vapour rising. Sauté the potatoes, turning occasionally with a spatula, until the edges crisp and they are tender inside. Remove to a plate lined with a cloth to absorb excess fat. Keep warm.

Clean the pan and add the butter. Beat the eggs and season with a little salt. Pour them into the pan and cook until a firm layer begins to form at the base. Use a table knife to draw the egg from the edges into the middle of the pan, allowing the runny egg to spill into the recess. Continue to do this until the omelette is high and rippled but there is still some runny egg. Tip in the potatoes and scatter over the basil. Use a spatula to fold the omelette in half (it will probably break up a bit), then tip onto a serving dish. Cut into huge slices and serve.

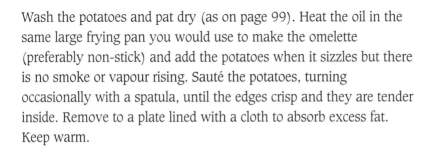

Kitchen note
Lara likes this with feta cheese, and with herbs such
as chives, basil and parsley.

Roast potatoes

A celebrity moment, but I was once asked by the *Daily Mail* to test a
roast potato recipe given by Michael Caine when he was interviewed for
BBC Radio 4's *Desert Island Discs* programme. Scribbling notes
frantically as I listened, I set about following the actor's instructions.
Tasting the result, all I can say, on behalf of some very happy children,
is that Caine is an honorary girl for creating a potato with loud crunch,
and parting with his secret so generously. It is all in the cold oil.

SERVES 4
1kg/2lb 4oz floury potatoes, peeled, washed and cut in half
salt
extra virgin olive oil
8 sage leaves
leaves from 1 rosemary sprig

Put the potatoes in a pan with plenty of water, add a little salt and
bring to the boil. Par-boil for about 7–9 minutes (so the potatoes are
half-cooked). Drain the potatoes and leave them to dry in the
colander. Shake the colander to roughen the edges of the potatoes.

Preheat the oven to 190°C/375°F/Gas 5. Pour about 5mm/¼in oil
into a roasting pan big enough to take all the potatoes without too
much crowding. Put the cooled potatoes into the cold oil with the
herbs. This is the revolutionary aspect; most recipes recommend
heating the oil. Turn them over so they get a good coating and
absorb the oil, then put in the oven. Roast for 1 hour, turning once,

until golden. You can roast at a higher temperature but it spoils the oil (see 'frites' on page 99).

When the potatoes are ready, remove from the oil with a slotted spoon or spatula and keep warm on a dish. They will not lose their crispness.

Caramelised carrots

And while the potatoes are in the oven (see opposite), up on the hob you can cook carrots that are a carrot, metaphorically, to the vegetable-shy. These are Jacqueline's – again (see page 98) and I can still bring their gorgeous toffee scent to mind any time I want.

SERVES 4

500g/1lb 2oz carrots, cut into sticks about 1cm/½in thick and
    2cm/¾in long
salt
1 tablespoon Demerara sugar
1 tablespoon butter

Boil the carrots in salted water for 5 minutes. Test to see if they are tender and cooked, then drain and replace in the pan. Add the sugar and butter and stir over the heat until they caramelise. I like it if you continue cooking until they catch and brown a little. I am sure they are not a dish for every day but definitely for an occasional roast.

Bacon sandwiches

The lure of the smell of bacon. Sometimes it is the only way to get them out of bed. I buy dry-cured bacon because it is less salty in the centre. Among the endless reasons to feel anxious are the newspaper reports about giving too much salt to children, especially those fed a lot of bacon. The real concern should be reserved for bacon (and ham) that is injected with brine. Labels will not identify this so look for the word 'polyphosphates' in the ingredients list instead. In the end, it is worth spending a little extra on dry-cured bacon. It shrinks less in cooking so can actually be better value.

I don't want to patronise anyone by showing how to make a sandwich, except to beg you to use good crusty bread, but sandwiches can be a means to introduce other interesting ingredients. Try putting in some young spinach leaves, for instance. I was amazed to see a teaspoon of sweetened mustard pass the taste panel, then some slices of avocado got the thumbs-up from another child. Mayonnaise followed. And cooked chicken. Goodness, it's become a club sandwich . . .

Buttered sweetcorn and grilled polenta

Sweet canary-yellow slabs made from dried maize, with a side dish of the fresh stuff. Rather conceptual, in a way, but comfort food of the highest order and, in later summer when corn cobs are cheap as chips, good value, healthy food.

SERVES 4 (WITH POLENTA LEFTOVERS)
FOR THE POLENTA:
1.8 litres/2¾ pints water – exactly
2 teaspoons salt
225g/8oz coarse-ground polenta meal

4 corn-on-the-cob
4 tablespoons butter
salt and black pepper
a handful of chopped parsley (optional)

Prepare the polenta in advance (it will keep for days in the fridge). Bring the water to the boil in a large pan, add the salt then slowly pour in the polenta meal as you stir with a whisk. Bring back to the boil, still stirring, then slowly whisk as it thickens. Cover and simmer for about 40 minutes, whisking from time to time. It will become thick but not solid. Dampen the inside of a loaf tin (about 20–25cm/8–10in in length) with water then pour the cooked polenta into it. Leave to cool completely – it will set firm so you can cut slices from it for the grill.

Boil the corn-on-the-cob in water for about 5 minutes, then drain. Put 1 tablespoon butter in a grill pan and brown the corn cobs in places. Remove and use a knife to cut away the kernels. Put the kernels in a pan with the rest of the butter, season with salt and pepper and heat gently. Stir in the parsley and keep them warm.

Turn the cooked polenta 'loaf' out onto a board and cut 4 thick slices (of about 1.5cm/¾in). Wipe the grill pan until the butter is removed then grill the polenta for about 5 minutes either side over a high heat. Remove from the grill and put on a serving dish. Spoon over the buttered corn kernels and serve.

Sticks and wings

To let you in on another confidence, the butcher often gives me chicken carcasses. Simmered with water they make stock (see page 390), and the excess meat and gristly bits are pulled off to feed the dog. Butchers willingly give these bonuses, excuse the pun, because they have to pay for bones to be removed and taken away. But in the odd bagful I find extra freebies: whole chicken drumsticks and wings. Unbelievable, but these are surplus to the butcher's requirements because most of his customers are interested only in buying filleted breast meat, as if the rest of the bird's superb structure were pointless.

I buy sticks and wings at the butcher's, too; they make sense if you are paying extra for free-range meat. They need little special treatment. Sprinkle with paprika and a tiny bit of salt; rub with olive oil and roast until crisp. Eat with rice, potatoes or polenta.

Baked beans

You will never get away with pretending you can imitate canned baked beans, but slowly casseroled, soft-textured beans, with a hint of pacifying sweetness, are worth a trial run and will not be an expensive mistake. Use canned haricots for speed and to guarantee they will be soft. Dried beans sold in the UK can be a let-down – if they are too old they will never cook.

SERVES 4
4 tablespoons cold-pressed sunflower oil (or extra virgin olive oil)
1 thick slice of smoked bacon, diced
1 onion, finely chopped or grated
1 garlic clove, finely chopped
1 teaspoon ground coriander seeds
2 cans haricot beans, drained (about 900g/2lb)
200ml/7fl oz passata, or 1 x 400g/14oz can tomatoes liquidised
    until smooth
1 tablespoon Demerara sugar
1 tablespoon Worcestershire sauce
salt

Heat the oil in a casserole and add the bacon, onion and garlic. Cook over a medium heat until soft. Add the coriander, beans, passata and enough water to cover the beans. Add the sugar, the Worcestershire sauce and bring up to a simmer. Simmer for 30 minutes until the flavours have come together and the beans are soft. You may need to add more water to prevent the beans drying out. Season to taste with salt.

Beefsteak burgers and all the trimmings

Given some minced lean steak, lettuce, tomatoes, cornichons, mayonnaise, ketchup and a baguette, I am my own burger bar.

To make 4 large beef burgers, mince or chop 450g/1lb lean rump or cheaper top rump of beef. Add 1 tablespoon celery salt, 1 tablespoon dried oregano and 1 teaspoon freshly ground black pepper. Mix well then form into 4 evenly sized patties, about 2cm/¾in thick – use a round biscuit cutter to shape them, if you have one.

Heat a ridged grill pan until it begins to smoke. Place the burgers on the grill, turning it down to medium immediately. Cook for about 4 minutes each side.

Split the baguette (or ciabatta roll) and toast the cut side lightly. Spread with a little mayonnaise on one side and add a few sliced cornichons (baby gherkins). Lay a couple of small romaine (or cos) lettuce leaves over the mayonnaise, follow with a slice of tomato, the burger, the ketchup and, finally, the second slice of bread.

Rich pancakes

Bribery in a pan – what child will resist pancakes? I sometimes swap food for conversation, when one is not talking to me. Pancakes do this nicely, quickly and cheaply. This is an adaptation of Jane Grigson's recipe for 'pancakes for the rich' and makes the most delicious pancakes of all: thin with edges like fine net. Being buttery they are heavier, so less easy to toss.

MAKES AT LEAST 15
175g/6oz fine plain white flour
2 large eggs
175g/6oz unsalted butter, melted and cooled
500ml/18fl oz creamy wholemilk
butter, for cooking
To serve: lemon and sugar, agave syrup (healthier than golden syrup
    and just as nice), maple syrup

Sieve the flour into a bowl and make a well in the centre. Add the eggs and gradually beat in the butter and milk until you have a smooth, creamy batter. Leave to stand for 30 minutes – this makes a better-textured pancake.

Wipe a crepe pan or heavy-based frying pan with butter paper, then place over a medium to high heat. Pour about half a soup ladleful of batter into the pan and tilt in a circular motion to spread over the bottom. Cook until the edges and underside are golden brown, then flip over with a palette knife. Cook for another 30 seconds or so, being careful not to burn the underside. It should have pale brown spots. Remember that the first will never be a great pancake. Make the rest, using a little more butter each time or if the pan seems dry, swirling a small piece around until it melts and foams. Keep all the pancakes warm in a pile, wrapped in a teacloth. Serve with lemon and sugar, agave syrup or maple syrup.

Kitchen note
Pancakes keep for about 48 hours, stored airtight with greaseproof or baking paper between each. Reheat on a dry frying pan over a medium heat.

Rich pancakes, stacked with a pear and fudge sauce

You need 5 pancakes. Put 85g/3oz butter, 85g/3oz Demerara sugar and 3 tablespoons golden syrup in a pan and simmer until they emulsify into a thick fudgy sauce. Peel, core and slice 4 pears and add to the sauce. Immediately spoon a quarter of the sauce onto a pancake, place a pancake on top; finish with the fifth pancake as the top layer. Serve warm.

Buttermilk 'snow' with caramelised apples

Buttermilk makes a delicate, lemony snow to pile on top of sweet caramelised apples, strawberries, raspberries, blackberries, cooked plums, apricots or rhubarb.

SERVES 4
FOR THE SNOW:
600ml/1 pint buttermilk
1–2 dessertspoons caster sugar, to taste

1 tablespoon butter
6 dessert apples, cored and sliced
2 tablespoons Demerara sugar

Put the buttermilk in a jug and add enough sugar to take the edge off its sourness. Pour into 2 ice-cube trays or a shallow dish and freeze until solid. Just before serving, remove from the freezer, leave for 5 minutes, then either put the cubes in a food processor and process to 'snow' or mash the iced buttermilk in the tray with a fork.

Meanwhile, prepare the apples, which can be served straight from the pan, or cold. Melt the butter in a pan and sauté the apple slices until they catch a little brown colour. Add the sugar and gently stir until it melts and caramelises. Serve in little bowls with some buttermilk snow spooned over.

Simmered apples, baked in rice pudding

A dish of sticky apples with a nice surprise of creamy rice pudding beneath.

SERVES 6
6 dessert apples: Cox's, Russet, Worcester or any nice smaller type
600ml/1 pint water
100g/3 ½oz caster sugar

FOR THE RICE PUDDING:
85g/3oz pudding rice, rinsed
1 litre/1 ¾ pints wholemilk, preferably gold top (Guernsey or Jersey)
pinch of cinnamon powder
pinch of nutmeg
a few drops of vanilla essence
2 tablespoons caster sugar
30g/1oz unsalted butter
150ml/¼ pint single cream
2 tablespoons Demerara sugar

Peel and core the apples, leaving them whole; put in a small casserole pan with the water and sugar. Bring to the boil and poach for about 10 minutes, turning them from time to time. They will be slightly soft. Remove to a plate and clean the pan.

Put the rice in the casserole with about half the milk, the spices, vanilla and caster sugar and bring to the boil. Turn down to a simmer and cook for about 20 minutes. Add the remaining milk, the butter and cream, and stir. Preheat the oven to 170°C/325°F/Gas 3. Place the apples on top of the rice, scatter over the Demerara sugar and bake, uncovered, for about 40 minutes. You may want to add a little more milk if the pudding becomes dry. The apples should be sticky and slightly caramelised.

Apple tart - quick

see PLATE 7

My sister Laura has always made this quick tart for my children when we visit, cramming it into a very small gas stove, which singes it in places, rather deliciously. In France they row about the colour of pastry (and why not?). The rustic pastry of the artisanal peasant is darkly burnished, reminiscent of traditionally fired ovens. Golden pastry is for wimps.

1 slab (approximately 500g/1lb 2oz) butter puff pastry
6 dessert apples (use juicy, tart-flavoured ones such as Gala, Cox's or
    Granny Smith), cored and thinly sliced
3 tablespoons apricot jam/apple jelly
1 tablespoon water

Preheat the oven to 230°C/450°F/Gas 8. Roll the pastry into a large rectangle and transfer to a buttered baking tray. Prick all over with a fork, so the entire surface is perforated at regular intervals. This stops the pastry puffing up in great bubbles during cooking, upsetting the rows of apple slices. Lay the apple slices on the surface of the pastry in neat-ish rows, each slice overlapping the one next to it. Bake in the oven until the pastry is crisp, brown (but not black-brown) and the apples are singed with colour. Remove from the oven and cool. Meanwhile, heat the jam or jelly with the water until it bubbles and breaks down into a liquid. Strain through a small sieve and use a pastry brush to paint a glaze onto the whole surface of the tart.

Plain, soggy chocolate brownies

It is not just me who hates brownies with nuts . . . A good recipe that makes a store of brownies to last the week. Eat as a pudding treat with ice cream and soft fruit.

MAKES 9–12
375g/13oz unsalted butter
375g/13oz plain chocolate
6 eggs
1 teaspoon vanilla essence
500g/1lb 2oz caster sugar
200g/7oz flour

Preheat the oven to 180°C/350°F/Gas 4 and line a high-sided baking tin (25 x 30cm/10 x 12in) with baking paper. Melt the butter and chocolate together over a low heat, then allow to cool. Beat in the eggs, one by one, then add the vanilla and sugar. Fold in the flour well, then pour the mixture into the baking tin. Bake for 25 minutes and no longer – or you will dry out the brownies. Cool in the tin before storing in an airtight box.

Birthday cake

see PLATE 8

The first cookbook I used was called *My Fun To Cook Book*, and was full of the most delicious illustrations and recipes that made extremely sticky food. Each recipe was drawn step by step; I vaguely remember a dog character that seemed to pop up and lick the bowl or help or something (I long to track down a copy, since mine is lost).

I spent hours cooking indoors, while the rest of the family were outside doing countryside things like riding and walking dogs. In Wiltshire, where my father lived, admitting you preferred to stay in and make cakes was akin to coming out. I was the only cook in the village . . .

I have bought birthday cakes, and it is true that it gets easier to buy a stunningly decorated cake, even one made with eggs laid by contented hens. But an iced sponge, studded with Smarties, remains the real thing. A love letter to your children.

Vanilla sponge

The following is a great basic: ideal innards for a birthday cake and good fairy cake material, too.

MAKES ENOUGH CAKE TO SERVE 12–16
280g/10oz unsalted butter, softened
280g/10oz caster sugar
5 eggs
1 teaspoon vanilla essence
280g/10oz self-raising flour
2 tablespoons ground almonds

Preheat the oven to 180°C/350°F/Gas 4 and prepare your cake tins – two shallow sandwich tins or a 12-hole muffin/fairy cake tin – greasing with butter and dusting with plain flour or lining with paper cases.

Beat the butter and sugar together until pale and fluffy-textured (an electric beater is helpful). Beat in the eggs, one by one, each with a teaspoon of the flour, then the vanilla essence. Fold in the remaining flour with the ground almonds.

Put into the tin(s) or cake cases and bake. Shallow sandwich tins will need 30–40 minutes; loaf tins about 1 hour and 5–15 minutes; fairy cakes about 15 minutes. Test the cake near to the end of the cooking time by sticking a skewer into it. If the cake feels firm and the skewer comes out clean, it is done.

Sandwich the cake together with raspberry or strawberry jam, then decorate with lemon icing.

Lemon icing

Because the egg white in this recipe is raw and a cake is often for children, I use 'Red Lion' stamped eggs from vaccinated hens, just to be safe.

200g/7oz icing sugar
1 egg white, beaten
juice of 1 lemon

Sift the icing sugar into a bowl and add the egg white. Add some of the lemon juice to the bowl, stirring all the time, until you have a thick smooth paste that will coat the back of a spoon well. Do not add all the lemon if the icing looks like it will become too runny. Pour over the cake, spreading to the edges with a knife. If you are adding any other decorations, do this now so they stick to the wet icing. Leave to dry for 45 minutes.

Mostelle – the dish that says goodbye and the end of my childhood

The day before we would leave my grandmother's house in France at the end of the summer, she would always ask what we would like to eat as our last meal. It certainly felt like a death sentence. Leaving this pretty family house, a place I'd known since a baby and the one house that had been constant. Leaving her, knowing we would not see her for months, and breaking up the party of cousins, aunts and uncles. No more sunny days, hot and heady smells of eucalyptus or centipedes on the bedroom floor. I went there every year from the age of nought to 28. I never went anywhere else on holiday. There had been no need to.

For my last meal I asked for mostelle, a mysterious fish that was sold in the local market. Looking it up in a seafood encyclopaedia, I discover it was likely to be mostelle de roche or mostelle de vase – the Greater Forkbeard. This is a gentle-flavoured, boneless white fish not unlike a ling – or from the same family. Jacqueline simply dipped the mostelle steaks in flour and fried them, then served the fish with homemade mayonnaise mixed with parsley, a few chopped capers and sliced cornichons. I did not know that the last time I asked for mostelle it actually would be the very last time. The house was sold before I could go back. It will always be the goodbye recipe.

'Stop trying to be a good mother.'
Jack Prince (when 14 years old)

'My mother gets cross, and then she has some wine.'
Lara Prince (when 4 years old)

Warm tomatoes, oregano and
feta cheese
Pearl barley and creamed button
mushrooms
Devilled prawns
Grilled bread
Top rump steak with tender herbs
and warm olive oil sauce
Ricotta with broad beans
Fast, warming bowl of soup
Léa's leaves and fried bread, with
a smoked-herring dressing
Giant baked mushrooms, on toast
Jacqueline's tomato and olive oil
Bread and tomatoes – the Tuscan
mothers
Chickpeas and rocket
Bitter leaves, parsley and warm
black pudding
Roast peppers
Salmagundi
Coronation chicken
Peas, more peas and fennel
mayonnaise
Celeriac remoulade with smoked
haddock tartare
Butter beans, olive oil, black olive
paste, parsley and courgettes

Tuna and coconut – Indian ocean
breakfast
Summer green vegetables with
olive oil
French bean vinaigrette with shallots
Piquant chicken-liver pots
Porcini pots
Hot haddock and saffron pots
Crisp smoked bacon, polenta
cubes, bittersweet chicory
Sausage with shredded spring
greens and apple
Pan-fried plaice with lettuce hearts
and lemon
Pan-fried parsnips and 'mountain'
cheese
The mother of all breakfasts –
scrambled eggs
Escalopes
Monkfish and bacon cakes
South coast stew of gurnard, cod,
mussels, saffron, new garlic and
butter beans
Chicken thighs stuffed with walnut
and watercress purée, cooked in
cider
Pudding in a pan
Poached summer fruit with vanilla
and allspice

FAST, GOOD-FOR-YOU LUNCHES AND SUPPERS

Looking at the clock as I get in, I realise I am home later than I thought. It is late afternoon and the roadworks on the bridge near home have turned the local traffic into a lava flow that moves only a few inches at a time. I am wondering what is in the fridge (I meant to pass that butcher near my meeting in town, but feeling tired I lost my shopping zeal). Once inside the door, I know what is coming next. A question I hear every day, ready or not: 'What's for dinner?'

I love to spend my time cooking, but that does not mean I always feel in the mood for it. Tiredness and attendant grumpiness kill the eagerness to pick up a knife. What is more, on top of getting a meal together I know I have other jobs to do before the morning, and there is a child sitting over a piece of homework, grimly looking for answers. It is going to be a long night.

I know. I should be better organised. I of all people should be able to plan ahead. But the truth is that this is not always the case. Real, human cooks often fall short of their hopes. The dilemma, and one that the next pages can deal with, is finding a formula for food that is quick to make and recharges batteries; light, energising, flexible cooking. There are ways to sort out a speedy meal for children (see pages 58–122), but what about you and how you aspire to eat?

All the pressures of modern life mean it is essential to look after yourself. Sure, I can make cheese on toast or eat pasta with a bought sauce, but in truth a bowl of pearl barley with the rich forest flavour of mushrooms will do so much more for the quality of the life I have; it is much nicer to sit down to a pan containing a piquant little stew of tomatoes, oregano and feta cheese, and scoop it up with crisp spoons of toasted flatbread. I want to reach the end of the day with everything (nearly) done and having enjoyed a little gastronomy. I do not want simply to refuel. Like a weary camel.

'Across the road' cooking

I live near a late-night newsagent-cum-grocery. Large areas of it are devoted to bottles of fizzy drinks, sweets, long-life breads and cleaning fluid. The freezer is full of pizzas with small squares of sweet pepper all over them like the houses and hotels on a Monopoly board. There is no fresh meat and the cooked and cured meats are low grade. But I can cook out of this shop. They bake baguettes from frozen sticks of dough, which can be handy for last-minute garlic breads, and they sell good canned vegetables like chickpeas, butter beans and tomatoes, as well as rice and red lentils. They now stock free-range eggs, decent European cooking cheeses, Emmental and Gruyère (over-priced), plus feta cheese, spices, onions, garlic and potatoes. There is always a supply of Greek yoghurt. I like our cobbled-together dinners from across the road. It is even quite relaxing not to have the plethora of choice that can make a supermarket trip so wearing.

Warm tomatoes, oregano and feta cheese

see PLATE 9

A favourite 'across the road' recipe, needing only basic ingredients.
I cannot count the times I have been grateful for the way British cities
have embraced feta cheese and pitta bread.

SERVES 2–3

4 tablespoons extra virgin olive oil
1 x 400g/14oz can chopped tomatoes
2 pinches of dried oregano
½ teaspoon ground coriander seed
225g/8oz feta cheese, drained and cut into 2cm/¾in cubes
¼–½ teaspoon smoked paprika
black pepper
chopped flat-leaf parsley (optional)
To serve: pitta bread, toasted and cut into strips, or other types of
    flatbread

Choose a pan with a well-fitting lid. Heat the oil until it is just
beginning to release white smoke and quickly add the tomatoes. Put
the lid on quickly – they will sizzle and splash. Leave the lid on the
pan until the sizzling dies down, then lift the lid and add the oregano
and coriander. Simmer for about 10 minutes, then add the cheese.
Swirl a little with a spoon. When the cheese begins to melt, remove
from the heat, sprinkle over the paprika and season with black
pepper. Scatter over the parsley, if using. Serve with the toasted
flatbread.

Kitchen note

You do not have to stick with the recipe as it stands. Substitute fresh parsley with coriander or a few fresh thyme leaves; you can also add some rocket leaves just as you serve, or some chopped capers, or perhaps pitted black olives, cut in half. You can also make this simply by adding the feta cheese to a pan of the sweet cooked tomato (see page 400).

Spontaneity

Hunger calling: a little contraction in the gut, a bodily alarm that is simply asking for some attention. It is a sudden need for fuel, a demand for nourishment, and what do so many of us do? Instead of sending in a crack team of ideally suited nutrients, we lob Jaffa Cakes at the situation. Traditional cookery deals well with the kind of food that is just right for a family meal in the evening, a weekend lunch or a show-off dinner party. But in actuality there are a number of times each week when meals are informal – and most often need to be taken in a hurry. To be fair to those with the Jaffa Cake solution, it is typical to be caught short of food away from home. Making better packed lunches and car picnics is a good habit to acquire, as is learning to cook the kind of spontaneous dishes you will find over the next pages.

The art of combining ingredients from a number that are always on your shopping list and cooking them in a way that maximises their quality – and by this I mean their nutrient element – is a good habit to have. It is fair to call it an art. Good spontaneous cooking is an instinct for what works well together and, if pleasing others, a sensitivity that tells you what they might enjoy. It can be full of colour and sensuous texture, good-for-you food that is a joy to eat, however simple. It is flexible food and, most importantly of all, it does a much better job of dealing with hunger than a circle of sponge spread with orange jelly and chocolate. Oh yes it does.

Pearl barley and creamed button mushrooms

Any time of the year, a dash to my local late-night shop will mean a wire basket containing a pack of pearl barley: the polished whole grains that become tender after just 15 minutes' cooking. Also, a bag of button mushrooms (slightly wrinkly, not the freshest, but good enough) and either some cream or creamy cheese. I always feel revived by this pan of elegantly pale food that insulates from the inside out.

SERVES 2–3
1 tablespoon butter or beef dripping
1 small onion or 2 shallots, chopped
1 garlic clove, chopped
leaves from 1 sprig thyme (optional)
225g/8oz button mushrooms, halved or roughly chopped
225g/8oz pearl barley
750ml/1 ¼ pints chicken or vegetable stock or water – or more
sea salt and black pepper
2–3 tablespoons mascarpone or other full-fat cream cheese, double
    cream or crème fraiche

Melt the butter or dripping and add the onion and garlic, and thyme if using. Cook over a medium heat until soft but not coloured, then add the mushrooms. Cook for another 2–3 minutes, stirring to coat them with the cooking juices. When they begin to shrink in the heat, add the barley and cook for another minute. Cover with the stock or water, bring to the boil, turn down to a simmer and cook, partially covered, for about 15 minutes until the barley is tender. Do not cook too long or it will become fluffy and soft, and the dish will be stodgy. If the liquid evaporates, add a little more – but do not make it soupy. Season with salt and pepper, then serve in bowls with a spoonful of the cream cheese or cream swirled in.

Kitchen note
You can use dried porcini mushrooms in place of the fresh mushrooms: use 100g/3½oz and soak in a small amount of boiling water first. Use the soaking liquid in the dish; it will be full of flavour. You can also use alternative mushrooms: crimini (tiny buttons), chestnut or cultivated exotics like oyster, king oyster and enoki. Tarragon leaves will be good in place of the thyme, especially with the crimini or king oyster mushrooms, which, while white and insipid-looking, have a stronger flavour than ordinary buttons.

Hurry

Time: the most precious commodity, the most misused; spare time is something I'd guess most people dream of, but sadly cooking has fallen lower and lower in the list of things people enjoy doing in leisure time. The only conclusion to take from this is that for many people it is a chore. That it is creative, and even an art, is lost on many who are overwhelmed by the thought of cooking one or two meals a day.

So let's be honest, cooking is a job, a duty, but let me quickly say that at least it is one with an artistic side. The crucial point is to find a way to do it that reduces the chore. The truth about cooking is that it needs to be done far too often to be a hobby. And the reality is that most of the meals we cook each week must be made quickly so they do not eat into the activities people prefer to do when not working. Or no one will come over to cooking. Learning to throw together a few good things – when menu-planning and recipes are too troublesome to follow – is a very valuable skill.

I would argue that knowing how to cook a dish quickly is as essential as being computer literate. This does not mean you cannot make bread or slow-cook a stew, but the hurried, stressed generation needs to be able to open the front door and get dinner out of the way. I believe we have no option but to cook. I fear what will happen to our children and our children's children if we don't. But few will be convinced to do it unless it fits in with life as it is. What does tend to happen, once a few delicious dinners have been made and plates licked clean, is that the enjoyment of cooking creeps in.

Devilled prawns

Very easy and brisk to make, a spiced dish of easy-to-buy North Atlantic prawns. To eat on toast, but also lovely with braised durum wheat grains, sometimes sold as Ebly, or pearled spelt, another wheat grain that can be boiled and eaten as rice. Or rice, of course.

SERVES 4

2 tablespoons extra virgin olive oil or butter
½ teaspoon yellow mustard seed
½ teaspoon black mustard seed
6 each of whole fennel seed, cumin seed and coriander seed
¼ teaspoon salt
¼–½ teaspoon cayenne pepper
2 medium onions, chopped
2 garlic cloves, sliced
400g/14oz cooked North Atlantic prawns, defrosted and drained on kitchen paper
4 firm plum tomatoes, quartered and pips removed, then sliced into strips

Heat the oil or butter, add the seeds, salt and cayenne pepper and fry until they make popping sounds. Add the onions and fry until pale gold, stirring. Add the garlic with the prawns (making sure all water is squeezed from them). When they are warmed through (remember, they are already cooked), stir in the tomatoes. Cook for another 1 minute, then serve.

Kitchen note

It is fine to be flexible with the seafood in this dish:

* Use raw tiger prawns, which are imported and sold frozen; there are serious sustainability, i.e. 'green', issues over these prawns, however. Organic tiger prawns are more costly but worthwhile. Cook until they become pink and opaque.

* Salmon – again, choose a fresh salmon from a trusted source. I buy wild Alaskan salmon from the supermarket, or farmed organic salmon: look for brands like Loch Duart or Glenarm who use sustainable farming methods. Cook the salmon briefly; I like it very slightly undercooked inside.

* Smoked undyed haddock – this easy-to-find fish will add a delicate smokiness.

* Fresh cooked, 'dressed' or picked brown crab – add the brown meat first and only stir in the white meat at the last minute.

Grilled bread

Good for many of the dishes on these pages, and especially for hungry people. Just one rule: use a good open-textured bread, either ciabatta, white or rye sourdough, or split baguettes. It is best to use a bread that will not collapse into a mush under something juicy, such as the devilled prawns above (see page 133). You will need a ridged grill pan. I invested in a small round one with a folding handle many years ago and have never regretted the £15 it cost.

Cut slices of bread about 1½cm/½in thick and brush with olive oil. Heat the pan and grill the bread on both sides until coloured and well toasted. Appetising charred lines should form: push the bread down with a spatula to make this happen. After grilling, rub each piece of bread with a halved garlic clove – if you wish. Keep it warm, wrapped in a cloth, until needed.

Goodness
It is easy, faced with thousands of different choices, to forget that food is sustenance – or fuel. There has been a long conflict in Western culture between nutritionists, who tell us what is good for us, and cookery writers, whose job is to tickle our senses. The two schools are not compatible. Cookery writers believe nutritionists to be killjoys, some of them highly bogus, and many nutritionists feel the liberal use of butter and red meat in recipes is irresponsible.

I read some nutritional advice with the same scepticism I view the existence of vampires in Transylvania. I just don't believe in 'superfoods', or accept that 'antioxidants' travel round the body zapping cancer cells. Much nutritional advice, the kind that brings on paranoia, is found in the women's pages of the media. It is no wonder with so many mixed messages that women feel uncomfortable about cooking. There is also well-founded suspicion over the relationship between science and big business, and that it stifles independent thought.

There is, though, such a thing as common-sense nutritional knowledge, which goes well with common-sense cooking. Slowly evolving food traditions, all over the world, can teach us much about what is really good for you. There is also a new school of free-thinking nutrition experts who have begun to question the old claims, and who have moved away from endorsing highly processed food in favour of whole ingredients. Every decent nutritionist will endorse a diet that is diverse, balanced and based on using fresh, raw materials. Even butter, one such ingredient, is getting a better write-up these days.

Not forgetting you

This chapter is also dedicated to your wellbeing, because you deserve good things, too – and quickly. The smaller, seemingly insignificant meals are the ones that literally shape us, and are much more important than the occasional 'showpiece' meal put on for guests. Yet we do not want to make a fuss about them. Parents' health can suffer, especially the mothers; putting others first, cooking for them and forgetting your own needs is an old tradition. Lots of parents suffer from this, tending to get the children's food out of the way, in a separate meal, then not feeding themselves properly – this is more so in Britain and the USA than elsewhere.

Likewise there are people who occasionally cook, dragging down a recipe book from the shelf and pulling off an awesome dinner party, yet who might exist on ready meals for the rest of the week, seeing cooking strictly as something to do for other people, or as a hobby. Acquiring the habit of shopping for a few essentials and cooking and eating something invigorating and delicious will make an enormous difference to the way you feel when you wake each morning. I think this is as much in our minds as it is genuinely physical – you are, quite simply, doing a kindness to you.

Top rump steak with tender herbs and warm olive oil sauce

see PLATE 10

A dish that will revive the iron levels of a flagging carnivore, and with an extra bonus. Top rump costs approximately half the price of a prime steak cut such as sirloin. Here it is cooked in the style of Italian tagliata: in a whole piece, left slightly underdone, then sliced, exposing the pink interior, and served beside a spinach salad and a fruity, green olive oil and caper sauce.

A 200g/7oz steak is plenty for each person; ask the butcher to cut slices across the grain of the rump, 2cm/¾in thick. There will be little fat but some membrane around the outer edge, which can be left on. Do not set out to make this thinking the sliced top rump will ever be as tender as fillet, but a well-hung cut will not give you too much to chew on. The thinner you slice the meat after grilling, the more successful this dish will be.

SERVES 2
2 x 200g/7oz top rump steaks (or rump, sirloin, skirt or feather steak)
black pepper

FOR THE SAUCE:
100ml/3 ½fl oz extra virgin olive oil
1 tablespoon green olive slivers, cut from green olives
1 teaspoon capers
juice of quarter of a lemon
2–3 tablespoons water, hot from the kettle and seasoned with salt to
    taste
2 small handfuls of baby spinach salad leaves, to serve

Warm a plate for each person. Season the steaks with a generous amount of pepper. Heat a grill pan and grill the steaks for 3 minutes each side over a medium-hot flame; you will see red droplets on the surface – indicating the inside is rare to medium rare.

Remove from the heat, place on a board and cover with foil. Rest for 10 minutes. Meanwhile, make the sauce, putting all the ingredients into a bowl and whisking to emulsify. Set to one side.

Cut the steaks into thin, 1cm/½in slices and arrange on the plates, side by side. The inner flesh of the steak slices should be pink. Scatter over the salad leaves and then zigzag a couple of tablespoons of the sauce over the top.

Kitchen note

Alternate the leaves with others, including herbs.

* Fresh dill leaves, and a salad made with thin slices of fennel marinated in lemon juice; add a teaspoon of Dijon mustard and a pinch of sugar to the dressing.
* Rocket – add shavings of a hard ewe's milk cheese (this is how these steaks are served in Italy, as tagliata). Choose from pecorino, Grana Padano and Lord of the Hundreds (a delicious, mature, English ewe's milk cheese).
* Microleaf salad – I can't help being fond of these infant herb and vegetable leaves, available from wholefood shops, specialist food markets, online and occasionally in supermarkets. They include red basil, Thai basil, borage, daikon, broccoli, shiso, rock chives, and – last but not least – good old mustard and cress.
* Grated roots and toasted nuts, marinated in lemon juice: either carrot, celeriac or beetroot. Add some toasted pine nuts, crushed

toasted hazelnuts or walnuts, or perhaps sautéed sunflower seeds.

* When it is cold, serve a hot vegetable: sautéed slices of Jerusalem artichoke, curly kale (be careful to drain it well and dress with butter), mange tout or green bobby or 'French' beans.

* If serving with hot vegetables, make a herb butter, combining tarragon, lemon juice and unsalted butter.

* Basil and coriander (if available, or use mustard and cress) – spoon a little sauce onto the side. A few parings of hard ewe's milk cheese, such as Lord of the Hundreds, will make a richer dish.

The mothers of speed

Like many people I was influenced by Nigel Slater, an honorary mother in my book, whose *Real Fast Food* (1992) was the first cookery book to address the dilemma of post-1950s cooks who wanted good food at a fast pace. Here at last was a book about the informal art of cooking, as impulsive as a picnic in the park on a hot surprise of a day; much, much more than baked beans on toast.

In *Appetite*, published eight years later (2000), Slater took his idea further, liberating cooking from the hard-and-fast rules of the prescriptive recipe writers and teaching readers how to use their instinct to substitute and improvise. The 'fast, warming bowl of soup for tonight, tomorrow, for now', with a base of chicken stock and noodles, might have a handful of spinach, but then you could add mustard greens, or tender cabbage. You choose. Add chicken, or don't; make a mushroom version if you like. This was cooking that was up to you. It had a blueprint, but it was one to build on.

Ricotta with broad beans

Ricotta was daring at the time but it has endured as a lovely ingredient to have in the kitchen for hurried, delicious, good-for-you food. In *Real Fast Food*, Slater wrote: '[Ricotta] must be very fresh if it is to be good, and there should be no yellowing around the edges, which indicates ageing. For me it is at its best when eaten as an accompaniment to baby broad beans. Just put the beans on the table with a lump of the ricotta, let everybody scoop up the cheese, and shell the beans, themselves.' This is dinner, stripped to nudity, but very pretty and nourishing. Not a recipe so much as a great idea.

Kitchen note

Outside the broad bean season, buy frozen broad beans, blanch in boiling water for no more than 1 minute, then drain and pop the individual green kernels out of the skins. It won't take long if you are feeding just 2 or 3 people, and, dressed with olive oil and put beside the ricotta, you can eat and dream of early summer.

Fast, warming bowl of soup

In *Appetite*, Slater called this a soup for tonight, tomorrow, for now, saying 'few suppers are so satisfying'. The base is chicken stock (see page 390) and noodles, and the seasoning comes from chilli and lemongrass. You can then add from a menu of good things. This recipe has been adapted so it can be done using one saucepan.

PER PERSON, USING THE BOWL AS A MEASURE
1 handful of dry egg noodles
chicken stock
small, red-hot chillies – 2–3 depending on your heat threshold
lemongrass – 2 thick blades from the stalk
1 handful of greens, either spinach, mustard greens or dark cabbage
salt

Boil some water in a pan and add the noodles. Cook until just tender
– about a minute or two for oriental noodles. Drain and drop into
cold water so they do not stick together.

Pour the desired amount of chicken stock into a pan. Use the bowl
you eat from as a measure, filling it full. Bring the stock to the boil.
Split the chillies in half and deseed to remove any aggressive heat.
Smash the lemongrass blades with the handle end of a kitchen knife
so they splinter but stay together. Add them to the hot stock with the
chillies. Turn down the heat so the stock bubbles gently. Cook for
about 15 minutes and taste to check that the lemongrass has given
up some of its flavour.

Fish out the lemongrass from the stock, and add the greens. Taste
and add salt. When the greens are soft – each type will take a
different time – remove the pan from the heat. Put some noodles in
the bottom of the bowl, ladle over the stock and serve.

AND MORE:
* Add shredded chicken or cooked prawns.
* Adjust seasoning: try chilli oil, lemon juice, nam pla (fish sauce),
  fresh coriander leaves, Thai basil.

* A very fragrant version: to the original recipe add a last-minute seasoning of torn basil leaves, mint leaves and lime juice.
* A deeper spicing: add star anise, sugar and nam pla (fish sauce).
* A mushroom soup: slice or quarter a few mushrooms per person. Fry in a wok (or in the pan before you use it to heat the stock) with garlic until nutty. Add to the noodles with the stock.

Les salades/Insalata

Now to the recipes of the mothers of France and Italy, who with the flick of a hand can throw classic ingredients into a bowl, add dressing or just a shower of olive oil and make an edible mosaic to eat for lunch or supper.

Léa's leaves and fried bread, with a smoked-herring dressing

see PLATE 11

A sustaining salad beloved of post-war Lyon where it was served in La Voute, the restaurant run by mère Léa. Léa is known as the last great mère de Lyon, the mother cooks whose home cooking was beloved not just by their families but by the customers who packed their restaurants. Léa did her own shopping in the market each morning, dragging round a hand cart, wanting everything 'just picked'. She would go into the dining room herself and announce the specials. She did not allow argument or criticism. Her motto was 'weak woman, powerful mouth', acknowledging – in the context of the time she lived in – that she may have been the weaker sex but in her palate she had a powerful ability to recognise good flavour. Her salade would have been made with pissenlits – dandelion leaves. I rarely see these slightly bitter leaves in shops, though I occasionally pick wild ones in spring, but any slightly fibrous salad leaf is fine.

SERVES 4
8 eggs
1 teaspoon butter
1 kipper fillet
2 tablespoons white wine vinegar
2 tablespoons extra virgin olive oil
8 slices of baguette, a day old, or slightly dry ciabatta
4 handfuls of salad leaves (rocket, spinach, mustard, chard, cos, frisee), washed and patted dry

FOR THE DRESSING:
1 garlic clove, crushed with the back of a knife and peeled
5 tablespoons extra virgin olive oil
pinch of sugar
1 tablespoon red wine vinegar
2 tablespoons flat-leaf parsley, chopped
sea salt and black pepper

Prick each eggshell carefully with a pin at the rounded end and put in a pan of cold water (this stops them cracking during cooking). Bring to the boil and cook for 5 minutes. Put the eggs in cold water to cool. Combine the dressing ingredients in a cup and set to one side.

Melt the butter in a pan, add the kipper fillet and cook on both sides until the flesh begins to flake. Remove from the heat and separate the flesh from any bone or skin. Mash to a paste on a plate with the vinegar.

Clean out the pan and add the oil, then fry the bread on both sides. When it is golden, lift it out and cut into rough cubes. Add the kipper paste to the dressing, and mix well. Remove the garlic clove and discard. Peel and quarter the eggs. Put the leaves in a bowl, add the dressing and mix. Scatter the fried bread and the egg quarters over the surface and serve.

Kitchen note

This salad can be made using anchovy and olives in place of kippers. Cook 8 anchovies and 12 halved, pitted black olives in the butter, mashing them with a fork once done.

Too busy not to cook

The favourite excuse, when someone explains to me why they do not cook, is always 'I'm too busy.' It has always been a difficult one to argue with. Managing the time you have, including that which is 'spare', that is, when not employed, is personal. At the first sign of being bossed into changing the way we live, most of us react badly. Our time is our time, to arrange in a way that suits us. The more persuasive argument for adding cooking to an already hectic life has to be one that does not make a busy person feel guilty. Cooking can in fact remove the guilt felt at not giving enough time to family. This was perfectly articulated to me recently by Drusilla Beyfus. A successful journalist for over fifty years, author and a former magazine editor, Beyfus is also a mother of three. She explained that, being married to the theatre critic Milton Shulman, cooking was the way to enjoy conversation with him at the end of the day. In other words, a cooked meal bought a bit of time, because he was at work most evenings. 'Supper for most daily newspaper theatre critics would be a glass of beer and a sandwich,' she says. 'But I would always cook at ten thirty in the evening, after we returned from the theatre, otherwise there would have been no time to chat.' Under pressure to achieve so much in one day, it becomes hard to know when to stop. Yet oddly, adding one more task – cooking – gives a quiet moment back to the day. I find this utterly convincing and persuasive. Beyfus admits she 'made lists' to make this and the other cooking she did for her children possible. She also had to find recipes that could be prepared in minutes, recipes that were much more than a cheese sandwich, like the following juicy mushroom encounter.

Giant baked mushrooms, on toast

Ideal for supper, any time of the evening, and made with easy to buy ingredients, these pan-cooked mushrooms make their own delicious dark savoury liquid as they cook, lovely when it soaks into the waiting, hot buttered toast. Add the parsley, Beyfus says, only if you have the energy and will. The same mushroom dish is good also with sausages, or grilled gammon.

SERVES 2
2 tablespoons olive oil
4 large flat mushrooms, wiped, with stalk trimmed but left on
4 heaped teaspoons butter
salt and black pepper
1 garlic clove, chopped
To serve: finely chopped parsley (optional), hot buttered toast

Heat the oil in a frying pan big enough to hold all 4 mushrooms. Put in the mushrooms, stalk up, with a teaspoon of butter on each. Season with a little salt and pepper. Scatter over the garlic, add 2 tablespoons of water, cover with a lid and cook for 5–6 minutes. Remove from the heat, and lift the lid. The mushrooms should be tender and quite translucent, and will have shrunk in size. If they need more cooking, place back on the heat and cook uncovered for another minute or two.

Jacqueline's tomato and olive oil

see PLATE 11

Back in the holidays of my childhood, in Jacqueline's kitchen. The secret of this tomato salad is to peel the tomatoes first, and remove the watery spawn of pips. It takes only a few minutes and not only will dull, not as ripe as they should be tomatoes be deified beyond expectation, the absence of skin allows the oil to work its way into their flesh. Lovely on bread, toast or pasta.

SERVES 4
16 medium tomatoes
8 tablespoons extra virgin olive oil
salt

OPTIONAL:
20 pitted black olives, chopped
2 tablespoons capers, rinsed, dried and chopped
2 shallots, sliced
4 tablespoons chopped herbs: chives, mint, parsley or basil

Nick each tomato skin with a knife, scoring a line around the circumference of the tomato but not cutting much deeper than the skin. Put in a bowl that will easily take all the tomatoes and pour boiling water over to cover. Leave for 2 minutes. If the tomatoes are very hard and a bit under-ripe, leave for another minute. The skins will begin to curl away from the flesh. Drain the tomatoes in a colander then peel and quarter them, and remove and discard the pips. Dress with the oil and salt, and additional ingredients, if using. Allow to sit for about 10–20 minutes before eating.

Bread and tomatoes - the Tuscan mothers

Shocking as it may be to the gap-year generation, I never travelled out of Britain or France until I was nearly thirty, preferring to spend my holidays at my grandmother's home. After she died, a trip to Italy was a shock of pleasure. I stayed with an English friend who lived on a farm in Tuscany. I was smitten, not immediately with Italy, since I still pined for the table on the terrace at La Ferme Blanche, but with the southern Tuscan bread, made without salt, that tastes only of the grain and wild leaven. Bought fresh and biteable each morning, it was approaching chewy by supper-time. The next day you had to attack with the bread knife, sawing powerfully, trying not to chop your own fingers off. Slices were then soaked into soups or this salad. Made by the Tuscan mothers in every house in the area, it is a good use for ageing bread.

SERVES 4

1 loaf open-textured bread, preferably a day old; use ciabatta, white
    sourdough or saltless Italian-style bread if you can get it
8 tomatoes, preferably peeled (see Jacqueline's tomatoes, page 146)
2 tablespoons capers, rinsed, dried and chopped
1 garlic clove, chopped
2 tablespoons red wine vinegar
8 tablespoons extra virgin olive oil
leaves from 2 sprigs basil

Toast the bread in the toaster until golden then tear into pieces. Put
in a bowl. Chop the tomatoes, retaining the seeds and juice, and add
to the bowl. Add the capers, garlic and vinegar and mix well. Dress
with the oil, scatter over the basil and mix again. Leave for 10
minutes to soak before eating. I like it just as much the next day.

Chickpeas and rocket

I am one of the many thousands who love the food writer Anna del Conte's recipes, and so she needs very little introduction. She is the mother of Italian cooking for British cooks who wanted to stray away occasionally from typical, classic Italian cooking into a new territory of ideas. I believe she has an artist's eye, because everything she makes is a picture. When she called her 1989 book *Secrets of an Italian Kitchen*, it perfectly expressed that sum of achievable, practical, creative recipes which I am always searching for. Recipes that work, but which either break new imaginative boundaries or which have been lost and need rediscovery. Del Conte came across lemon risotto, now very much in the Anglo-Italian cooking vernacular, and panzanella, a peppery version of the bread salad above (see page 147). She made a famous apple cake using olive oil – this became the most food-splattered page in my old copy of her book.

Her chickpea and rocket salad was ahead of its time. Rocket was hard to get in the late 1980s and very expensive, but now it is easy to buy along with conventional lettuce. With the yellow, nutty flavour of chickpeas and a kick from the garlic, this is a reviving salad I turn to again and again.

SERVES 4
2 x 400g/14oz cans chickpeas, drained
5 tablespoons extra virgin olive oil
2 garlic cloves, crushed with the back of a knife and peeled
100g/3½oz rocket leaves (about 2 handfuls)
sea salt and black pepper

Squeeze the skin off each chickpea – this, Conte says, is quicker and easier than it sounds (with practice) and makes a difference to the way the peas taste, removing a slight bitterness, and helps with the absorption of the oil. If you do not have the time, it is not a crime to leave the skins on.

Heat the oil with the garlic in a pan. When the oil simmers and begins to give off the fragrance of the garlic, remove the garlic and discard it. Add the chickpeas and warm them in the oil. Remove from the heat and leave to cool. Transfer to a bowl and mix with the rocket; add salt to taste and some freshly ground black pepper.

Kitchen note
You can add other ingredients to this, including some fresh ricotta cheese or fresh goat's curd, chopped pitted black olives or good-quality skipjack or albacore/yellow-fin tuna fish from a tin or jar.

Bitter leaves, parsley and warm black pudding

In winter I love to eat leaves from pink and green chicory, radicchio and other wan endives that have been grown in the dark. They are a good seasonal choice as they are grown all over northern Europe, and they last for a long time, stored in the fridge. This salad, a poem of delicate colours, is one I make often. Based on another French mother-cook standard, salade Lyonnaise, you can be quite flexible about the base ingredients. The mustard in the dressing is, I believe, essential. The potato is optional but makes the salad economical as it can be served as a main dish.

SERVES 4

FOR THE DRESSING:

1 heaped teaspoon Dijon mustard

½ teaspoon sugar ·

¼ teaspoon sea salt

1 garlic clove, crushed with the back of a knife and peeled

1 tablespoon red wine vinegar

6 tablespoons olive oil

2 tablespoons water

4 medium potatoes, boiled in their skins until just tender

4 rashers smoked streaky bacon

a length of black pudding about 20cm/8in long, or two small Spanish 'morcilla' – look for non-fatty ones

4 handfuls of leaves from chicory (pink and/or white), endives, radicchio (look for 'treviso' type) or Italian 'puntarelle'

2–3 tablespoons chopped flat-leaf parsley

Put all the dressing ingredients in a jar with a tight-fitting lid. Close the lid and shake until you have a smooth, greenish-yellow dressing. Taste and adjust the salt or vinegar to your preference. Leave for about 15 minutes to infuse the garlic. Remove the garlic clove before using.

Cut the potato into cubes and put in a large bowl. Dry-fry the bacon rashers in a pan over a low heat until crisp, then remove and drain on paper or a cloth. Split the black pudding open lengthways and remove the skin. Sauté the whole piece (or cut in half to fit the pan) in the bacon fat over a low heat until quite crisp. Remove from the heat and drain. Cut into chunks and tear the bacon into shards and put in a bowl with the potato. Cut or tear the leaves into strips then add to the bowl with the parsley. Finally, pour over the dressing. Mix well and serve immediately.

Roast peppers

There was a moment in the early 1990s when everyone was crazy about roast peppers. On every menu, dressed with olive oil, they introduced the concept of a sweet pepper that actually lived up to its name. There was a small problem in that they tended to be delicious in restaurants but were less easy to cook at home. The classic method of charring them on a flame is not practical, and the Dutch peppers that seem to monopolise shops did not roast well when left whole. I fiddled about with them after cooking, furiously picking out seeds that had become embedded in burnt, sticky flesh; they also seemed extremely difficult to peel. But then I experimented at little.

By cutting each red pepper in half (yellow and green are not so good for roasting), removing the stalk and seeds and then placing them inner-side down in a roasting pan, on a sheet of oiled foil, I found they took just 20 minutes to roast in a high oven and that the thin flesh of the Dutch peppers did not dry out. Putting them into either a plastic bag or container with a lid afterwards helped the burnt outer skins to lift. Removing them from the bag, it is a quick job to pull the burnt skin off with your fingers. The result: vibrant orangey-red fillets of pepper, with slight dark flavoursome bruisings from the heat of the oven.

My mother loved roast peppers, and would lay them on a dish side by side until it was completely blanketed with soft, silky fillets of pepper. She then dressed them with extra virgin olive oil, and scattered chopped hard-boiled egg white over them. Next she added the hard-boiled egg yolks, crumbling them finely by pushing through a sieve (the French call this 'mimosa'), followed by a handful of chopped flat-leaf parsley. If you like eggs, I still think this is the nicest of all ways to eat roast peppers. It gives them a soothing richness. My, they seem so old-fashioned, now . . .

Salmagundi

Just to reassure that English provincial cookery can be as good as French or Italian, I look back at seventeenth- and eighteenth-century British cookery writers. Plainness in British cookery has been a curse, an excuse for other nations to giggle and point, but the pre-industrial and pre-agricultural revolution cooks were adventurous with flavour. Hannah Glasse was the saviour of many eighteenth-century cooks. Her published recipes were artful yet simple, relying on good fresh produce and many were designed not to wear out a busy home cook. Poor Glasse had a fraught life. She was the illegitimate daughter of a gentleman; she knew fine food but she had to earn a living. She married a feckless penniless man and endured terrible financial difficulties, including bankruptcy, and was sent to a debtors' gaol. Her best book, *The Art of Cookery Made Plain and Easy*, is wonderfully clearly written and full of recipes which were far from plain in aromatic terms, and often simple to do.

Glasse was acutely tuned to the struggle that other women faced in the kitchen, and came to the rescue with recipes that were both possible and often visually delicious. Salmagundi is a beautiful layered salad of leaves, herbs, boiled eggs and cold meat dressed with a piquant dressing. A definite precursor to Caesar salad, yet you can be more flexible in what you add to it. 'You may always make a salamongundy [sic] of such things as you have, according to your fancy,' wrote Glasse. My version can be varied, too, and I always add anchovies to the dressing, rather than leave them whole in the salad.

SERVES 4
FOR THE DRESSING:
8 canned anchovies, drained of their oil and very finely chopped
2 teaspoons Dijon mustard (or other that you prefer)
pinch of sugar
1 garlic clove, crushed with the back of a knife and peeled
juice of 1 lemon
8 tablespoons olive oil
¼ teaspoon sea salt

FOR THE SALAD:
4 handfuls of salad leaves – cos (romaine), spinach, watercress,
    mustard leaf, rocket, chard, mizuna or a mixture (in winter use
    chicory, endives, very finely shredded red cabbage)
cold meat from 4 whole roasted or poached chicken legs or breasts,
    sliced – substitute smoked chicken, roast duck, roast pheasant, roast
    mallard, roast quail halves
2 tablespoons herb leaves: tarragon and/or basil, chives, dill, chervil
2 tablespoons capers, washed and left whole
2 tablespoons cornichons (or larger gherkins), sliced
2 tablespoons golden sultanas
4 whole eggs, boiled for about 6 minutes then cooled, peeled and
    halved – substitute quail eggs, duck eggs, pheasant eggs
To serve: edible flowers (optional: a Glasse touch)

Put all the dressing ingredients in a jar and shake until well mixed.
Leave for a few minutes for the garlic to infuse, and remove the
clove before using.

Layer the salad on a big plate, beginning with the leaves, following with the rest of the ingredients, except the eggs and flowers. Pour over the dressing – after discarding the garlic – finish with the egg halves and place the flowers, if using, around the edge.

Cooks to grow up with

Its dusky, pink cloth cover with sloping gilt writing on the spine still haunts my own kitchen. Constance Spry's cookery book's 1230 pages contained more recipes than could probably be cooked in a lifetime. Nor would you want to try some of the aspics and chaud froid chicken (a buffet dish glazed with jellified béchamel). But my mother picked out a number that she liked, and we lived by them. The Belvoir ginger cake came on every picnic, the drop scones were a tea-time treat; the sweetcorn fritters a part of the wonderfully indulgent Maryland chicken, the Victoria sponge, the toffee pudding . . . I have used these recipes in my previous books, but forgot about that old curiosity, Coronation chicken.

Coronation chicken

I make no apologies for loving this faux curried chicken salad served cold. It is one of those dishes, like kedgeree, that is somehow right, though ought to be wrong. Created for Queen Elizabeth II's coronation, CC has morphed into a sickly horror, when in fact the original has a lighter, tarter sauce and is totally free of soggy sultanas. A little goes a long way – I like a little heap of the creamy spicy mixture served on shredded crisp lettuce, a sort of chicken cocktail . . .

SERVES 6–8

1 large cooked chicken – poached or roasted, and cooled
1 tablespoon groundnut or sunflower oil
1 onion, finely chopped or grated
1 dessertspoon curry powder (medium or hot, as you wish)
1 teaspoon tomato purée
1 wineglass red wine
1 wineglass water
1–2 tablespoons chopped dried apricots
1 bay leaf
pinch of salt
pinch of sugar
¼ teaspoon ground white pepper
juice of half a lemon
250ml/9fl oz mayonnaise (homemade or good ready-made fresh
    mayonnaise)
3 tablespoons whipping cream
leaves from 2 sprigs coriander
1 teaspoon nigella seed (optional)

Remove the meat from the chicken and set to one side. Heat the oil
in a pan and add the onion. Cook gently for 3 minutes, then add the
curry powder. Cook for another 2 minutes. Add the tomato purée,
wine, water, apricots and bay leaf and bring to the boil. Add the salt,
sugar and pepper plus the lemon juice then simmer for 5–10
minutes. Strain and cool. Add the curry essence slowly to the
mayonnaise, then fold in the cream. Taste and add more salt if
necessary. Add the chicken, and stir until well coated, then serve
with the coriander and nigella seeds scattered on top.

Peas, more peas and fennel mayonnaise

Another delicious retro salad which is filling enough to eat on its own, or serve it with ham. Sometimes I serve it in a 'bowl' made by opening out a round lettuce.

Slice 1 fennel bulb thinly then chop roughly into bite-sized pieces. Place in a large bowl with some lemon juice. Boil a large pan of water and add 2 handfuls of mange tout. Boil for 1 minute, leave them in the pan and add 450g/1lb frozen petits pois. As soon as the water comes back to the boil, drain the peas and mange tout and immediately refresh with cold water under the tap. Put in a salad bowl and add enough mayonnaise (homemade or good-quality fresh ready-made) to make a rich sloppy salad. If you can find pea shoots (sold in some supermarkets or available online), scatter a handful over the top. A few fennel leaves from the bulb will also be pretty. I sometimes pick up a pot of bronze fennel and plant it in the garden. It shoots up into a 1-metre/3-foot-high source of coppery, frothy leaves – lovely in salads. Substitute fennel leaves or pea shoots with mustard and cress.

Celeriac remoulade with smoked haddock tartare

The classic French salad of grated celeriac, tarragon, capers and mayonnaise, twisted with the wood-smoke flavour of cured raw haddock.

SERVES 4

1 celeriac, grated
250ml/9fl oz mayonnaise (homemade or good ready-made fresh
    mayonnaise)
2 tablespoons whipping cream
2 tablespoons capers, rinsed, dried and chopped
leaves from 6 sprigs tarragon
450g/1lb undyed smoked haddock, off the bone
juice of 1 lemon
slices of pumpernickel bread, to serve

Combine the celeriac with the mayonnaise, cream, capers and tarragon. Slice the haddock as thinly as possible and mix it in a small bowl with the lemon juice. Add to the salad and eat on slices of nutty dark pumpernickel.

Butter beans, olive oil, black olive paste, parsley and courgettes

I can usually buy all the ingredients for this earthy, sustaining salad in my local late-night shop – fresh courgettes are a must.

SERVES 4

2 courgettes
juice of 1 lemon
¼ teaspoon sea salt
1 x 400g/14oz can butter beans
1 heaped tablespoon black olive paste (tapenade)
6 tablespoons extra virgin olive oil
leaves from 6 sprigs flat-leaf parsley, chopped

Trim the courgettes and cut them in half lengthways, then slice each one across very thinly with a potato peeler to make thin half-moon shapes. Put in a bowl with the lemon juice and salt and leave for a few minutes. Drain the butter beans and combine with the olive paste and the oil. Mix well and add the parsley with the courgettes. Mix again, turning everything in the bowl over and over so all is well coated with the dressing.

Tuna and coconut – Indian Ocean breakfast

This time it is the secrets of Maldivian fishermen to share, picked up when on an assignment for the *Telegraph* magazine. We ate this for breakfast on a dhoni (fishing boat) while hunting for yellow-fin tuna. In vain, as it turned out. Eat it rolled up in roti, chapatti or flour tortilla wrap. Toast the breads in a dry frying pan first, to freshen.

SERVES 4
2 limes
250g/9oz canned tuna meat, drained of oil or brine and flaked
either the grated meat of 1 fresh coconut or 150g/5½oz desiccated
    coconut, soaked in 200ml/7fl oz boiling water
2–3 red or green chillies, deseeded and finely chopped
leaves from 3 sprigs mint, chopped (optional)

Pare the peel from the limes with a peeler and cut out and chop the segments, holding the fruit over a bowl to catch the juice. Add the segments, the tuna meat, the coconut, chillies and mint to the bowl, mix well and serve.

Summer green vegetables with olive oil

A dish to make in a pan then eat at room temperature, on grilled bread with perhaps a spoonful of fresh goat's curd.

SERVES 4

4 tablespoons extra virgin olive oil, plus more for finishing
1 courgette, cut into small dice
1 celery stick with leaves, chopped very small
1 bunch of asparagus, chopped into bite-sized pieces
1 garlic clove, chopped
1 wineglass white wine
2 handfuls of podded broad beans
2 handfuls of podded garden peas, defrosted frozen peas or petits
    pois
salt
leaves from 2 sprigs mint

Heat the oil in a pan and add the courgette, celery and asparagus. Sauté for a few minutes but do not let the vegetables brown. Add the garlic and cook for half a minute more then pour in the wine and cook for 3 minutes until the asparagus is just becoming tender but not quite cooked. Add the beans and peas, simmer for 2 minutes and remove from the heat. Tip into a bowl, add a splash more olive oil to cool the dish. Season with salt. Dress with the mint leaves when the vegetables reach room temperature.

French bean vinaigrette with shallots

I listen out for cooking advice, one ear on elastic even when a totally different conversation is taking place. Sometimes another cook will tell, in perhaps one vital phrase, the right way to do something. Miss it, and you will never know. That is what I worry about. Once I was watching the chef and food writer Simon Hopkinson, of *Roast Chicken and Other Stories* fame, preparing a dish of French beans to go with – yes! – a roast chicken. He nearly threw away a line, but I have been forever grateful to have picked it up. 'Cook French beans until they no longer squeak when you bite them,' he said. Like mice, I thought. And have never forgotten. Some vegetables are always served undercooked, to preserve the greenness; others are boiled far too long. Hopkinson's secret is the middle way.

SERVES 4–6
FOR THE VINAIGRETTE:
1 tablespoon Dijon mustard
1 teaspoon sugar
6 tablespoons extra virgin olive oil
1 garlic clove, crushed with a back of a knife and peeled
1 tablespoon water or single cream (to temper the strength of the
     dressing)
pinch of salt
pinch of ground white pepper

1kg/2lb4oz French beans
1 teaspoon salt
6 small pink shallots
a few microleaf herbs, or some mustard and cress, to serve (optional)

Put all the dressing ingredients into a jar and shake until well amalgamated. Leave for 30 minutes and then remove the garlic clove, discarding it.

Snip the stalk ends from the beans, but leave the pointy tips alone. They are edible, and I think the beans look nicer prepared this way. Put the beans in a pan of boiling water, add the salt and cook for 6–8 minutes, depending on thickness. They are done when just tender and do not 'squeak' when bitten. Drain and refresh with cold water. Tip onto a clean teacloth so all excess water is absorbed, then put in a bowl. Add the dressing and mix well.

Cut the shallots in half lengthways and peel off the skins. Cut into quarters and then slice very thinly. Scatter over the beans, followed by the microleaf herbs or cress (if using). Eat immediately or later – it doesn't matter.

Pots

Men and women have very different ideas about presenting food, especially if it is their profession. I am always struck that the more macho the chef and the worse his bullying, the louder he shouts and swears, the more camp the décor and garnish on the plate of food he presents. This is very typical of the type of chefs who chase Michelin stars. Their kitchens are highly stressed and this stress is translated into the food, with every teetering, wobbling leaf, delicate tuile, smear of sauce or dribble of bubbling foam. Women cooks, even the best, tend to say to hell with that, let's not gussy it up – then throw the herbs at the plate. It is also true that male chefs who prefer to cook the kind of food women find practical in the home, yet which can be wonderful to eat in restaurants, tend also to let well alone, and allow the food to 'decorate itself'.

Often women take this to a new place with their love of pretty china and pottery. Most women who love to cook enjoy buying utensils (while it is true to say that electric gadgets and swanky gas barbecues seem to speak to men). I speak for myself when I say that we gravitate towards the window displays of kitchen shops like flies to a bug zapper. Nothing is nicer to have in my hands than a new pot. There is a warm pleasure in serving a simple dish on a special plate.

I collect pots and china. I do not buy sets but pick up one or two at a time if they are 'new' or nose about in charity shops and markets looking for old. I have never owned a set of china. I tried, when we married, by putting some china on our 'wedding list'. A gravy boat, four side plates and a teapot arrived. The shop tried to make us spend £400 to complete the set. I am afraid I sent the lot back and swapped them for some flower pots.

I like to imagine, when I find things, what I will put in them. I have memories of certain pots that are associated with the food of my childhood. If I see a ramekin, I think of potted shrimps or egg mousse, grown-up dinner parties and bridge tables. If I see those little pot-bellied white ones, I can picture a little chicken liver pâté and a silver toast rack.

Pots of goodness

But little pots of food are not necessarily overtly grand. There is sense in making a rough chicken liver pâté (see below) and packing it into individual pots, because they keep well, untouched, until needed. These are things to delve into, gratefully, longing for something more interesting than eggs and bacon. With a pile of hot buttered toast, these pots of goodness are just as happy on a tray on your knee as on the double damask cloth.

Piquant chicken-liver pots

A rough pâté, similar to a famous Tuscan appetiser; incredibly easy to make and delicious with the rounded, intense flavour of the anchovy and capers. Try to buy free-range chicken livers.

MAKES 4–6 SMALL POTS, EACH FOR ONE PERSON
2 tablespoons butter
6 shallots, finely chopped
12 chicken livers, trimmed of ducts and left whole
10 anchovy fillets
2 tablespoons capers, rinsed
1 wineglass red wine
sea salt and black pepper

TO FINISH:
4 tablespoons salted butter, softened
2 tablespoons finely chopped flat-leaf parsley
1 tablespoon finely chopped chives

Melt the butter over a medium heat, add the shallots and cook for about 5 minutes until pale gold and sweet. Add the chicken livers and cook, stirring, until browned. Add the anchovies and capers and cook for a further minute, then add the wine. Allow the wine to boil for about 30 seconds, stirring the contents of the pan, then season with a pinch of salt and some pepper. Tip the contents of the pan onto a wooden board and chop finely (any liquid should be absorbed as you chop the ingredients).

Fill the pots with the mixture, packing it down inside, leaving at least 5mm/¼in space at the top. Clean the board, then put the softened butter on it and use a knife to blend it with the herbs. Spread a little of this butter on top of each pot. It will help preserve the contents and you can take a little to spread on hot toast with the pâté ` underneath. Cover the pots with clingfilm or foil to store them. They will keep for up to a week.

Kitchen note
You can use duck liver, rabbit liver and pork liver, but always make sure the liver is either very fresh, or was frozen when very fresh, otherwise the pâté will be dry.

Porcini pots

A wonderful pâté with forest aromas, nice to eat on hot bread but also good to heap onto a grilled steak or piece of chicken. The pots keep in the fridge for up to 10 days.

SERVES 4

100g/3 ½oz dried porcini mushrooms, soaked in boiling water
6 tablespoons extra virgin olive oil
2 garlic cloves, finely chopped
leaves from 1 sprig thyme
½ teaspoon dried oregano
½ teaspoon ground coriander seed
sea salt and black pepper

Drain the porcini, reserving the liquid, then chop the mushrooms finely. Warm the oil in a pan and add the garlic, porcini, thyme, oregano and coriander. Fry over a low temperature, so as not to spoil the oil. When the mixture becomes fragrant and the garlic has softened, add 4 tablespoons of the mushroom liquid and cook until it is reduced by two-thirds. Season with salt and pepper then spoon the mixture into 4 small pots. Allow to cool, and serve. Or refrigerate, covered with clingfilm, until needed.

Hot haddock and saffron pots

Inspired by the widow of a Brighton fisherman who drowned at sea.
Much later Linda married her husband's closest friend, Jack Mills.
Together this adorable couple run a smokehouse on the beach below the
esplanade, where they hand out heavenly grilled smoked mackerel
sandwiches (easy to make, incidentally). When I returned home after
meeting the Millses, I made these heart-warming little pots for supper
and ate them with fried bread.

SERVES 4

20 new potatoes
450g/1lb undyed smoked haddock fillet
450ml/¾ pint crème fraiche
8 saffron strands
4 rashers smoked streaky bacon, sautéed until crisp, then roughly
    chopped
1 tablespoon chopped chives or chervil (optional)

Preheat the oven to 200°C/400°F/Gas 6.

Boil the potatoes until just tender, then refresh in cold water and
slice. Pack into 4 medium-sized ramekins or pots. Cut the haddock
into bite-sized pieces and put on top of the potatoes. Heat the crème
fraiche with the saffron then divide it among the pots. Bake for
15 minutes, until bubbling. Serve, scattered with bacon and herbs.

Pans

When my children leave home, I will buy each a good frying pan.
I can see them now, scarlet-faced, unpacking it in front of new room
mates. They will thank me, in the end. So perhaps will their friends.
The secret of successful sautéed dishes relies on a heavy base. Put
another, nicer way, the thickness of the base of a pan evenly
distributes high heat, making it possible to cook quickly without
scorching the food. 'Hard anodised' pans, which have a non-stick
surface baked onto chunky inexpensive metal, have now made pans
that perform well affordable. They are a perfect first pan for any new
cook.

The simple idea of sautéing needs a step-by-step approach. It is not a
good idea to sauté all the ingredients at once. Imagine you are
building the meal in the pan, beginning with the ingredients that
need the longer cooking time, then adding more, finishing with those
that need the least time. It is all quite obvious, really, but this way
everything will be correctly timed, and cooked perfectly.

I make many fast meals this way. The challenge is to choose
ingredients that need only a little trim before going, raw, into the
pan. If you have to start parboiling items, you will be at the cooker
for longer, and have more than one pan to wash.

Crisp smoked bacon, polenta cubes, bittersweet chicory

see PLATE 12

Strong, contrasting flavours of precious endives with the comfort and economy of polenta.

SERVES 4

8 rashers smoked streaky bacon, cut into small pieces
2 tablespoons extra virgin olive oil
450g/1lb ready-cooked polenta (see page 55), cut into 2cm/¾in dice
2 chicory (red or green), cut lengthways into strips
leaves from 2 sprigs flat-leaf parsley
salt and black pepper

Sauté the bacon until crisp in a frying pan over a medium heat, allowing it to cook in its own fat. Remove from the pan with a slotted spoon and place on a warm plate. Add the oil to the pan and sauté the polenta cubes, turning them carefully with a wooden spatula so they crisp a little. Add the chicory towards the end of cooking, and return the bacon to the pan. Stir-fry a little, and serve the dish when the leaves have begun to wilt and soften. Add the parsley, season and serve.

Kitchen note
You can use other bittersweet endives – choose from witloof chicory, chicoria, puntarelle, frisee . . .

Sausage with shredded spring greens and apple

Use a meaty, well-seasoned spicy or garlic sausage. Cumberland or Toulouse sausages are ideal for this inexpensive dish, which can be eaten at any time of year.

SERVES 4

4 tablespoons extra virgin olive oil

4–8 large sausages, skinned and sliced

a few rosemary leaves

4 garlic cloves, chopped

2 heads of spring greens or hispi cabbage, shredded into very thin strips

2 dessert apples, cored and sliced

4 tablespoons dry cider, wine or stock

Heat the oil and stir-fry the sausage meat with the rosemary over a medium-high heat. Remove from the pan with a slotted spoon and keep warm. Add the garlic, greens and apple to the pan and cook over a lower heat until the greens are tender. Add the cider, wine or stock and bring to the boil. Pile the sausage meat on top and put the whole pan on the table. Good with boiled potatoes (see page 47).

Pan-fried plaice with lettuce hearts and lemon

see PLATE 13

The gentle, easy flavour of plaice, with the sweet taste of sautéed lettuce hearts, sharpened a little with lemon. Use cos or romaine hearts, or the lovely, ever so English, soft and floppy butterhead lettuce.

SERVES 4
2–3 tablespoons butter
8 skinless fillets cut from 2 plaice (ask the fishmonger to do this)
salt and black pepper
4 lettuce hearts, cut into quarters
juice of 1 lemon

Have ready 4 warmed plates. Heat the butter in a large frying pan until it foams. Season the plaice fillets with salt and pepper and lower each one gently into the butter. Add the lettuce hearts to the pan, cut-side down – finding space for them between the fillets. Cook for 1–2 minutes then turn the fish and the lettuce. When the fish is opaque and slightly firm, remove from the pan and divide among the plates. Continue to cook the lettuce in the butter for a minute or two more; lift out of the pan with a slotted spoon and divide among the plates. Add the lemon juice to the pan and heat through. Spoon a little over each plate.

Kitchen note
Substitute the plaice with any of the sole family, or use fillets of white fish like ling, hake or pollock.

Fast

Pan-fried parsnips and 'mountain' cheese

Parsnips cook well from scratch, in a pan. Serve with a smooth-textured, nutty-flavoured 'mountain' cheese like St Gall from Ireland or a European equivalent (see below). A winter supper that warms from the inside out.

SERVES 4
4 medium parsnips, cut into sticks no more than 1cm/½in thickness
4 tablespoons extra virgin olive oil
1 sprig rosemary
225g/8oz St Gall cheese (you can use Cantal, Comte, Gouda, Emmental or Gruyère)

Sauté the parsnips in the oil with the rosemary until golden and cooked through. Put the parsnips in a dish; shave the cheese into strips using a potato peeler and lay on top. The contents of the dish should be hot so the cheese melts. Eat straight away.

The mother of all breakfasts – scrambled eggs

Breakfasts on Saturdays, when there is less of a morning rush and the phone is quiet, are the time for the best scrambled eggs in the world.

My stepfather Teddy used to cook them this way, to eat as part of the mother of all breakfasts. The secret is in melting the butter with the eggs.

Make sure you have the toast on the go, and all other accompanying breakfast foods are ready to serve. Scrambled eggs need to be served slightly runny. They continue to cook until spooned out of the pan, so do not expect them to sit happily waiting for the bacon to crisp up or the toast to pop.

I allow 2 eggs or more per person. For every 2 eggs add about 1 teaspoon of butter. Put the eggs and the butter in a non-stick pan – do not add water or milk to bulk the quantity. It is cheating and you will be caught out as, once cooked, a thin whey-type liquid seeps from the egg onto the toast. Disgusting.

Beat the eggs with a small whisk, taking care not to scratch the pan, then place the pan over a low heat. Stir until all the butter melts. Add a pinch of sea salt. When you are ready to scramble, turn up the heat. Continue to stir the eggs. As they cook and thicken on the bottom of the pan, scrape and stir at the same time. The eggs will scramble to a thick rich mass. While they are still reasonably runny, spoon them onto toast, or plates.

Kitchen note

Scrambled eggs are not just for breakfast but can be eaten in imaginative ways at other times of the day.

* Cold as an appetiser on toast, with chopped chives.
* With sautéed chillies, and a few rocket leaves.
* With smoked fish, warmed in a pan, and a watercress salad.
* With sautéed white pudding, and cooked, buttered spinach.

Escalopes - hammered meat

Not every cut of meat will be tender after sautéing both sides. The method rules out many cheap cuts. The Italians have got around this problem. Markets sell meat hammers to tenderise meat, and kitchens ring with the sound of the mothers bashing a cut between two sheets of greaseproof paper. I exaggerate a little – butchers and supermarkets in Italy sell the meat already hammered to a 5mm/¼in thickness, no more, ready for the pan. In France you see minute steaks and veal escalopes everywhere. We have a poorer escalope culture, due, I believe, to having had forty years of low food inflation and the loss of cooking skills. With prime cuts like rump steak affordable, humble cuts have been ignored.

It is important to trim sinew or gristle from the meat if you are to cook it this way, and – of course – to buy pieces off the bone. Cut slices of the meat – or ask a butcher to do this – across the grain. Even tender meats like poultry benefit from the treatment. I take boneless chicken thighs, hammer them thin using sheets of greaseproof paper (or clingfilm) as a shield, and dip them in egg and breadcrumbs before frying (see page 100). With a squirt of lemon juice, they are transformed, and very satisfying dipped into mayonnaise seasoned with capers and herbs (parsley, dill, basil).

MEAT CUTS TO MAKE INTO ESCALOPES
* Beef – chuck steak, top rump, topside, skirt, neck, blade steak, flank steak. The method works all the better if the meat has been well hung, on the bone. Veal escalopes are cut from the rump, incidentally.

* Lamb – most cuts of lamb are tender, but neck fillet and shoulder steaks will have an almost melting texture if treated this way.
* Pork – neck fillet, shoulder chops.

TO SAUTÉ ESCALOPES, THEN MAKE A SIMPLE, UNIVERSAL JUICE IN THE SAME PAN

Slice the meat across the grain, cutting pieces which are about 1cm (just under ½in) thick. Trim away any gristle. Place them a few centimetres apart on a sheet of greaseproof paper or clingfilm. Place another sheet on top and use a meat hammer or rolling pin to thin them no more than 5mm (just under ¼in), or as thinly as possible. I do not season escalopes but put salt on the table when we eat.

Heat some butter mixed with a little olive oil in a pan until it foams. Sauté the escalope for 1 minute on each side – the meat is usually perfectly done, very slightly pink inside, when you can see tiny droplets of pink liquid on the surface of the meat. Remove from the pan and rest on a warm plate. Lightly cover with a sheet of foil. Add wine or stock, or some lemon juice combined with water, to the pan: about 1 full wineglass for 2 escalopes. Let it come to the boil, while stirring and scraping the bottom of the pan with a wooden spatula. Allow the juices to reduce a little, by boiling. Add two walnut-sized lumps of butter and whisk with a fork, then serve as a juice, or gravy, with the meat. To make the sauce rich and fragrant, add a couple of tablespoons of cream in place of the butter, and a few leaves of tarragon. This is especially good with pork, veal and chicken. My mother used to add vermouth to sauces such as these, which gives the sauce a heady flavour and old-fashioned luxury.

Monkfish and bacon cakes

see PLATE 14

The quickest fishcakes you can make. Monkfish, when processed to a paste, has a slight cartilaginous quality which helps it bind easily with the other ingredients. Serve with buttered peas. I always look for Cornish monkfish, because it has fewer sustainability issues.

MAKES 8 CAKES, SERVING 4 AS A MAIN COURSE
4 rashers thinly cut smoked streaky bacon
500g/1lb 2oz boneless monkfish fillet
100ml/3 ½fl oz full-fat crème fraiche
1 heaped tablespoon plain white flour
1 large egg, beaten
salt and black pepper
olive or sunflower oil for shallow-frying

FOR THE COATING (PUT INTO SEPARATE SHALLOW BOWLS):
2 tablespoons plain flour, seasoned with salt
1 further egg, beaten
6 tablespoons dry breadcrumbs

Sauté the bacon until crisp, drain on paper, then chop or break into small pieces. Trim any membrane from the monkfish and put it in a food processor. Blitz to a paste then put in a bowl. Add the bacon, crème fraiche, flour and egg. Season and mix well. Form into 8 cakes, dip them in flour and then in the beaten egg. Finally, coat them with breadcrumbs and refrigerate.

Just before you eat, shallow-fry in the oil over a medium heat until golden on both sides.

Kitchen note
Eat with mayonnaise, or mayonnaise with chopped tarragon, capers and gherkins (see page 416).

South coast stew of gurnard, cod, mussels, saffron, new garlic and butter beans

A quick-to-make stew that can match the glories of the famous French bouillabaisse any day.

SERVES 4

2 heaped tablespoons butter
1 bulb wet garlic, roughly chopped
1 celery stick, finely chopped
8 saffron strands
2 teaspoons ground coriander seed
½ teaspoon ground cumin
2 fillets from a large gurnard, skinned and cut into bite-sized pieces
450g/1lb cod fillet, skinned and cut into bite-sized pieces
1 litre/1¾ pints mussels
2 wineglasses white wine
2 teaspoons tomato purée
1 x 450g/1lb tin butter beans, drained
toasted bread, to serve

Melt the butter in a casserole dish and add the garlic, celery and spices (including the saffron strands). Cook over a medium heat, stirring, until soft but not coloured. Add the fish, and turn it in the butter before it flakes. Throw in the mussels, then pour in the wine. Cook until the wine bubbles, then add the tomato purée, the butter beans and just enough water to cover.

Bring to the boil and cook gently for a few minutes until the fish is cooked and the mussels are wide open. Discard any that do not open. Serve spooned into bowls, with toasted bread on the side.

Chicken thighs stuffed with walnut and watercress purée, cooked in cider

A good use for the cheaper brown meat on a chicken. Lazily, and with absolutely no guilt, I buy ready-boned free-range chicken thighs from the supermarket – they are the best-value cuts on the shelf. Eat with buttered noodles, or boiled or baked potatoes and butter.

SERVES 4
8 boned, skinned chicken thighs
2 bunches of watercress
200g/7oz shelled walnuts – fresh if possible
2 garlic cloves, peeled
1 heaped tablespoon fresh breadcrumbs
2 tablespoons olive oil, plus a little more
8 thin slices prosciutto or pancetta
300ml/½ pint dry English cider

Place the chicken thighs between two sheets of greaseproof paper and hammer until about 1cm/½in thick. Lift off the paper carefully and lay the meat out on a worktop. Chop the watercress and walnuts in a food processor with the garlic, breadcrumbs and 2 tablespoons of oil. Lay a slice of prosciutto or pancetta on top of the chicken, put about 2 heaped teaspoons of the watercress mixture on top, then gently roll (so that not too much of the purée escapes) and secure with a cocktail stick. Using a little more oil, brown on both sides in a pan, then add the cider and cook, turning the rolls once, for about 15 minutes.

Pudding in a pan

Faced with the task of producing something sweet in no time, there is a simple solution with a bunch of bananas and a couple of oranges. Spilt the bananas lengthways and sprinkle with a little ground cinnamon. Heat 2 tablespoons Demerara sugar in a pan with 2 tablespoons butter and add 2 cardamom pods (if you wish). Add about 3 tablespoons orange juice. Bring to the boil; cook until you have a thick syrup then poach the bananas in it until soft. Remember to pick out and discard the cardamom before you serve the bananas, with crème fraiche or vanilla ice cream.

Poached summer fruit with vanilla and allspice

The prettiest, almost instant pudding, which brings to mind summer markets and stalls heaped with soft fruits. I especially love the rosy hue of the peaches, once cooked. Good with clotted cream or vanilla ice cream.

SERVES 4–6
4 heaped tablespoons caster sugar
water
½ vanilla pod, split in half
2 allspice berries
4 peaches or nectarines, used whole
4 plums or greengages, used whole
4 figs – black or green will do
mint leaves, to serve

Put the caster sugar in a saucepan that is wide enough for the fruit to fit neatly inside in one layer. Add water to the depth of about 3cm/1¼in, with the vanilla pod and allspice. Bring slowly to the boil. Once simmering, put in the peaches or nectarines. Cook for 3 minutes, then turn them over. Add the plums or greengages and figs and cook for about 10 minutes. The syrup should boil up and around the fruit. Tilt the pan occasionally while cooking, and spoon some syrup over the fruit. Once the fruit is soft, but not collapsing, remove from the heat and transfer to a bowl to cool. Scatter over a few mint leaves and serve.

A word about eating less

Would I have written about losing weight, ten years ago? Probably not, but a decade of eating for a living has meant a search for a sensible approach. Cookbooks do not often cover the issue of temperance, but from time to time I tune into the body's need to take it easy. I like to say I do not diet, in that I do not deny. If I crave, I tell myself it will always be there to eat again, once I am in good health.

I tried a lot of diets in my twenties, and all failed. But in the course of these subsequent failures, in among reading healthy doses of sensible Susie Orbach, I learned more about appetite and its connection to our state of mind. The mind and stomach work in tandem. We hear bad news and feel it in the stomach. It is impossible to control our appetite, one way or the other, unless we are content. Because most diets dictate a hatred for food and ban everything, they are impossible to stick to.

The following plan for cutting down was published in the *Telegraph* in the first weeks of 2010. Readers responded enthusiastically, writing to say how it had changed their attitude. I take no credit, because this way of eating is simply a person, any person, finally understanding true nutrition. I simply offer the facts about diet, and it is over to you. It is a total rejection of concepts such as low-fat or meat-only diets, or calories or other scoring systems that make one more and more obsessed, and more likely to fail.

My diet has rules but I prefer to think of it as an understanding; something that in time makes perfect sense because it brings about the end of a dysfunctional relationship with food and certain bad habits. So, when I am on the diet, I follow an uncomplicated code:

✳ I do not drink wine (or other alcohol) from Sunday to Thursday. This means I am full of energy on Monday and through most of the working week. Lunchtime on Friday, I look forward enormously to my fingers enclosing a glass of icy white Bordeaux, wet with condensation. Heaven in its infrequency.

✳ I have learned to love pulses and seeds as a replacement for white carbohydrates. This is a very important part of the plan – and makes for more elegant eating than you might first imagine. Pulses and seeds contain complex carbohydrates which give you a steady energy feed. So I make a breakfast with linseeds in the morning (nicer than it sounds) and eat green lentils at least once a day (see recipe on page 53, for example). Likewise, I make delicious risotto-type dishes from whole grains such as pearl barley, oat groats, spelt (farro) or durum wheat (sold as Ebly).

✳ I do not eat refined white carbohydrates, so no white flour or white sugar, and that means no white bread and very little bread with added white flour, no biscuits or cakes and staying away from any convenience foods with carbohydrate 'fillers' such as maize starch (often found in cheaper ready meals like curries and gravies). White carbohydrate is nutritionally pointless. It gives a short burst of energy then charges up the appetite again. I also avoid snacks containing brown sugar, which has only trace nutrients. After a few days I do not miss them. And – so sorry – but you must also cut right back on potatoes. The carbohydrate in potato triggers the appetite and you can obtain the good nutrients in potatoes, like vitamin C, from other foods.

✳ On either Saturday or Sunday I do have toast, however, with eggs, scrambled or boiled in all their loveliness. I might eat white toast but increasingly I find I want to eat a really good sourdough or spelt bread instead, toasted and buttered, simply because I genuinely respect well-made bread.

* I eat fruit or drink fruit juice only at breakfast. Munching on apples or nibbling dried fruits through the day is a trigger for hunger.
* I eat butter. Butter is a wholefood that has plenty of good nutrients and that our bodies burn with ease. There is convincing evidence that eating butter increases metabolism. I do not 'splash it all over', however, but some saturated fat is essential to the human diet. I eat a little butter melted on vegetables and use it in soup and risotto.
* I only use wholemilk and eat full-fat yoghurt – the vitamins in the fat help you digest the calcium. There is little nourishment in low-fat foods.
* I make and use a lot of fresh chicken stock (see page 390). Not only is it satisfying, it adds a mass of flavour to food, especially soup, without the need for salt, cutting water retention in the body. It also helps spread the higher cost of naturally reared or organic meat.
* I drink lemon water (a quarter lemon in hot water) at breakfast and various herb teas during the day. Ideally it is good to limit ordinary tea and milk. For me there is something rather narcotic about tea with milk; it is a 'drug' associated with other addictive things, like biscuits and chocolate brownies.
* I believe in dieting when busy with other things in life, because there is always a boredom factor. The extra energy you get from the foods I recommend helps concentration. I get a lot 'done' when I eat this way.
* I cook food that needs little preparation, and does not need too much thought. I do not want to obsess about recipes when trying to bring my appetite under control. For the same reason I have always found that counting calories or Weight Watchers' points is a neurotic form of dieting and far removed from real nourishment. Many of the recipes in this chapter are suitable for this way of eating.

* Lastly, but very necessarily, I do 20 minutes of aerobic exercise a day, or 40 minutes every other day. Food is fuel and needs to be used. It is only 20 minutes a day. Do it. Whether getting off the bus or tube a couple of stops early and fast-walking in trainers, or swimming, or jogging – whatever makes the pulse quicken. Dieting rarely works without exercise.

A typical day

* Breakfast – a muesli made with 3 dessertspoons oats, 1 grated apple, 2 dessertspoons of golden linseed (part-ground in a food processor to release the oils), a dessertspoon of raisins, a teaspoon of honey or molasses sugar. Add milk, apple juice or yoghurt. This keeps you going until lunchtime.
* Lunch – a soup or a dish of Puy lentils (or other grain) plus some protein like cheese, charcuterie, a fried sausage or some bacon, smoked or canned fish plus fresh herbs or leaves with olive oil. I add chilli for interest sometimes. See the lentil recipe on page 53.
* Dinner – basically any recipe you like as long as it contains no white carbohydrates. I eat a larger lunch than dinner.
* Snacks – pieces of favourite cheese, crudités and mayonnaise and hummus, salami or ham, cornichons, olives. Occasional pieces of dark, 70%-cocoa-solid chocolate – nice before bed, and very good for you.

Because nothing is as easy as it sounds

Real life will still threaten the best-laid plans. It helps to anticipate.
* The long drive – nothing undoes me like hunger in the car. Fuel stations rarely sell healthy food, although an increasing number of larger motorway services sell fruit or snacks like hummus. Take a

picnic. Allowed foods include oatcakes, cheese, raw vegetables
and any salad; nuts, seeds, smoked fish, pickles, ham and salami.
Make a flask of soup. Not allowed: bread, pastry (pies/pasties),
anything sweet.

* Leftovers from tea – try introducing dishes to the children/
teenagers that are less mouth-wateringly tempting than food that
has been fried, or dishes like macaroni cheese. It is not 'terminal'
if you end up picking at risottos and pilaffs, or noodle soups,
coconut curries or casseroles made with chicken or lamb (see
pages 68–76).

* Eating out – restaurants are surprisingly tolerant of people who
order two starters. Oddly enough, eating out in gastronomic
restaurants has little impact – good places are sensible about size
of helpings. But sit on your hands when bread is put on the table
(ask for olives if possible); do not order puddings (there might be
cheese, a few nibbles of which will keep hunger at bay) and leave
the potatoes.

* It is rude not to – I know people who accept a drink when they
are not 'on the booze' then keep the glass full or take a sip or
two. I'd so like always to be one of them, but, if you are in a
situation where it is rude not to accept hospitality, it can be the
only way out.

* Beyond your control – that long-planned bit of fun, a friend's
birthday, dinner somewhere you had to book weeks in advance.
Just go and have fun. One day's holiday from the diet will not do a
great deal of harm, and I have found a feast will actually boost the
metabolism. But be discriminate. It is only worth breaking a diet
for something good. If the party canapés are not worthy of your
sacrifice, however, don't eat them.

Eighty degrees beef:
  With olives
  With pickled walnuts
  With sliced aubergines
  With black grapes
  With golden sultanas or Muscat
  raisins
  With butter beans and herbs
A blueprint for a beef stew – more
  than one cut, more than one way:
  With orange, garlic and thyme
  With smoked lardons and garlic
  With split pig's trotter
  With carrots
  With kidney
  With fresh oysters
Festive boiled dinner – bollito misto
Oxtail stew
Simmered pork belly, new season
  root vegetables under a suet
  crust
Young lamb shoulder, shrugged
  off the bone
Pork cheeks with cider and white
  beans

Braised gammon, with fried apple
  and pumpkin seeds
Pork shoulder cooked with
  yoghurt, cardamom and apple
Potted pork and rabbit
Potted pork with radish salad
Pot-cooked spring chicken with
  young veg
Poached chicken and a supply of
  stock
Pot-roasted partridge with leeks,
  cider and smoked bacon
Braised beans:
  Haricots with garlic and tomato
  Flageolets with butter, celery,
  lettuce and wine
  Butter beans with aubergine
  and mint
  Mexican black beans with
  pepper
Baked Hungarian beans with
  smoked pork
Ribollita
Dual-purpose marmalade

A SLOW-COOKED POT

The lid of the pot settles into place with the dong of an untuned bell. Cast iron meets cast iron, but it is a sound I am relieved to hear. I spent fifteen minutes preparing the contents of the now simmering pot and, aside from the odd peep or taste, my work is done. Under the lid, a kind of magic is happening. Meat clinging firmly to a shank will be shrugged off, its texture melting into the rich juice. The flavour of bay will invade, the glass of wine add deep sweetness. Not for the first time I remind myself that the quick answer to providing big, economical food is one word: slow.

Welcome to the world of the slow pot, a way to cook that has its roots in the Iron Age but is still so relevant to aspiring cooks today. This is a part of the 'lost kitchen' where the past holds the best solutions, and I do not mean the recent past. Sometimes I look back at fifty-year-old recipes and think, 'I'd never add flour to a sauce like that now, or margarine to a cake . . .' But a slow-cooked pot is different.

Often I find that the older the recipe, the better it turns out. For me it is quite a testing sphere of cooking. I have high hopes: chunks of beef that part obediently with the slightest tease of a fork; rich, dark, smooth juices. But I can't count the times where I have been disappointed in a stew that I dutifully nurtured. I wanted to know why, and that is what you will find over the next pages.

Digging around in old books, asking advice, the answers are there, and no surprises who has them. This is territory that is utterly feminine, tied into a traditionally structured society. Can it belong in our lives today? Perhaps not every day. If you haven't got a pot permanently on the bubble, don't worry, you are not failing in some way. But slow cooking – and please do not run for cover at the sound of the S word – is something to enjoy and reap benefits from. It is not hard work. It simmers. You do ... well, whatever you like.

It is the cheapest meat cookery, and done the right way, slow cooking is good for you, too. I like to take a ladleful of braised beef, stored in the fridge, warm it, scatter it with herbs and eat it with lentils, buttered ribbons of pasta or a stick of grilled polenta. I like to put an oval dish of perfectly poached silverside on the table, to eat with a green, capery sauce. Now and then I make a pie, or a suet crust, and view the results with a little sigh of pride. Made right, these things restore the equilibrium of those who eat them. Eating this food is a form of ancestor worship.

Rethinking the S word
Can we talk about 'slow' in hectic times? No thanks, you say. I can't come in from work and make stew. Of course you shouldn't – make it the evening before. Recipe books need a small telling off about this. It is almost as if no one wants to admit that a meal can take more than two hours, or that it tastes nicer if made the previous day. You can make a stew in two hours, but it is unlikely to be as good. More expensive stewing cuts will become tender after two hours' cooking time, but that rather defeats the economical purpose of slow cooking. And it is necessary, in order to convince would-be slow cooks how delicious stews and braises can be, to mention that when I say slow, I mean very slow is best. I set out to write the first words of this chapter, having just made a beef stew. It took over four hours. OK, it took five. There, I have said it. But it is so, so delicious. I now have a supply of something good, and the friendly ghost of a mother cook in the kitchen.

Slow-cooked dishes might not be something to do often. Many are better suited to the colder months of the year. But they are problem-solvers for stressed, busy people even though they need a long cooking time. Planning ahead and making stew means that in an especially busy week I know I have some good food I can simply reheat. There is relief in knowing it cost very little, and also a promise of comfort when it is most needed. Reheating ready-made stews delivers none of this. Over-priced, over-salted, over-rated.

The science of slow

Cooks and scientists argue endlessly about the various ways in which a stew can fail. Mrs Beeton's unfriendly writings on the matter would send slipshod cooks running to hide in the understairs cupboard. If we are not topping up the liquid in our pans adequately, or are neglecting to skim off rising scum, hard, tasteless, innutritious meat will be sent to the table! Well, I am not a believer in scaring people. But while skimming off impurities at the beginning is important, and of course you do not want the juice to evaporate, it is how the pot boils, or rather doesn't, that matters most of all.

There is little wrong with many of the basic recipes for stewing, except a glaring omission: temperature is everything. Stewing was invented when the dying ashes of a fire and economy of fuel was a way of life. Today's cookers are over-powered; the lowest setting is just low enough. When a recipe says 'simmer', it would be better to say keep well below boiling point at about 75–85°C/165–185°F, the temperature of a well-made espresso coffee. This is the temperature Mrs Beeton rightly recommended. The very lowest temperature of my oven is 80°C/175°F, so I tend to slow-cook on the hob. Food thermometers, something I always thought a serious tool for anoraks, actually take the headache out of slow cooking. A simple food thermometer can be left in the stew, or £20 will buy a thermometer with a probe to dangle in the pot. This does not mean you have to stand over the oven, checking all the time. Once the heat is regulated, the pot can be left. Heat diffusers are also helpful if you need to temper the power of more aggressive hobs. Agas have a low oven which is ideal for stewing, and electric slow cookers can do a good job, too.

Patience

Be prepared for the extra time it takes to make a really good stew. Peep under the lid after an hour and it will seem like not much is happening. But at above 85°C/185°F, the proteins in the meat will gradually break down and it will become tender. You have to have faith in the process. Odd as it may seem, cooking at too high a temperature, even in a pan of liquid, dries the meat out. This is the main reason why stews fail or whole cuts like poached brisket can be tough. You cannot rescue dried-out meat. If you cook it for longer, it becomes harder and drier.

Low temperature cooking times

* Beef – whole pieces (silverside, brisket), diced steak, shin, 'ox' cheek and tail – minimum 4 hours at 80°C/175°F.
* Lamb – shoulder, neck chops, chump chops, shanks – minimum 4 hours at 80°C/175°F.
* Pork – shoulder, leg, hand (on bone), belly and cheeks – minimum 3 hours at 80°C/175°F.
* Ham – rolled leg fillet, ham hocks (on bone) – minimum 2½ hours at 80°C/175°F.

The pot

Slow cooking can be done in ordinary saucepans but is safer (from burning or spoiling) when done in a pot made either from cast iron or a specially treated ceramic that can be used on the hob and inside the oven. The pot needs a well-fitting lid. It is hard to find a good-sized pot costing less than £50, though an online trawl might throw up a bargain. A proper pot is a good, life-long investment (unless you become the second person, after me, to smash a Le Creuset by dropping it); it was a present from my mother. I now own a small and a large cast-iron pot, and both have earned their keep many times over.

Bucket dinners

Traditionally, when the fire was too hot, stews were made in pottery crocks set inside a pan of boiling water. Inside them, the liquid would murmur, barely moving, rather than boil. This produces perfectly cooked meat, but it is a slower process than most recipes reveal. I once tried out the recipe for a bargee's (barge worker's) dinner, a meal cooked in a crock set in a bucket of water over smouldering coals, that I took from Dorothy Hartley's *Food In England*. It still remains one of the most delicious suppers ever (see page 211).

This method can be replicated on a cooker, putting a ceramic pot inside a pan, or with an electric slow cooker. I used to sniff at this gadget, thinking it belonged to my grandmother's generation, but they are a genuine contemporary solution for busy people. A slow cooker will safely take care of the work while you are out or busy doing other things. Unless, of course, you want to buy an Aga . . .

The meat

So you timed the stew right and cooked it at the lowest temperature, but it was still disappointing. Again it is surprising that a style of cooking that everyone tells you is so simple leaves you wondering where you went wrong. The third factor, after time and temperature, to bring success is the meat itself. Easy, says convention, any cut will tenderise after slow cooking. Surely this fact cannot be altered when pots of beef have been bubbling for a millennium? But it has. For the last five decades the British have turned meat production on its head. We now eat almost exclusively young animals. Beef cattle are rarely more than a couple of years old when slaughtered; lamb and pork only a few months and chickens reach only a teenage number of weeks when ready for the pot (ostensibly – because most end up as fillets that will be cooked quickly).

The fact that modern meat is too young for the pot was revealed to me by a lady farmer with a huge knowledge of food and especially the meat industry. I met Caroline Cranbrook in 2000, and worked with her on a Westminster Committee of Enquiry into the 'misregulation' of the meat industry (a topic and investigation that was more fun than it sounds, believe me). A farmer in Suffolk, Caroline knew more about livestock farming than the rest of us committee members put together. She remembered meat before production of the vast majority was industrialised, a time when animals were largely slow grown on a forage (grass and hay) diet. She also loves to cook (see her recipe on page 232) and when I visit her we often discuss cooking and recipes, while eating delicious meals made with the Alde Valley lamb her son Jason now rears in Suffolk, and vegetables from her garden.

Too young to stew

'Of course, meat today is too young to stew,' Caroline said to me one day, and opened my eyes to an unsolved problem. Fast or 'intensively' grown livestock do not have fully developed connective tissue or bones. They are fed grain supplements, including protein-rich soya, which helps them gain muscle weight. The resulting meat has a higher water content (which is why this type of meat appears to shrink a lot during cooking), and, paradoxically, dries out during a slow braise. The meat of older animals that are forage-fed – mutton, for example – contains a lot of connective tissue. On hearing this, the immediate concern is that this will mean tougher meat – which it will be if roasted. But stewed, the connective tissue breaks down into gelatine, which gives stew richness and unctuousness. The fibre of the muscle is better developed and has a different appearance, too (though meat fibre also varies, breed to breed). During cooking the muscle from older animals shrinks less, breaking down into broader strips instead of fine threads.

It is possible, despite the predominance of intensively reared meat, to buy meat from slow-grown beef cattle, pigs and sheep. Traditional or 'rare' (sometimes called native) breeds tend to reach maturity at a slower rate, as do animals that are solely grass fed. Mutton, meat from older ewes up to five years in age that have had lambs, is often exported to appreciative customers in southern Europe. Successful campaigns in Britain to bring it back into our cooking have made it more widely available. All the above meat will be sold with a free-range (or sometimes organic) tag, and will be more expensive than that which has been reared intensively. But it is true that the cheapest cuts on those more expensive animals are the best of all for stewing; shin or neck joints give beautiful results at prices that may be higher than supermarket prices but are still affordable.

Exceptions to the very slow rule

When there is little option but to buy meat from younger animals, I recommend buying cuts on the bone, like neck of lamb, or buying the more cartilaginous joints, such as shin of beef, to guarantee a juicy outcome. This is difficult when shopping in supermarkets where almost all meat is filleted from bones, but butchers – who tend to have customers with traditional tastes – will be able to supply what you need.

The rule goes that the cheaper the cut, the more connective tissue in the meat. The more connective tissue, the longer it will take to break down to become tender. Don't be put off by this: this tissue will gradually turn to gelatine, making the most delicious braise. Leaner and therefore more expensive meat will tenderise at a faster rate, but I find the outcome never has great texture and I avoid using it. Diced lamb shoulder meat is the safest bet for a stew in a short, two-hour cooking time at a higher temperature, simmering at 95°C/205°F. Lamb shank (shin) or pork 'hand' will also tenderise within two hours and have that sought-after unctuousness.

Unwritten secrets

'Let me tell you a secret,' said Adonis Babelakis, a fisherman and chef, as he began to prepare a beef stifado, the classic Greek stew. 'My mother taught me to cook meat in water flavoured with bay, juniper and cinnamon, at eighty degrees Celsius – you can braise beef or lamb faster than this, but she never had more than a few sticks of charcoal for energy. She could not afford to let the pot boil. She never added olive oil until the meat was cooked, because long cooking spoils the goodness in the oil. But in the end we ate the most beautifully cooked meat, we were well nourished – and we saved fuel. I still do it the same way today.'

Hand-me-down methods are swiftly becoming lost because cooks like Babelakis's mother rarely wrote down their methods. They just told their children or a curious guest. The hope is that they will pass it on. But it would be typical, now, for a daughter of a traditional southern European cook, not to marry young but to study further, take a white-collar job and shun all thoughts of cooking. She hasn't time. Even if she has a family there are better things to do than make her mother's stifado. And just like that, a skill is uprooted and blown away into the air. But, like everything that floats in the air, it has to land. With luck, it will settle somewhere receptive to its true value. A chance conversation, like mine with Adonis, brings it back and plants it once again in the mind of a cook.

Eighty degrees beef

see PLATE 15

A braise for beginners, and an enlightening experiment for experienced slow cooks, too. The Cretan mother turns stew (or stifado) cooking on its head. The typical order for adding the basic ingredients to the pot is: oil, onions, meat, water (or stock). In this recipe the first ingredient is water, then meat, and finally onions and oil. The Cretan mothers and their sons and daughters value the goodness in olive oil highly. Adding it after the slow cooking is done preserves the nutrients. The total cooking time is between 6 and 7 hours at approximately 80°C/175°F. You can adapt this dish to lamb, hare and rabbit. The meat literally melts into a juicy mass – there will not be much liquid. It is lovely eaten with buttered egg noodles or roasted or sautéed potatoes. Below the recipe is a list of ingredients to add during or after cooking. This is a perfect recipe for a slow cooker but the dish must be finished in a pan over a higher heat.

SERVES 4

1kg/2lb 4oz shin of beef (or other braising cut like blade or neck), cut into large 4cm/1½in cubes

1cm/½in cinnamon stick

8 juniper berries

3 bay leaves

4 tablespoons olive oil

8 small onions or shallots, peeled and left whole, or 2 onions, finely chopped

1 wineglass red or white wine

salt and black pepper

Trim any excess amount of fat or gristle from the beef. Place a heavy-based casserole or cast-iron pot over the heat and fill with water to a depth of about 5cm/2in. Heat the water to boiling point. If possible, tie up the spices in a piece of muslin and drop into the water. Otherwise add them loose, but remember that you must later pick them out of the braise, once the meat is tender. Add the meat to the pan and allow the water to come to the boil. The meat will immediately shrink and harden on contact with the hot water. Skim off any foam or impurities that rise to the surface. This is very important as it ensures the juices are clean and clear and will improve the end result.

Set the pan over a very low heat, minimum 75°C/165°F or no more than 85°C/185°F. You do not need a thermometer. Watch the liquid; it should just swirl slightly, and there should be no visible bubbles. Leave to cook like this, partially covered by a lid, for approximately 6 hours or until the meat is very tender. Lift out the meat with a slotted spoon and place on a plate. Pick out the spices or spice bag from the liquid and discard. Pour the liquid into a separate bowl and set to one side (there will only be a small amount left).

Turn up the heat and add the oil with the onions. Cook until they are lightly brown, then add the beef. Do not let the oil reach smoking point, because it destroys the nutrients and – just as essentially – the flavour. Brown the beef lightly in the oil. Add the wine and allow to come to the boil, then add the remaining cooking liquid. Simmer with the oil and other juices in the pan just for a few minutes. Taste for seasoning and add salt and pepper, then serve.

You can add a number of different ingredients to the stew at the end.

* Pitted Kalamata olives and fresh marjoram – add with the onions and 1 teaspoon tomato purée.
* Pickled walnuts, with 1 tablespoon of their pickling juice – slice and add at very end.
* Sliced aubergines and fresh thyme sprigs – sweat the aubergines first with salt, rinse and pat dry. Then add the aubergines and thyme with the onions and 1 tablespoon tomato purée and cook until soft.
* Black grapes – add at the very end.
* Golden sultanas or Muscat raisins and rosemary – add with the onions.
* Butter beans and herbs – add after the beef has been browned.
* Alternative meats: use cubed lamb shoulder, jointed rabbit, jointed hare or cubed venison.
* Alternative cooking liquid: substitute the water and wine with either beer (ale), dry cider (good with rabbit) or meat stock.

The mothers of slow

Early memories of slowly braised meat began with page 546 of *The Constance Spry Cookery Book* and the oxtail stew my mother would often cook for Saturday lunch. Spry's essential secret lay in blanching the meat in boiling water first, resulting in a stew that had reassuring, clear juices which would seep into the buttery contents of the baked potatoes on our plates.

From there I turned to Jane Grigson, whose meat chapter in *English Food* taught me the most about the lost traditions of braising; how the liquid in the pot should barely move – only 'burp,' as she delightfully put it. Grigson was unafraid to admit that slow meant really slow. 'Leave the whole thing in a cool place for four days,' she said drily, in one of her recipes for mutton. Now that is what I call an unfashionable truth, news that the 'quick and easy' brigade must take sitting down. She also wrote about the lost breeds and styles of traditional livestock farming, and how important these elements are if you want great results.

I made my first bollito misto (mixed boiled meats) following a recipe for a cheaper version of the festive dish in Elizabeth David's *Italian Food*. The outcome, with very little work but a substantial amount of simmering, was unutterably glamorous: a tender piece of gammon, rolled brisket and a whole chicken, served with the dark blond cooking broth and a dazzling green herb and caper sauce. But I was equally passionate about a recipe for a humble hand of pork braised with water, herbs and garlic, and much later on with Rose Gray and Ruth Rogers' easy recipe for pork cooked in milk with lemon and sage. Many encounters with slow pots in the kitchens of friends and family remain the best in my memory. A huge bowl of game and pork rillettes made by a friend, Charlotte Moore, in her Buckinghamshire farmhouse kitchen; Julia Moore, another talented, natural cook (but no relation), made an unforgettable pot of poached chicken with ten thousand fathoms of flavour. This is beginning to sound like a claim that men never braise, but they do. They were taught to by their women, of course!

A blueprint for a beef stew - more than one cut, more than one way

A conventional beef stew made the British way, with influences from Jane Grigson's 'shin of beef stew' and a decade of experimentation at home. It can be adapted to any type of cubed braising steak or unusual cheap cuts like 'ox' cheek. Grigson wrote that her favourite cut for this stew was shin of beef on the bone; she would ask the butcher to cut the shin into slices, sawing through the bone, so that the marrow would make the stew even better. It is rare to find a cut like this in butchers, but if you call ahead a helpful butcher will do it for you. You can adapt this basic blueprint using a number of added ingredients (see page 204).

SERVES 6–8

2kg/4lb 8oz shin of beef (add an extra 500g/1lb 2oz if buying
    slices on the bone), or other braising steak
2 tablespoons beef dripping or butter or olive oil
4 onions, finely chopped
2–3 tablespoons plain flour
salt and black pepper
200ml/7fl oz ale or red wine
1 litre/1¾ pints beef stock, plus a little more

If using beef that is off the bone, cut it into 4cm/1½in cubes.

Melt half the dripping (or butter or oil) in a large casserole or heavy-based pan over a medium-high heat. Fry the beef in the dripping in four batches, removing them to a plate once browned, adding the remaining dripping when needed. You will need to turn the heat up quite high so the meat browns well and gives the stew extra flavour – expect a little smoke to rise from the pan. Once all the meat is browned add the onions to the pan and brown them quickly in the remaining fat.

Add the beef back to the pan, sprinkle with the flour and give the whole lot a good stir to coat the contents of the pan with flour and fry it a little. Season with salt and then cover with the ale or wine. When the liquor boils, add the stock. Bring to the boil, skimming off any foam that rises to the surface. As soon as the contents boil, set the pan over a much lower heat – about 80°C/175°F if you are using a thermometer – the liquid in the pan should gently swirl and move. Do not let it boil, though you may see the odd bubble rising. Place a lid on the casserole, leaving it very slightly open. It is unlikely that much liquid will evaporate during cooking, but if it does, add a little more.

Cook for about 4 hours or until the beef is tender and the juices have become gelatinous (this is more the case when using shin of beef). Once the meat is cooked, taste and adjust the seasoning. The end result is a simple stew to eat with boiled, baked or mashed potatoes.

ADAPTING THE STEW TO OTHER INGREDIENTS

* With orange, garlic and thyme – make the stew without the flour – you will have a thinner juice rather than a thickened sauce. Add 8 garlic cloves, peeled and crushed. Peel the zest of half an orange and add it at the wine stage with 4 sprigs thyme. Simmer until you have a fragrant daube of tender beef.
* With smoked lardons and garlic – brown the lardons (cubed salted, smoked bacon) with the meat. Add 6 garlic cloves, peeled

and chopped, with the onion but try not to burn it or the flavour
will be ruined. Add a bay leaf.

* With split pig's trotter – a good way to add richness. Add a whole
  pig's trotter, split in half, to the pot once the browned beef has
  been added back.
* With carrots – add whole young carrots to the pot about halfway
  through the cooking time.
* With kidney – slice 500g/1lb 2oz ox kidney and trim away any
  ducts or membrane. Dust with one of the tablespoons of flour and
  brown in the pan after you have browned and removed the meat,
  but before you add the onions. Use red wine in this recipe –
  adding an extra splash. Simmer as usual until all is tender. Finish
  as a pie, if you wish (see page 271 for the pastry recipe).
* With fresh oysters – make the stew with chuck steak and no
  onion. Open 12 oysters and add the juice inside the shells with the
  wine. Set the oysters aside in the fridge while the stew simmers.
  Add the fresh oysters at the end, and serve the stew with triangles
  of fried bread.

How to poach

Tender slices of meat, tasting cleanly of themselves and a hint of the
spice that flavours the water they simmer in, to eat with a little
pickle, mustard or chutney. Poached meats can be very elegant, the
soft suede gloves of cooking as opposed to the sheepskin-lined that
is stew. Following the same principle as slow-cooked stews,
poaching one whole cut of meat is a case of a pan of water,
murmuring at 80°C/175°F, and a good long time. Cuts suitable for
poaching include brined silverside and ox tongue, fresh rolled
brisket, gammon and large mature chickens.

Cooking times vary, depending on the size of the cut. One hour per 1kg/2lb 4oz is the guide I follow for smaller joints (under 3kg/6½lb). Cook larger pieces for less time and use the doneness test, below. It is not a difficult cooking process. As long as you do not let the water boil, the meat will remain juicy even after a long cooking time. To test if the meat is done, insert a skewer into the thickest area of the cut and then pull it out. If the meat 'clings' to the skewer tightly, the meat inside is still underdone. If the skewer comes out with ease, the meat is cooked. I usually test 30 minutes before the meat is due to be cooked and am prepared to stop the cooking early, following the result of the test, rather than sticking to the cooking time guide.

Festive boiled dinner - bollito misto

Echoes of dinners with my mother, who loved platters of sliced boiled meat with buttered spring vegetables, parsley and a big pot of mustard on the table . . . And also a salute to the mothers of northern Italy and their festive bollito misto. But this is nothing like as grand a dish as it sounds. Just three pieces of meat cooked together, a feast for eight people, plus hopes of leftovers to last a few days. The sauce is not authentically Italian but one that works well. Braised lentils (page 53), boiled new potatoes or spring vegetables are good to have on the side.

SERVES 8, WITH LEFTOVERS

1 brined ox tongue, soaked overnight in cold water
water or 2–3 litres/3–5 pints beef or chicken stock
2 onions, finely chopped
4 garlic cloves peeled and smashed with the back of a knife or a
   whole head of green garlic
2 carrots, finely chopped
2 celery sticks, finely chopped
10 fennel seeds
1 bay leaf
2 sprigs thyme
1.5kg/3lb 5oz fresh rolled brisket
1 chicken, trussed with string

FOR THE SAUCE:

2 tablespoons capers, rinsed, dried and chopped
1 tablespoon pitted green olives, chopped
yolks from 4 hard-boiled eggs, grated
2 fresh egg yolks
1 shallot, finely chopped
8 sprigs flat-leaf parsley, finely chopped
1 teaspoon red wine vinegar

Put the ox tongue in a very large pan and cover with water or stock.
Add the vegetables, fennel seeds and herbs, and bring to the boil,
skimming off any foam that rises. Turn down the heat – the water
must not boil but just swirl and occasionally bubble (80°C/175°F).
Leave like this for 1 hour. After 1 hour add the brisket and bring to
the boil. Again turn down the heat to about 80°C/175°F so the
liquid is not boiling and cook for another 2 hours before adding the

chicken. Simmer for 1 further hour, by which time the chicken will be cooked.

To make the sauce put all the ingredients except the vinegar into a jar and mix well. You can make this sauce in a food processor if you wish, but perhaps not overly whizzed such that it loses its texture. Season to taste with salt and stir in the vinegar just before serving to prevent the parsley discolouring.

To serve the meat, lift out and place on a board. Make sure to have some hot plates or shallow bowls ready. Cover lightly with foil while you strain the stock through a sieve, discarding the vegetables and herbs. Reheat the stock in the pan so it is piping hot. Remove the skin from the tongue using a knife. Cut a slice or two of each type of meat for every person, and serve with a little of the juice and the sauce.

Kitchen note

Alternative meats to serve in place of the tongue or brisket include the Italian cured boiling sausages zampone (40 minutes to cook) and cotechino (20 minutes to cook), both available from Italian food shops. Rolled gammon is also a good alternative to the tongue, and will also need to be soaked in water overnight before boiling to remove excess salt (1.5kg/3lb 5oz piece cooks in 2½ hours). If you use either of the Italian sausages, serve with mostarda di frutta, a pickle made with fruits, mustard oil and sugar, which is also available in jars from Italian food shops.

Oxtail stew

see PLATE 16

Knobbly and odd, oxtail bones look challenging to cook but this is a stew that never fails. The meat, which is always mature, falls from the bone with gelatinous submission. Rich flavour, poor food. I make it Constance Spry's way, just as my mother did, and eat the stew with baked potatoes and plenty of butter.

SERVES 4
1.5kg/3lb 5oz oxtail pieces
2 tablespoons beef dripping or butter or olive oil
2 rashers smoked streaky bacon, chopped
2 onions, sliced
2 carrots, sliced
2 celery sticks, sliced
1 tablespoon plain flour
1 bay leaf
2 sprigs thyme
1 wineglass red wine (optional)
2 litres/3 pints beef stock
12 young carrots, scraped but left whole
salt and white pepper

Soak the oxtail for about 2 hours. Put it into a casserole and cover with fresh water. Bring to the boil, skimming away any foam that rises, then turn down to a very low simmer (the water should swirl and bubble occasionally). Cook for about 15 minutes then drain.

Place the casserole over the heat and add the dripping (or butter or oil). Fry the meat in the dripping, browning it lightly all over. Shake the pan to turn the oxtail pieces (Spry's tip, and always works).

Remove the meat from the pan and set it aside, then add the bacon, onion, carrot and celery and brown the vegetables lightly in the remaining fat. Add back the meat and dust with flour. Shake again to coat with the flour then add the herbs, red wine and stock and bring to the boil. Remove any foam that rises as it comes to the boil then turn the heat right down so the water simmers below boiling point, again swirling and bubbling only occasionally. Cover the pan with a sheet of foil then put the lid on top. Cook for about 4 hours. Be careful to keep the temperature low. A pot that is not boiling when uncovered will build up heat when you put the lid on. You could braise in the lowest oven if it is possible to set it to 80°C/175°F.

Half an hour before the oxtail is due to be served, remove the pieces from the pan. Strain the stock to remove the stewing vegetables. Add the stock back to the pan with the meat and put in the whole young carrots. Season to taste with the salt and pepper and cook for another half hour or until the meat is tender and the carrots cooked.

Simmered pork belly, new season root vegetables under a suet crust

A curiosity, yet a slow-cooked pot explaining the concept of cooking with one vessel placed inside another – a slow cooker in other words. Based on a recipe from Dorothy Hartley's *Food in England*, the stew is cooked inside a ceramic crock, placed inside a bucket of simmering water. The recipe shows how a meal with every possible nourishing ingredient can be simply left to cook, needing only a little attention midway through the cooking process. I experimented with Hartley's recipe, leaving out the built-in apple pudding, thinking it was going a step too far. Expecting the exercise to be no more than a bit of fun, the extraordinary texture of the meat and sweet flavours of the root vegetables were something to take seriously. The suet crust is a must and seals in the flavour. Eat with a watercress salad.

SERVES 4–6

Fill a large pan with boiling water and find an earthenware pot, crock or casserole that will fit inside it. A large pudding basin will also do.

To feed 4, cut 1 swede or large turnip into 1.5cm/½in dice and place in the bottom of the crock. Season with black pepper and a sprig of thyme.

Remove the rind from a 1kg/2lb 4oz piece of fresh pork belly, filleting it off with a knife, then cut the belly into 4 pieces. Place inside the crock on top of the swede. Chop a thick slice of smoked bacon and add it, with more black pepper and thyme, to the pot.

Slice 2 parsnips and lay on top of the pork. Follow with a layer of sliced carrots (2–3 depending on size). Add about 2 tablespoons butter and another thyme sprig.

Mix together 100g/3½oz beef suet with 200g/7oz self-raising flour and add a pinch of salt. Add enough cold water to make a firm dough. Take half of it and roll out to 1.5cm/½in on a floured surface, making a disc that will fit over the vegetables. Place the pastry in the crock, cover the crock with a cloth, secure with string and put in the pan.

Place over the heat, bring the water to a simmering boil, cover the pan with a lid and cook for about 1½ hours. Remove the crock and the cloth cover. Place about 12 mid-sized new season potatoes (red-skinned are delicious) inside the pot over the pastry, which should have puffed up nicely.

Roll the remaining pastry into a disc and place on top. Cover with the cloth again and cook for a further 1–1½ hours. You can leave it longer if you wish on a low setting.

Young lamb shoulder, shrugged off the bone

see PLATE 17

I love this dual method of roasting for one hour, and then braising for one hour. When you lift the covering of foil from the pan at the end, the meat will be almost molten and the aroma sensational. This is a dish to slow-cook in the oven, however, because the first hour is designed to crisp the outer surface and the second will tenderise the meat underneath. Serve with redcurrant or apple (or other orchard fruit) jelly.

SERVES 4

1 medium-sized lamb shoulder – 1–1.5kg/2½–3½lb
3 tablespoons olive oil
sea salt and black pepper
clusters of leaves pulled from 2 sprigs rosemary
2 wineglasses white wine
300ml/½ pint meat stock
6–8 medium-sized potatoes, peeled
8 garlic cloves, crushed but left whole and unpeeled

Preheat the oven to 230°C/450°F/Gas 8. Rub the shoulder front and back with olive oil and season with salt and pepper. Place in a deep roasting dish. Make small incisions in the skin and insert tiny sprigs of rosemary. Roast for 15 minutes, then turn the heat down to 175°C/350°F/Gas 4. Roast for another 45 minutes.

When the hour's roasting is complete, pour the wine and stock into the pan and add the potatoes and garlic. The potatoes will not be as crisp as normal roast potatoes, but will absorb all the delicious flavours in the pan. Cover with foil and roast for a further hour or until the meat tenderises and begins to fall away from the bone. Serve each person a helping of lamb and potatoes, and the roasted garlic squeezed out of its skin.

Pork cheeks with cider and white beans

Pork cheeks are a lost cut. So many of the interesting cheaper cuts have been obsolete for too long since butchers and retailers had a collective imagination bypass and went about mincing every cut that could not be roasted. But a campaign by traditional cookery enthusiasts has brought the cheek back into the stew pan, a cut with plenty of connective tissue that dissolves into almost sticky-sweet lozenges.

SERVES 6

2 tablespoons butter
1kg/2lb 4oz pork cheeks
1 rasher smoked streaky bacon
2 onions, finely chopped
8 garlic cloves, finely chopped
1 teaspoon dried oregano
1 tablespoon tomato purée
450g/1lb white haricot beans, soaked overnight in cold water then
     drained
1 wineglass ale, cider or white wine (or sherry, for a richer taste)
1.5 litres/2½ pints chicken stock or water
salt and white pepper

Melt the butter in a casserole and brown the pork cheeks lightly. Add the rasher of bacon and the onion and garlic and cook, stirring, for a few minutes. Add the oregano and tomato purée with the beans. Pour in the ale or wine, then add the stock or water. Bring to the boil, allow to bubble for 5 minutes then turn down to a simmer. Cook at about 90°C/195°F – the liquid should just bubble – for about 3 hours until the pork and beans are both tender. Season to taste.

Braised gammon, with fried apple and pumpkin seeds

Choose either a cured ham hock or rolled boneless piece of British gammon, buying a little more than you need so as to have some leftover cold meat. Smoked gammons are a little less salty. A good dish to eat with baked potatoes.

SERVES 4 MINIMUM
1–2 ham hocks, or a 1.5kg/3lb 5oz piece of gammon
1–2 tablespoons English mustard, made from mustard powder
4 tablespoons powdered palm sugar (or Demerara)
3 tablespoons butter
4 Cox's or other English apples, cored and sliced
4 tablespoons green pumpkin seeds
a little hot chicken stock (optional)

Put the hock or gammon into a large pan, cover with water, bring to the boil, then drain immediately, discarding the water. Cover with fresh water and bring to the boil a second time, then simmer very slowly for 15 minutes per 500g/just over 1lb.

Preheat the oven to 200°C/400°F/Gas 6. Remove the joint from the pan, untie any string, peel away the rind (using the tip of a knife to lift it), then spread with the mustard. Sprinkle with the sugar and put in the oven for 10 minutes. Meanwhile, melt the butter in a frying pan and fry the apple slices and pumpkin seeds until golden. Slice the meat and serve with the fried apples and seeds. You can add a little hot chicken stock if you wish.

Civilised kitchens

When my sister Sam left university with a languages degree after a flawless school career and announced that all she wanted to do was cook, my mother was a little horrified. Cooking was something you did if you were, you know, not very academic. My mother, who loved cooking and who was essentially a housewife, would not have wanted a job in a kitchen herself. The girls of her generation learned to cook because they needed to feed their husband and families. In the 1950s the feminist movement began its campaign to destroy this stereotype but cookery remained a subject for girls (and sometimes boys) who did not get a kick out of maths or physics. This is, of course, quite irrespective of the fact that cooking encompasses every academic subject.

Sam is my half-sister. We share a mother but Sam's name was Clarke. She went to work for the Eagle Pub in Farringdon, east London, cooking relaxed, Mediterranean food made from fresh seasonal ingredients. She met her future husband working in the kitchen in the Eagle, the sweet-natured and talented chef Samuel Clark. Samuel, who belongs in my 'honorary mothers hall of fame', had arrived at the Eagle after a long stint working for chefs Rose Gray and Ruth Rogers at the River Café. On his recommendation, my sister Sam headed over to work there for three years. Eventually Sam and Sam opened their own restaurant, Moro, to great acclaim. A combination of brains and creativity made Moro what it is today, proving that food is a great career for the brightest as well as the most artistic students.

Rose Gray had an enormous influence on both Sams, and hundreds of young chefs who went to work for her and Ruth at the River Café, not least Jamie Oliver, to whom both are still an obvious inspiration. When Gray died of breast cancer in 2010, the announcement on the BBC news followed that of a major earthquake in Peru. A sad moment but I am glad such a fuss was made. She and Rogers moved restaurant food away from the finicky fussiness that had previously won accolades, and gave a high profile to a style concentrated on good, sometimes humble ingredients and lightness of touch.

Rose Gray in particular instituted a culture of kitchen management that looked down on bullying. She made the professional, high-end restaurant kitchen, which before 1990 had been an almost exclusively male domain, a place where women could work and assert their own style and talent. Thanks to her, and others including Sally Clarke, and now Sam, restaurants have once again become places where women can use their natural instinct with food, and do not have to mimic the conventional style of men chefs – who can be much greater divas – to compete.

At home the two Sams' commitment to food carries on in the most natural way. Both are keen growers and the spare time on their allotment, and the food they cooked over an open fire there, for their children, friends and fellow allotment holders, became the subject of a book, *Moro East*. Sometimes, though, she will ask a neighbour who makes a great dal to make a potful. We once ate nearly a bucketful at one sitting. Even chefs need time off, and love to eat the food of others.

Pork with milk

A River Café dish that caught everyone's imagination when *The River Café Cook Book* was published in 1995 was an amazing braise of pork and milk, flavoured with lemon zest, garlic and fresh sage. It was a very typical River Café dish. As the pork simmered, covered in a bath of wholemilk, the liquid curdled to a thick caramel sauce. I have made this dish many times, using pork shoulder rather than the loin that Rose specified. A 2.25kg/5lb piece of shoulder will take 3 hours to cook.

Meanwhile, Sam and Sam had applied much River Café philosophy to a restaurant of their own that celebrated the Arabic influence on Spanish food. At Moro they cooked a Spanish version of pork in milk too, but flavoured with bay and cinnamon. But yoghurt is the dairy ingredient you find most often in their kitchen, made at the restaurant. They use it in sauces to eat with grilled meat, in a famously soggy cake and as a marinade. They also make divine vegetable soups with thick creamy yoghurt and ladle them into earthenware bowls with spiced butter. The following recipe is a nod to both them and the good and lasting influence of Rose Gray.

Pork shoulder cooked with yoghurt, cardamom and apple

The yoghurt will cook down to a thick, sweet mass, leaving not so much a juice as lemony-flavoured curds. Eat this dish with butter beans braised in stock and olive oil, or just with good artisan bread.

SERVES 4

1.8kg/4lb pork shoulder, boned and rolled, or 4 generous-sized pork shoulder chops
sea salt and black pepper
2 tablespoons butter
black seeds from 4 crushed cardamoms
1 teaspoon cumin seeds
2 garlic cloves, peeled and left whole
8 saffron strands infused in 2 tablespoons boiling water
1 litre/1¾ pints wholemilk or Greek-style yoghurt
To serve: 4 dessert apples, cored and sliced, plus 2 further tablespoons butter

Season the pork well; heat a large casserole and add the butter. When the butter foams, brown the pork well on all sides. Add the cardamom seeds and cumin and let them fry in the butter for a moment before adding the garlic, saffron and yoghurt. Bring to simmering point. The yoghurt will likely split but do not worry about this. Simmer very slowly for about 2–2½ hours (about 1½ if using shoulder chops), until the pork is tender. Leave the lid of the casserole half off while you cook the pork, so the sauce will thicken.

When the pork is ready, sauté the apple slices in some butter, in a small frying pan, until soft and slightly caramelised. Serve scattered around the pork in the dish.

A pot to store

Not every slow-braised dish has to be a hot one. The French slow-cook pork, sometimes adding game, until the meat falls into threads. They pack the meat juices and fat into pots and serve it as rillettes. More of an unctuous spread than a terrine, melted onto hot bread with pickles, this is French comfort food at its best. I had never potted my own pork until inspired by a delicious evening in a warm kitchen, one freezing December night. I had heard that Charlotte Moore was a wonderful cook from her daughter-in-law, Summer Nocon, who I worked with at the *Daily Telegraph*. Living in the Buckinghamshire countryside, where pheasants and wild rabbit swarm like locusts, Charlotte is always looking for ways to use up the meat. When I visited her on that cold night, she offered a huge bowl of rillettes made with pork and wild rabbit meat. She had cut out a recipe from a Saturday paper (reminding me very much of my mother's ways) from British chef Mark Hix's column in the *Independent*. His recipe for rabbit rillettes can be adapted to pheasant, too. We ate the whole bowl, and a stack of bread. I have rarely felt better.

Potted pork and rabbit

Always serve rillette-style dishes with cornichons or another pickle.

SERVES 4–6

1 wild rabbit, meat removed from the bone
100g/3½oz smoked pork belly, rind removed
5 garlic cloves, halved
½ teaspoon ground nutmeg
½ teaspoon ground Spanish paprika (optional)
2 teaspoons freshly ground black pepper
2 teaspoons Maldon sea salt
2 bay leaves
½ tablespoon fresh thyme leaves
½ teaspoon chopped rosemary leaves
200g/7oz goose or duck fat

Preheat the oven to 150°C/300°F/Gas 2. Put all the ingredients into
a small casserole: cast iron or ceramic is perfect. Add 150ml/¼ pint
cold water and gently bring the contents of the pan up to a simmer.
Cover with a sheet of foil and then with a lid and put into the oven
for 3–3½ hours. Stir occasionally, and add a little more water if the
liquid has evaporated. The meat is done when it is falling apart.
Empty the contents of the pan into a colander or sieve placed over a
bowl. Allow to cool a little and remove the bay leaves. With a fork or
very clean fingers, break up the pieces of meat into shreds, then
chop any large remaining pieces of fat. Transfer into a clean bowl
and mix in enough of the drained fat in the bowl to form a creamy
paste. Add more salt and pepper if required.

Transfer the mix into a bowl or sterilised jar. Spoon a little more fat on top, especially if you plan to keep it for some time. Store in the fridge – it will keep for up to 2 weeks, but check for signs of deterioration.

Kitchen note
To make a pheasant or duck version, substitute the exact quantity of the rabbit with either meat. You do not need to remove the meat from the bone but can strip it off afterwards, once it is cooked.

Potted pork with radish salad

This is my own version of plain pork rillettes, made with shallots.

SERVES 4

FOR THE POTTED PORK:

2 tablespoons duck fat

4 red shallots, finely chopped

5 thin slices smoked streaky bacon or pancetta, cut into 2cm/¾in
   pieces

250g/9oz fresh pork belly, cut into large dice

500g/1lb 2oz fresh pork shoulder, cut into large dice

½ teaspoon ground mace

small pinch of ground cloves

180ml/6fl oz dry cider, rosé or white wine

chicken stock or water

2 sprigs fresh thyme

1 bay leaf

salt and black pepper

Preheat the oven to 150°C/300°F/Gas 2. Put half the duck fat in a
heavy-based casserole over a medium heat and add the shallots with
the bacon, fresh pork and spices. Cook until pale golden, then add
the cider or wine. Cook for 1 minute, scraping the bottom of the pan
with a wooden spoon to remove any caramelised 'bits', then cover
with stock or water. Add the thyme and bay leaf. Bring to the boil,
turn down to a simmer and cook for 2–2½ hours or until the meat
breaks apart easily. Strain into a bowl, reserving the cooking liquid.
Remove the bay leaf and mash the meat with a fork to make a rough

paste. Put in a dish with a total of about 250ml/9fl oz of the cooking liquor (you can use up any remaining stock for soup or gravies).

Season with salt if necessary (note that the bacon already contains salt) and add pepper. Melt the rest of the duck fat and pour over the top. Cover and leave to set in the fridge.

RADISH SALAD

2 bunches of radishes, washed and thinly sliced, plus a few radish
  leaves (in good condition) to add to the salad
1 red shallot, thinly sliced
2 tablespoons red wine vinegar
5 tablespoons olive oil
sea salt

To make the salad, put the radishes and the leaves in a bowl with the shallot. Add the vinegar and oil and mix well. Season with salt before serving. If you make this salad too far in advance, the radishes lose their colour and heat. You can prepare them in advance, but then dress the salad at the last minute.

Kitchen note

Serve with pickled walnuts in place of the radish salad, or a mixture of cornichons and tiny capers (rinsed and drained).

Too good

The trouble with cooking well is that people want more and more of your food. Then having had more, they want more – and yet more. A popular chef will hire more staff, and you can only hope the goodness of the food is not diluted. Knowing when to ask for help, or halt the demand, is vital. Exhaustion kills enthusiasm very quickly. The cooking of a famous mère de Lyon, Eugénie Brazier, was so loved and famed she had to retire early through fatigue. Eugénie Brazier opened a tiny restaurant in Lyon, a porte pot, the Lyonnaise term for a bistrot, a place where you could eat a workday lunch and share a pot of wine. Brazier's fifteen seats were packed each day and had to expand and expand. Her most famous dishes were the simplest of all: gratinée lyonnaise (onion soup with grilled cheese), bread and milk soup. She was an expert with poultry and would carve the birds she had cooked at the table. Like all French women of her time, she made pot au feu. A grand version with black truffles slipped under the skin was another famous Brazier dish, but – never mind restaurant dining – a simple poached chicken is a dish every home needs. You can eat the meat for one meal, use the poaching stock in another, and feed off the leftovers for days.

Pot-cooked spring chicken with young veg

see PLATE 18

Serve with baked or boiled potatoes. Mére Brazier served her pot-cooked chicken with Dijon mustard and cornichons on the table – I recommend it.

SERVES 4

1 spring chicken – weighing about 1.4kg/3lb 4oz
1 sprig thyme
1 bay leaf
1 tablespoon butter
2 small shallots, peeled and left whole
16 young carrots, stalks removed, and/or other new season vegetables: green beans, peas, fennel, young new potatoes, small turnips
sea salt and black pepper
500ml/18fl oz chicken stock or water
chopped parsley, to serve

Preheat the oven to 200°C/400°F/Gas 6. Pull out any fat on the opening of the chicken cavity and discard. Put the herbs inside the cavity, truss the chicken tightly with string and rub with butter. Put it in a casserole and tuck the shallots and carrots around it. Season with salt and pepper and pour the stock or water around it. Cover with a lid and roast for 45 minutes. Remove the lid and cook for a further 20 minutes. Taste the cooking juices and season with a little more salt if necessary. Serve with chopped parsley.

Poached chicken and a supply of stock

An even more basic version and ideal for busy people. I make this when I need to have a few days of healthy living. Sometimes just a cup of the hot broth with a pinch of chopped parsley can do more than a cup of tea to give me a boost in the afternoon.

Put a whole corn-fed chicken in a pot and cover with stock brewed for 1 hour from a few roasted carcasses (the butcher will give you carcasses if you ask; just roast them for 20 minutes until browned – see page 390). The chicken will take 1 hour to cook. Eat with vegetables and herbs then put the carcass back in the pot with more water and give it another boiling to make more stock. Do this as often as you want.

Pot-roasted partridge with leeks, cider and smoked bacon

More pot-roasted game, this time a very full-flavoured recipe with wild red leg partridges, which are available from 1 September and usually abundant until the end of November. Pot-roasting suits partridge because you can extract every bit of the meat and not waste a thing.

SERVES 4

4 wild red leg partridges
4 garlic cloves, peeled and left whole
4 sprigs thyme
2 bay leaves, torn in half
1 star anise, broken into pieces
4 juniper berries
8 peppercorns
salt
2 rashers smoked bacon, chopped, or 1 heaped tablespoon smoked
    lardons
1 leek, sliced
1 walnut-sized piece of butter
150ml/¼ pint cider
250ml/9fl oz chicken stock or water
1 tablespoon chopped prunes
2 tablespoons double cream

Inside each bird put 1 garlic clove, 1 sprig of thyme, ½ bay leaf, 1 piece of star anise, 1 juniper berry and 2 peppercorns, then truss with string. Season with salt.

Preheat the oven to 180°C/350°F/Gas 4. Lightly brown the bacon in a casserole into which all 4 partridges can fit. Add the partridges and brown on all sides in the bacon fat, then add the leek and butter. Cook over medium heat for a few minutes, then add the cider. Simmer for 1 minute, then add the stock or water and prunes. Turn the heat right down so the liquid is barely moving and bubbles only occasionally. Cover and cook for 1–1½ hours or until the meat is tender and beginning to fall off the leg bones. Add more stock if necessary. Remove the partridges and keep them warm. Add the cream to the sauce and bring to the boil. Stir and add back the partridges. Leave to rest for a few minutes, and serve.

Slow-cooked vegetables

While the greater number of slowly made pots are designed to give economical cuts of meat the time to develop delicious textures and flavour, there are vegetables which cannot be prepared in a hurry. There are dozens of types of dried bean, grown all over the world, which are the nuts and bolts of everyday economical eating in the countries that produce them. In the UK most bean eating is centred around cans of baked beans, but not braised bean soups and stews. I am an enthusiastic buyer of canned reconstituted beans, and get cannellini, haricot and flageolet often. But when I want to slash the food budget down to just a few pence a head, I buy dried beans and restore them to toothsome softness myself in a casserole or soup pot.

I braise white haricot (navy) beans slowly back to life with garlic to make a dish that is good hot or cold, dressed with olive oil. Pale green flageolets, rich and delicate, can be cooked then finished with celery leaves, lettuce, white wine and butter. Big flat butter beans make a lusty supper when mixed with sautéed aubergines, onion and mint, and I also like to make a dark muscular pot of Mexican black beans with sweet pepper, coriander seed and paprika.

Soaking beans

Most beans are ready to cook if soaked overnight in cold water. This water must be discarded and the beans rinsed, because it can be toxic. There is such a thing as a bean that is too dry and will never reconstitute. Always use dried beans fairly soon after buying them because if they are too old, they will never cook, no matter how long you simmer them. There are hundreds of types, some of them dappled with pink or purple, some spotted, others tiny and white. Caroline Cranbrook, the farming expert mentioned earlier in this chapter, is a committed grower of beans from all over Europe and Latin America, and even grows a black bean that the Cherokee tribe travelled with, used as currency and called 'necklace of tears'. You see, there is romance with the cheapest foods in the world.

Boiling beans

Simply cover with water and bring to the boil, skimming off any foam that rises. White cannellini, haricots and flageolet will take about 1½ hours to cook, possibly 2. Butter beans take 1–2 hours, black beans approximately 1–1½ hours. Do not salt the water or the beans will be hard.

After cooking, drain the beans and rinse. You can then finish with fat, vegetables, spices and herbs.

Braised beans

The following ideas can be applied to the reconstituted dry weight of 200g/7oz beans, enough to serve 4.

* Haricots with garlic and tomato – heat 4 tablespoons olive oil and add 6 chopped garlic cloves, the cooked beans, 2 teaspoons dried oregano and 300ml/½ pint passata. Bring to the boil and add water just to cover the beans – but only just. Simmer for 20 minutes. Add salt, pepper and a teaspoon of sugar. Eat hot, or cold dressed with olive oil.
* Flageolets with butter, celery, lettuce and wine – heat 4 tablespoons butter and add a handful of chopped celery (or lovage) leaves, a handful of lettuce leaves, the cooked beans, a pinch of salt and a wineglass of white wine. Simmer for 5 minutes.
* Butter beans with aubergine and mint – cube 1–2 aubergines, put them in a colander and salt them for 1 hour (do this while the beans are boiling). Rinse the aubergines and pat dry with a towel. Heat 4 tablespoons olive oil and fry the aubergine until it takes on some colour. Add 3 chopped garlic cloves, 1 teaspoon ground coriander, a pinch of cinnamon, 3 deseeded chopped tomatoes and stir. Add the beans with a little water to loosen, if necessary. Simmer for 5 minutes. Season with salt and add a handful of chopped fresh mint.
* Mexican black beans with pepper – heat 4 tablespoons olive oil and add 2 chopped garlic cloves, 1 chopped onion, 1 teaspoon ground cumin, 1 teaspoon ground coriander and 2 red peppers, deseeded and chopped. Cook until the pepper is soft then add the beans, cook for a few more minutes, then season and serve with extra olive oil.

Baked Hungarian beans with smoked pork

Caroline Cranbrook, a mentor (see page 195) and a gifted grower and cook, grows three varieties of beans from Eastern Europe, collected from markets in the 1980s. She explained to me that in autumn, market stalls in Hungary are piled high with beautiful, multi-coloured beans – purple, mauve, brown, black and white – just the type that Jack-and-the-Beanstalk might have exchanged for his mother's cow. They are either eaten fresh, like borlotti beans, or dried – sometimes on their own, sometimes with meat.

SERVES 4
450g/1lb dried beans
1 tablespoon olive oil
1 small onion, chopped
1 garlic clove, chopped
1 teaspoon dried mustard powder
1 bay leaf, a little chopped parsley and thyme
black pepper
225g/8oz smoked pork
1 tablespoon molasses
3 tablespoons sugar
salt

Dried beans must always be soaked before use. Cover the dried beans with plenty of water and soak overnight. They will absorb most of the water. Drain them in the morning and put them in a saucepan of fresh, cold water and boil for 10 minutes. Drain again and throw the water away.

Heat the oil in a casserole and sweat the onion and garlic in it. When these are softened, add the beans, stirring well so they are covered in the oil. Add the mustard, herbs, black pepper and enough water so the beans are well covered with about 2cm/¾in of water above them. Add the pork, molasses and sugar and stir again.

Do not add the salt until the beans are cooked. If added earlier, the beans will be hard. Cover the casserole, bring to the boil and then cook in the oven very slowly for an hour or more. (Ideally, they should be cooked in the oven in a covered, earthenware casserole but they can also be cooked on top of the stove in a covered saucepan at very low heat.) Check the water level from time to time – they should not dry out. The beans are done when they are soft and the skins are starting to come off. Add salt to taste. The length of cooking will depend on the age of the beans – recently harvested dried beans cook in 1 hour. Older beans take much longer, but most take between 1½ and 2 hours.

 Ribollita

A vegetable stew-soup with a lovely rolling name, a word once heard most in the kitchens of humble country women in Italy. 'Reboiled' cannellini beans, broth, black cabbage, tomatoes and pearled spelt or farro. This is a soup I make and keep a supply of in the fridge, to heat when needed. Black cabbage, or cavolo nero, is now grown in Britain in winter and is increasingly easy to buy in farmers' markets and supermarkets.

SERVES 3–4
400g/14oz dried white cannellini beans
3 tablespoons olive oil, plus extra to serve
2 onions, chopped
2 carrots, chopped
2 celery sticks, chopped
4 garlic cloves, chopped
1 sprig sage
2 potatoes, diced
150g/5½oz pearled spelt or farro
1 x 400g/14oz can chopped Italian tomatoes
1 litre/1¾ pints water
6 leaves of black cabbage (cavolo nero), or green cabbage, chopped
salt and black pepper
4 slices ciabatta or other open-textured bread, cubed

Soak the beans overnight and then boil them in water for 1½ hours until tender. Drain in a colander and set to one side. Heat the olive oil over a low heat in a large pan, add the onions, carrots, celery, garlic, sage leaves, potatoes and spelt or farro. Cook for a minute or two then add the chopped tomatoes. Cover and simmer for 20 minutes. Add the boiled beans with the water and cavolo nero leaves and simmer for 1 hour. Season with salt and pepper. Remove from the heat and add the bread. Leave the soup to sit for half an hour. To serve, reheat what you need and ladle into bowls, generously drizzled with olive oil.

One last slow recipe - dual-purpose marmalade

This recipe is for a marmalade with a crystal-clear jelly and a substantial amount of thinly sliced peel. It is not one of those pulpy 'food processor' marmalades that I would classify as a jam. I call it dual purpose because once made, I reserve some of the syrup without the peel so I can use it in puddings. Making it involves time but much less labour than others. It needs your presence in the house more than anything else. Boiling the oranges whole softens the skins ready for slicing and makes it easy to remove the flesh and pips. You will need a muslin nappy or bag for the second boil.

15 bitter oranges (Seville)
2kg/4½lb preserving sugar

Put the oranges in a large pan and cover with 4 litres/7 pints water. Bring to the boil then simmer for 1 hour until the oranges have softened.

Lift out the oranges, leaving the cooking liquid in the pan. Allow the oranges to cool then cut into quarters and scoop out all the flesh and pips. Hold over a bowl to catch surplus juice. Transfer the pulp to a muslin bag or tie up in a muslin nappy. Put back into the pan with the cooking liquid.

Slice the orange quarters to the thickness you like – I like mine cut to 2mm/⅛in. They will be so soft and easy to cut that you can more or less pile 4 quarters on top of each other and slice all together. This speeds up what is ultimately the most tedious part of marmalade making. Add the sliced peel to the pan.

Add the preserving sugar to the pan and heat gently, stirring with a wooden spoon until the sugar has melted. Boil quite hard – what cooks call a 'rolling boil' – for about 1 hour until the mixture has reduced by at least one-third. To test for doneness, spoon a small amount of juice on to a dry plate and put it in the fridge. If a skin forms on top, it is ready to pot. If not, give it another 10–15 minutes boiling and test again.

Remove the muslin bag, squeezing as much juice from its contents as possible. Divide the mixture and pot some classic marmalade. Strain the remaining mixture for a supply of orange syrup and candied peel. Keep the syrup in bottles and the candied peel in plastic boxes.

Fifteen bitter oranges will make about six 450g/1lb pots of marmalade, or three pots plus two jars of orange syrup to use in sponge puddings, with pancakes (see page 113), in cookie or biscuit dough or for glazing hams or sausages. You can make a sublimely rich pudding by dipping brioche slices into a cream custard (made with egg yolks and single cream then heated, not boiled), then pouring over warmed orange syrup. A few shredded, unsalted, toasted pistachio nuts make this very elegant indeed.

Roast chicken

Roast duck

Roast beef

Yorkshire pudding

Argiano pork with herbs and garlic

Two-person pork or lamb roast

Fennel sauce for roasted meat

Potato, garlic and cream gratin

More root gratins: beetroot, parsnip, turnip, salsify

Onion soup gratin

Mother's aubergines

Baked marrow, chard and Gruyère cream

Fennel and potato gratin

Tomato, garlic, basil and crème fraiche

Tartiflette – baked cheese, bacon and potatoes

Rich pie pastry

Leek and tarragon flamiche

Picnic pie

Puff pastry pie filled with squash and washed-rind cheese

Baked pork terrine with figs

More terrines: duck, rabbit, veal, pheasant or partridge, chicken

Baked pork and saffron rice

Roast duck legs, stuffed with apple and black pudding

Baked buttered white cabbage

Baked trout and spring greens

Brown trout stuffed with mushrooms

Roasted flatfish with parsley mayonnaise

Overnight bread, including pizza dough and fruit bread

Gluten-free chestnut, maize and tapioca bread

Notepaper bread

Instant soft flatbreads

Lemon tart

Victoria sandwich

Banana and almond cake

Christmas cake

Christmas stollen

Sweet chicory lattice tart with old season orchard fruit

A POT
TO BAKE
IN THE
OVEN

Sometimes it feels like baking belongs to other people. Homebodies with all the time in the world to fulfil the domestic goddess fantasy; people with experience and confidence whose mothers taught them to make beautiful, golden cakes and glistening roasts. Kitchen orphans, experimenting with cookery and feeling their way, are too scared to shut the oven door, uncertain what will be going on inside. But let me tell you a secret: with good recipes, an oven can produce some of the easiest dishes and meals that memories are made of. If you are new to cooking, a roast is a great place to start. The oven, far from being a terrifying beast, is the mother of kitchen tools; give it the raw materials and, after a specified time nurturing them in the warmth, it delivers a lovable result. Once you have the inside information, baking is for everyone.

Roasting and baking, two words synonymous with a guarantee of happiness. Of course, not every cake rises or joint of meat will be perfectly done, but with a little practice and an eye on the heat, it is one of the least alarming ways to cook. I recommend any new cook to begin with learning to roast. There is plenty of science to explain what happens when you put something in the oven, and different ingredients react in various ways. Heavy cake batter is transformed into light sponge, doughy pastry becomes brittle, the skin of a chicken becomes crisp and golden while vegetables sweeten and catch a little colour.

Oven cooking covers such a vast range of much-loved foods: roasts, pies, gratins, breads and cakes – you could eat out of this chapter alone. And the following pages are about food and happiness. Typically, people will talk about their mother's roasts, their grandmothers' pies or their aunties' cakes. The memory of women's triumphs in the kitchen is tied up in ovens, or sometimes trussed, I should say. We are not lovers of gadgets, but we love our ovens. I once interviewed nearly forty male chefs for the *Telegraph* magazine about their home kitchens. Many admitted they never cooked at home and some even confessed they did not know how to work their cookers.

What ovens do

'What do ovens do?' I asked a pastry chef, Charlotte Oppe, who I worked with in a bakery when I was 21 years old. 'They dry things out,' she said. It sounds disastrous, baking the equivalent of drought – but she is right. No matter what you put in there, something drier will come out. Devotees of pan cooking get nervous around ovens. It's lack of control, probably. Taking the tongs or wooden spoon away is like losing the steering on the car. I always thought this is why ovens have windows, and men like barbecues . . .

I grew up in the countryside, where we had a cast-iron Aga and you never knew what on earth was going on inside. People who make soufflés in Agas have an awesome nerve. I remember the swearing when my mother's cast-iron, enamelled beast acted up and cakes were burnt. Or when it would nearly go out and the Christmas turkey took a day to roast. My father and stepmother had an ancient solid-fuel cooker which could get overzealously hot after a feed of coke. My stepmother once put a chicken in to roast to be eaten cold next day, forgot about it, and it actually disappeared.

I identify with the anxiety of giving up a dish of prepared ingredients to the closed workings inside an oven. I can still remember the

Bake

suspense, waiting for the timer to ding with the news that my early cooking experiments were ready. If you are a nervous cook, this chapter is for you as well as those who already love to cook. It is a celebration of pots to bake in the oven: hot, bubbling vegetable gratins that speak of the French style of cooking in my childhood; joints of meat, big and small, roasted with herbs, or foil parcels of whole fish, baked then eaten with buttery sauces. Soggy banana cakes are among a list of easy sweet things to bake in the oven, along with sweet tarts and a number of breads, some for every day, others for an occasion.

Fragrant roasts

Asked to recall a mother's cooking, the greater proportion of people will always remember a roast. Even those who never cook will attempt a roast at Christmas, and will likely please all who eat it, not just because a roast comes with a troop of other good things, like gravy, roast potatoes, bread sauce or Yorkshire pudding, but because a roast is so often a signal of love to others. We become nostalgic, recalling a certain group of people around a table eating a roast – slices of meat in pools of hot gravy are not easy meals to eat on laps in front of the TV.

Not that all our Sunday lunches reflected the Waltons' loving family routines in the American TV show. But the occasion instigated harmony of a sort. Like soldiers, we'd fall in, familiar with the rituals of dinner and a weekly ceremony that began with the carving of the meat. Already the room had filled with the persuasive aromas of the roast meat and the gravy, simmering in the roasting pan. We'd behave ourselves, more or less.

No-fuss roasts

At home our Sunday roasts tended to be beef, pork or lamb. Red meat was expected. For me, roast chickens will always have a European connection. The French, for example, respect poultry to the point that, from conception to the table, every moment of a hen's life is dedicated to our pleasure. Even the chickens from French supermarkets taste better; have crisper skins when roasted and stronger bones that make better stock. The side of my family who lived in continental Europe, or had been brought up there, could be relied upon for the best roast chicken. My grandmother's cook Jacqueline and my great-aunt Peggy served perfectly roasted, corn-fed chicken with very little but a jug of cooking juices and some sauté potatoes.

Dariel Garnett, an aunt who was raised in Italy and France, roasts a similarly good chicken at her home in London: all sticky, golden skin and firm-textured flesh that squeaks with tone when you bite. Ask her how she does it and at first she is not sure. It turns out that it is what she does not do, that counts. 'I use very little fat, just rub a tiny bit of olive oil onto it and put in a hot oven,' she says. She buys a decent, medium-price free-range chicken from a butcher, and does not make gravy, just drains off a little of the cooking fat and adds a glass or two of white wine. Dariel worked full-time when her children were young, but always cooked every day. 'I think it is a Latin thing, left over from my own childhood,' she says. 'Food is an essential part of living and when you cook for those you love, your husband, children or people you invite to your house, you are showing them a gesture of affection.' She believes that if food is simple, it is do-able when life is busy. 'I think there is too much fuss, too much worry about presentation,' she says. Unsurprisingly, when I visit her daughter Sophia, she roasts an equally perfect bird. It is just as it should be.

Roast chicken

There is a taste difference between naturally reared (free-range) and indoor (intensively) reared chicken, quite apart from the ethics of it all and animal welfare concerns over the latter – and there are many. And the extra cost, from about one-third of the price more, is justifiable if you put the bones in a pot afterwards and make a stock for use in other meals (see page 390).

SERVES 6
1 free-range chicken, approximately 1.5kg/3lb in weight
1 tablespoon olive oil
salt
1–2 wineglasses white wine
1 walnut-sized piece of butter

Preheat the oven to 220°C/425°F/Gas 7 and rub the chicken all over with the oil, almost massaging it onto every part. Tie the chicken legs together, if you wish, sprinkle with salt and put the chicken in a roasting pan. Roast for 1 hour to 1¼ hours. After 1 hour, test for doneness by sticking a skewer deep into the thickest part of the thigh and watching to see if the juices run clear. If the juices are pink, it means the chicken is still underdone. Allow another 15 minutes' cooking time and test again.

When done, put the chicken on a serving plate. Tip away excess fat from the pan and place the pan over a medium heat. Add the wine, and bring to the boil, stirring. Add the butter and stir into the juices, then take it off the heat, taste for seasoning and pour it into a jug to serve.

Cut the chicken up using scissors, or carve it if you wish. With scissors, cut down either side of the breastbone, then cut this long piece into two so you have 2 rectangles of breastbone with breast meat attached. Cut the side pieces in half to make two wing joints and two leg joints, both with a little breast meat attached. You can snip off the back ribcage, for reasons of tidiness, but there is some meat attached to this, too, including two lozenges of meat tucked behind the wing joint, called 'oysters'. This way 6 people can get the most out of one chicken. Serve with roast potatoes (see page 106) and the jug of cooking juices.

Kitchen note
It is possible to slow down the cooking of a chicken and buy time to do other things. Turn the oven to 150°C/300°F/Gas 2 and cook for 2 hours. The potatoes can go in at the same time and will be just as crunchy and good.

Roast duck

When roasting a duck, apply the same principles. You will need to roast it for longer, about 1 ½ hours for a 1.5kg/3lb duck, and use a fork to prick the skin around the edge of the bird to release the fat. Cut it up in the same way as a chicken. It is always better to roast a duck on a rack that fits inside a roasting dish, and to collect the fat in the pan halfway through cooking and use it for frying or roasting potatoes.

Roast beef

Never mind its lofty position as England's national dish, beef is easy to roast. Look in the old recipe books, Eliza Acton, Isabella Beeton, Constance Spry et al, and there is no fuss to doing it. Seasoning a piece of dry-aged, well-hung meat and roasting it is easy. Buying the best beef can be more of a challenge than cooking it. The maturation (hanging) is very important, because it has an enormous impact on tenderness and flavour. There is extra bonus in buying beef that is mature also at the time of slaughter, and grass-fed and native breeds have the perfect fine-grained texture for roasting. It will cost more, though. Choosing lower-grade beef from the UK is not like buying broiler-house chicken or the cheapest, imported pork, however. Concerns about welfare and feed are nothing like as serious, though there is a taste difference. When I buy more expensive beef, I buy it on the bone, or ask for the bones if it is filleted and rolled (the butcher will give you them). I make stock with the bones for other meals and use up leftover beef, too, to spread the cost.

TESTING FOR PERFECTLY DONE MEAT

For beef that is pink in the middle, well done on the edges, yet tender all the way through, you need a good sharp skewer, which you can buy yourself or beg from your butcher. Use this test, taught by my sister Sam Clark, and which I often quote:

✳ To roast any joint of beef on or off the bone (forerib, topside, silverside, whole sirloin), weighing 1.5kg/3lb 5oz (serves 6–8) to 2.5kg/5lb 8oz (serves 9–12): season the joint and sprinkle over some thyme sprigs or leaves, then roast at 220°C/425°F/Gas 7 for 20 minutes. Turn down to 160°C/325°F/Gas 3 and roast for 1½ hours.

✳ Test for doneness: take the joint out of the oven and stick a skewer into the deepest part of the centre of the meat. Leave the skewer in the meat for 1 minute, then remove and feel the part of the skewer that has been in contact with the centre of the joint. For meat that is pink, not too rare, inside, the skewer temperature should be just above blood temperature. If it has reached this temperature, leave the joint out of the oven, covered with foil, for 30 minutes to rest. If it needs further cooking, put the joint back in the oven and test again after 15 minutes.

✳ Make gravy simply by draining the fat from the pan into what will become your dripping bowl, then adding an optional tablespoon of flour (for thicker gravy) to the roasting pan, stirring it to a paste, and adding 300ml/½ pint beef stock. Serve with roast potatoes (see page 106) and Yorkshire pudding.

Bake

A NOTE ABOUT CARVING BEEF AND OTHER JOINTS

You must carve beef across the grain: not in line with the muscle fibres but at right angles to them. If you have any concerns about how to carve different cuts, buy your meat from a butcher and ask for guidance.

Kitchen note
If you buy beef on the bone, remember you can use the bones for stock (see page 390).

Yorkshire pudding

Tip a little of the dripping from the beef as it roasts and use it for the Yorkshire pudding. Allow about 45 minutes for the pudding to cook, keeping in mind the resting time for the beef and the time that the potatoes take to crisp up. Double ovens are a help when roasting beef, so that you can time the potatoes and pudding, which need hotter temperatures, perfectly. If you have a single oven, put the beef in earlier at the lower temperature specified in the recipe above. When ready, remove and rest it, covered in foil to keep it warm, then turn up the heat and cook the Yorkshire pudding.

SERVES 6
225g/8oz strong white flour
pinch of salt
3 eggs
400ml/14fl oz wholemilk
100–200ml/3½–7fl oz water
a little dripping

Put the flour and salt in a big bowl, make a well in the centre and add the eggs. Using a whisk to stir, gradually add the milk and water, beating it in until you have a batter with the consistency of single cream. If your eggs are very large, you will need only 100ml/3½fl oz of the water.

Melt some dripping in a large roasting tin over the hob until you see the first smoke rise off the fat. Pour in the batter and put the tin in the oven with the roast. Cook for about 45 minutes, until it is well puffed up – don't keep peeping, you will only let that valuable heat out of the oven. Serve immediately.

Crackling

The speciality of Italy, roast pork loin tucked into the roasting pan with herbs, cooked until the skin crackles. This recipe came from Sarah Sesti, an old friend, who cooked it in a wood-fired oven for a harvest celebration. We discussed whether or not to rub oil onto the rind, and both agreed that 'to oil' was better than not. I have tested pork roasting joints since, rubbing oil on one end and not the other. Time and again the oiled section comes up with a better 'honeycomb' crackle effect.

Argiano pork with herbs and garlic

see PLATE 19

Ideally, pork should be hung, or matured, to get really good crackling, and should come from a slower-grown animal that has had access to fields as well as shelter. Independent butchers are more likely to 'hang' pork to mature it.

SERVES 8–10

1 pork loin on the bone weighing about 2.5kg/5lb 8oz, the rind
   scored with a knife
8 tablespoons olive oil
8 sprigs sage
8 sprigs thyme
8 sprigs rosemary
salt and black pepper

Preheat the oven to 240°C/450°F/Gas 8. Boil a kettleful of water. Put the pork loin in the sink and pour the water over the rind then pat the joint dry with a towel. You will see the surface contract and the scores in it will open slightly. This helps with the crackling process. Take a long piece of string, tie it at one end and wind it around the pork, between each rib bone. Tie it tight at the other end. Put the meat in a roasting pan and rub the whole joint with the oil – on both sides. Tuck the sprigs of herbs under the string and season. Roast for 20 minutes then turn the oven down to 190°C/375°F/Gas 5 and roast for another 1½ hours. Take the meat out of the oven and rest it. If the crackling has not crisped and bubbled, possibly because of the reason given in the introduction to this recipe, do not worry, it will still be delicious. Eat with new potatoes roasted in the oven with oil and a few extra herbs. A big dish of olive oil-roasted aubergines, tomatoes, courgettes, garlic and fennel is perfect next to the pork.

Kitchen note
Shoulder is a more economical cut, but benefits from
a long slow roast, as does pork belly.

Two-person pork or lamb roast

Sometimes, just for two, I buy inexpensive fillets of pork or lamb, taken from the neck, for a small, ready-in-half-an-hour roast to eat in a variety of ways (see below). These cuts are easy to buy in butchers and are filleted off the bone. They can dry out, so be careful to time them correctly.

SERVES 2

1 neck fillet of lamb, or pork fillet (weighing approximately
    350–500g/12oz–1lb 2oz)
1 tablespoon olive oil
2 teaspoons dried oregano
salt and black pepper

Preheat the oven to 170°C/325°F/Gas 3. Rub the fillet with the oil
and season with the oregano, salt and pepper. Place the roasting pan
over a high heat on the hob and quickly brown the fillet on all sides.
Place the pan in the oven and cook for 25 minutes. This is quite a
low temperature for roasting and the meat should not dry out. If you
like lamb pink, remove it after 20 minutes, and allow to rest under a
sheet of foil. Rest the pork after roasting, too. To serve, slice quite
thinly.

THINGS TO EAT WITH PORK OR LAMB FILLET

* Lamb with mint, broad beans and lentils – buy frozen broad
  beans, plunge into boiling water for 1 minute and pop them out of
  their skins. Mix with braised Puy lentils (page 53), olive oil and
  chopped fresh mint.
* Lamb with mother's aubergines (see page 259).
* Lamb with warm tomatoes, oregano and feta cheese (see page
  127).
* Pork with butter beans, olive oil, black olive paste, parsley and
  courgettes (see page 160).
* Pork with French bean vinaigrette with shallots (see page 163).
* Pork or lamb with chickpea and rocket salad (see page 149).

* Pork with pearl barley and creamed button mushrooms (see page 130).
* Hot, grilled meat sandwiches – wrap either the pork or lamb in a toasted baguette and serve with fresh salad leaves and a pickle, sauce or chutney.

Fennel sauce for roasted meat

Grilled fennel and the flavour of sesame in a creamy yoghurt sauce – if you are barbecuing the meat, roast the fennel and quarter of a garlic bulb (skin left on) over the coals until dark but not burnt.

SERVES 4
2 tablespoons olive oil
2–4 garlic cloves (depending on preference), unpeeled
2 fennel bulbs, sliced, the green leaves reserved
300ml/½ pint Greek-style yoghurt
2 tablespoons tahini
juice of 1 lemon
salt and black pepper
more olive oil, to serve

Heat the oil in a grill pan and grill the garlic cloves and fennel slices, allowing them to become brown in places, which improves the flavour of the sauce. Peel the garlic and put in a food processor with the fennel. Add the yoghurt, tahini and lemon juice and blend until puréed. Season to taste, then put in a bowl and shake a little more oil on top. Scatter the reserved green fennel fronds on top.

Gratins

If there is one good aspect to washing up, it is the privilege of picking the delicious golden-brown bits from the edge of a dish that has baked in the oven. The French word for scrape is gratter, hence the cooking term 'gratin', which is now more or less in international use. Anything in a reasonably sloppy sauce, topped with cheese or breadcrumbs, falls into the gratin family. Irresistible dishes, they are the ones – along with baking bread and roasting coffee – that fill homes with the most potent, appetising smells.

Gratins include classics like pommes dauphinoise (potatoes with cream and garlic) and lovely, sticky, French onion soup. There are fresher-tasting concoctions on the list, made with the colourful vegetables of southern Europe: tomatoes, courgettes and aubergines. For colder days eat wintry, creamy rib-stickers, made with sliced parsnip, little turnips and a Schiaparelli-pink beetroot number. Children love gratins – think macaroni (see page 64) and lasagne – and mothers know this. Food that looks and smells so good has a calming effect.

It is not that gratins belong in the home or are exclusively a mother's speciality. Chefs love to serve dauphinoise in their restaurants, but what do they go and do? Cut little turrets of the layered potato dish with a round biscuit cutter and put them by the lamb cutlets. What a fuss, though I hope their sweating kitchen porters get to gratter all those wasted bits . . .

Gratin-ware

Shallow, straight-sided earthenware or heatproof porcelain dishes
are ideal for this kind of cooking. A 20cm/8in round dish will serve
four but it is good to have a larger one because a gratin is a
practical dish for making in advance to feed lots of people. A
shallow cast-iron gratin pan is also very useful, because it can be
used on the hob as well as in the oven. Lastly, two individual
dishes can be a romantic addition to the cupboard. Remember, this
is very loving food.

Potato, garlic and cream gratin

see PLATE 10

Pommes dauphinoise to the French, who invented it: thinly sliced potato
in a dish rubbed with garlic butter. Nico Ladenis, a great classic chef,
gives a good, true recipe for this in his cookbook-biography *My
Gastronomy* (1987, Ebury Press), then spoils it, admitting he likes to
serve it in little rounds carved out with the dreaded biscuit cutter. But
give over, the book was written in 1987 when fuss was fashion, and
Ladenis has to be forgiven. His description of the image he holds of his
Greek mother is one of the most touching ever written by a chef. He
describes her at the cast-iron stove at his childhood home in Tanzania,
'Wooden spoon in hand, her apron covered in flour, she would move
around the kitchen, tugging at the dough to make filo . . . I remember
the beautiful aroma of chicken stock made from whole chickens killed
that very morning which wafted through the house.' Ladenis was a
great, intuitive chef. For him, every moment of his time in the kitchen
was ruled by a single word: 'simple'.

Bake

Choose good white potatoes that will hold their shape, such as King Edwards or Maris Piper. Slicing them is easier if you have a mandolin (available from kitchen shops), but with a sharp, smooth-bladed knife it is not too difficult to slice the potatoes by hand. I find most double cream sold in our shops very bland. When this dish was invented it would have been made with ripened cream. I use crème fraiche to boost the flavour, so only a little salt is needed, and a sprig of thyme, which seems to restore the beta-carotene herbiness that old-fashioned milk and cream once had.

SERVES 6
8 medium-sized potatoes
150ml/¼ pint wholemilk
150ml/¼ pint crème fraiche
pinch of grated nutmeg
small pinch of salt
1 garlic clove, cut in half
1 tablespoon butter, softened
sprig of fresh thyme (optional)

Peel the potatoes then slice into rounds just 1–2mm/⅛in thick, at most. Soak the slices in cold water, which removes the starch, preventing the dish becoming stodgy. Heat the milk, crème fraiche, nutmeg and salt together, bringing it up to the boil in a pan then removing from the heat. Rub the sides and bottom of the gratin dish hard with the garlic, then use a piece of paper to butter it. Drain and dry the potatoes on a towel, then spread in layers adding a little of the milk mixture as you go. You do not need to be tidy about this. Keep back a little of the milk mixture to pour on top. Tuck the thyme sprig in the centre of the dish – it will add a subtle but grassy flavour to the milk. Bake for 45 minutes until the top is golden brown and the potato layers tender when pierced with a sharp-pointed knife.

Kitchen note
Purists never top a dauphinoise with cheese, mainly because
it is often the partner for roast best end of lamb or beef.
However, if you eat this gratin for supper with a green salad,
a little grated Cheddar or other hard cheese is wonderful.
You can cook and reheat this gratin successfully
(sometimes it's even nicer).

MORE ROOT GRATINS
Raw sliced roots can be treated in the same way as potatoes. No need to wash and soak them, however.

* Beetroot – make as for potato. Choose small, young beetroot and slice thinly (wearing rubber/plastic gloves). Prepare for astonishing colour.
* Parsnip – make as for potato. You may need a little extra milk as parsnips seem to absorb more than potatoes.
* Turnip – make as for potato, choosing smallish firm turnips, and add a small sprig of rosemary.
* Salsify – not easy to buy, but if you find it, peel the long thin root and cut into spears. Blanch in salted water first. The French often use canned salsify in their gratins, which is not bad at all.

Bake

Onion soup gratin

The dynamic Mère Brazier of Lyon was famous for this dish, which embodies practicality and economy. Soup is a rather loose term for her beautiful version, which contains egg yolks and can almost support a standing spoon. Give her a medal, I say, having never loved the fast-flowing type. Good fresh chicken stock (bought or see page 390) is a must.

SERVES 4
200g/7oz white or pale pink-fleshed onions, halved and finely sliced
2 tablespoons butter
1.2–1.5 litres/2–2½ pints chicken stock
1 day-old baguette, cut into rounds
200g/7oz grated Gruyère cheese
4 egg yolks
150ml/¼ pint red wine or port

Preheat the oven to 180°C/350°F/Gas 4. Put the onions and butter in a casserole and cook for 10–15 minutes, until they turn a golden colour. Be careful they do not burn. Add the stock, reserving one ladleful in a bowl, bring the onion mixture to the boil and simmer for 15 minutes, then pour the soup into a container and reserve. To finish the soup, toast the bread then put two layers of it in the bottom of the casserole, putting a layer of half the grated cheese between the bread layers and another on top. Spoon the soup over the bread slices, until just covered, then place the casserole in the oven and bake for half an hour, until the bread swells and the surface of the casserole is golden. Whisk together the egg yolks with the wine in the bowl with the reserved stock. Use a spoon to open the crust on the surface of the soup in several places, and pour the egg mixture into these openings. Gently shake the casserole from side to side, so everything blends. Put it over the heat for a minute or two, but do not let it boil. Then serve very hot, spooned into warmed bowls.

Mother's aubergines

see PLATE 20

This remarkable aubergine gratin was my introduction to a Greek, or rather Cretan, chef, Adonis Babelakis, whose stories of his mother's ingenious cooking inspired me to write a book about women's contribution to cooking. Babelakis serves it every day in his taverna, in Elounda, Crete. It was his mother's way to cook aubergines, and he credits her in naming the dish.

A measure of its greatness begins with the fact that my husband, an aubergine sceptic, will eat it. Other reasons include the faint flavour of goat butter, the way that Babelakis's mother prepared the aubergines for frying, the spearmint, the clever way water is used to allow the tomatoes to sweeten without drying out in the pan, and that olive oil is used to cook but then drained off so the dish is not a target of the usual complaint about Greek food – oiliness. Choose firm, long, slim aubergines. They have fewer seeds and a meatier texture.

Bake

SERVES 4

6 aubergines

2 tablespoons fine salt

8 tablespoons olive oil

2 onions, chopped

1 garlic clove, chopped

200ml/7fl oz water

1 tablespoon goat butter

leaves from 8 sprigs spearmint (or ordinary mint), chopped

1 teaspoon ground cumin

5 tomatoes, grated

1 tablespoon tomato paste

pinch of salt

pinch of sugar

leaves from 4 sprigs parsley, chopped

3 tablespoons grated hard ewe's milk cheese (Lord of the Hundreds,
    Somerset Rambler or pecorino are perfect)

Prepare the aubergines in advance. Peel and slice them, sprinkle with the salt and put in a plastic bag with holes punched in the base. Shake the bag and leave in a large bowl to catch the bitter water for 1½–2 hours – no more or the aubergines will dry out. Wash and dry the aubergines, then fry them quickly, in batches using half the oil. It does not matter if they are not fully cooked because they will be baked again later. Drain on a towel and set to one side.

Preheat the oven to 150°C/300°F/Gas 2. Heat the remaining oil in a casserole and add the onions and garlic. Cook for 2 minutes, then add 100ml/3½fl oz of the water. Bring to the boil, then add the goat butter, noting the lovely change in aroma. Add a handful of the chopped spearmint leaves and the ground cumin, then simmer for 5 minutes.

Add the tomatoes, tomato paste, salt and sugar. Simmer for 10 minutes until thick. Add the remaining 100ml/3½fl oz water, then cook for another 5 minutes. Tilt the pan and spoon out the excess oil, which can be discarded, then tip the tomato mixture into a bowl. Layer the aubergines in the pan, alternating with the tomato mixture, more chopped mint, little handfuls of chopped parsley and scatterings of the grated cheese. Finish with a little more grated cheese and bake for 45 minutes. This is good either hot or at room temperature, and it reheats beautifully.

Kitchen note
You can make this dish into a moussaka, using either fresh lamb mince or (better) minced leftover roasted lamb. For 4 people, use about 500g/1lb lamb, raw or cooked. Fry the lamb with a little garlic in a small amount of olive oil and set it to one side. Layer the dish exactly as explained in the recipe, but starting with the mince in a single layer, and excluding the cheese. Make a topping, mixing the cheese in the ingredients list (3 tablespoons) with 200ml/7fl oz double cream and 3 egg yolks. Pour it on top of the moussaka and bake as for the recipe.

Bake

Principle cooks

All the while the food of superchefs emerging in the late 1980s became increasingly fiddly, Sally Clarke was being very sensible in her Kensington restaurant. When she opened, and posted a no-choice menu – three courses and no alternatives on the door – it was shocking enough to be newsworthy. The food had a colourful parentage, provincial Franco-American, like a girl who had fled from bourgeois France into the arms of a long-haired Californian boyfriend (with an organic farm). This is not a metaphor for the very English Sally Clarke herself, but she had lived and worked in California kitchens and was heavily influenced by the cook, campaigner and writer Alice Waters of the Bay Area restaurant, Chez Panisse.

For 40 years Waters has gently spearheaded the US counter-culture against the burger-steakhouse diet. She triggered the organic-farming and food revolution on the West Coast, pioneered working kitchen gardens in local schools and even a prison, and through her restaurant taught French and Italian country cooking to North California, making it as well, if not better. I visited Waters in 2006 and I, too, fell under her spell.

Sally Clarke shares the same ethos in her own restaurant, but humbly complains she will never be as good as her friend. In many ways, given we do not have California's long growing season and that she has kept her organisation small, Sally has triumphed in a similar, enduring way. Eat her food and the understanding is that the ingredient is king. In 2009 she celebrated the restaurant's twenty-fifth anniversary. On that day, she cooked a marrow gratin that gave real dignity to a tricky vegetable.

Baked marrow, chard and Gruyère cream

Sally Clarke approaches Britain's most often vilified vegetable with determination. She deals with its marshy inner texture by giving it a brief boil, then slices it with the precision of a pâtissier making a tarte aux pommes. The final stroke of brilliance is the match with chard, a sturdy, briny leaf that itself needs a cohort, never being much good on its own. The end dish is elegant yet comforting, purring with the flavour of herbs.

SERVES 6
1 litre/1¾ pints wholemilk
2 bay leaves
salt and black pepper
1 tablespoon butter
1 tablespoon flour
4 tablespoons grated Gruyère
2 slices day-old bread, crusts removed
2 tablespoons chopped parsley
2 teaspoons chopped thyme
500g/1lb 2oz chard, including the stalks
¼ small–medium marrow, halved lengthways
olive oil

In a small pan, heat the milk gently to almost boiling with the bay leaves and some salt and pepper, then take off the heat and allow to infuse for about 10 minutes. Melt the butter in a small pan and add the flour, stirring over a medium heat until it starts to resemble sand. Pour the milk gradually into the pan, including the bay leaves, stirring until it thickens. Remove the bay leaves, sprinkle a tablespoon of Gruyère over the sauce to prevent a skin forming, and leave on one side, covered with a lid.

In a food processor, grind the bread until fine. Place in a bowl and add the herbs and a little seasoning.

Remove the white stalks from the chard and cut into 3cm/1¼in lengths approximately 1cm/½in wide. Bring a pan of salted water to the boil and blanch the stalks until tender – approximately 4–5 minutes. Remove, season and set aside to cool. Then blanch the marrow halves for 2 minutes, or until the flesh has just lost its 'rawness', remove and set aside to cool.

Place the chard leaves in a pan, drizzle with olive oil, salt and pepper, and steam, covered with a lid, until wilted – approximately 2–3 minutes. Drain and cool and chop very roughly if the leaves are large.

Once the blanched marrow has cooled, scoop out the large seeds, if any. With the flat surface on the board, cut across with a sharp knife into fine slices, keeping the shape together.

Preheat the oven to 170°C/325°F/Gas 3. Lightly butter a gratin dish and scatter the blanched white chard over the base. Sprinkle with a tablespoon of Gruyère. Next, cover with the green chard, adding another tablespoon of Gruyère. Finally, fan the marrow over the top, spreading the slices out slightly. Stir the sauce to loosen and pour over the vegetables evenly. Scatter the remaining cheese over the top, then the breadcrumbs and bake in the oven for 30 minutes or until golden brown and crisp at the edges.

Fennel and potato gratin

When I began to cook in earnest, taking a greater interest in food as I cooked in a café at the back of a cookbook shop in Portobello (Books for Cooks) in 1992, I bought Alice Waters's handsome cookery book, *Chez Panisse*. It cost me £25, which seemed a huge amount at the time. The book changed my mind about another vegetable I had always had difficulty with – fennel. I had never liked the coarse texture of the outer layers of the fennel bulb but it became so tender in her gratin recipe. This is an adaptation, which goes beautifully with fried fish, roast chicken and lamb. Or eat it on its own.

SERVES 4
500g/1lb 2oz new potatoes
3 fennel bulbs, sliced, the frothy leaves reserved
large pinch of salt
2 garlic cloves, peeled
juice of half a lemon
300ml/½ pint crème fraiche
4 tablespoons grated Parmesan
4 tablespoons fresh sourdough breadcrumbs (optional)
1 tablespoon butter

Preheat the oven to 175°C/350°F/Gas 4. Cook the potatoes until tender, then slice and set to one side in a gratin dish. Put the fennel into the pan with the salt, garlic and lemon juice and bring to the boil. Simmer for 15 minutes until the fennel is tender. Lift out the fennel and scatter it over the potatoes in the dish. Remove and discard the garlic. Boil the liquid in the pan until it is reduced to about 4–5 tablespoons. Add the crème fraiche and bring to the boil, pour over the fennel and potato, then scatter the cheese over, and breadcrumbs if using. Dot with little pieces of the butter. Bake until the surface is golden and the garlic cream is bubbling. Scatter the remaining fennel fronds over the top, and serve.

Kitchen note

Bronze fennel leaves are never sold in food shops but the plants are often available in garden centres. The leaves are exceptionally pretty, and unusually coloured. Scattered on fennel dishes, they are pure, delicious art.

Tomato, garlic, basil and crème fraiche

The last and simplest gratin in my list brings the blissful scent of tomatoes, garlic and basil, simmering in butter, into your kitchen. Cherry, plum or beef tomatoes are ideal for this, because there is more fibre to them. Eat with meat, on its own, spooned over pasta or on toasted bread.

SERVES 4
10 tomatoes, or 500g/1lb 2oz cherry tomatoes
2 tablespoons butter
leaves from 2 sprigs basil, torn into shreds
2 garlic cloves, chopped
300ml/½ pint crème fraiche
1 tablespoon grated Parmesan

Preheat the oven to 220°C/425°F/Gas 7. Cut the tomatoes in half, discarding the watery pips, then slice them. If you are using cherry tomatoes, just cut them in half. Melt the butter in a shallow cast-iron gratin pan that can be used on the hob (or use a frying pan and transfer to a gratin dish before baking). Add the tomatoes and basil and cook until the tomatoes begin to soften. Add the garlic and cook for another minute or two until fragrant.

Spoon the crème fraiche over the tomatoes and scatter with the Parmesan. Bake until spotted gold, then serve.

Kitchen note

Courgettes can be substituted for the tomatoes, yet cooked in the same way. Occasionally, I have made both for a feast and put them side by side on the table.

Word of mouth

If proof were needed that baking is possible even when it feels like you are out of time, it is in Louise (Haines), my editor. Her situation is unusual, in that one member of her family cannot eat wheat under any circumstances. Gluten-free ready-made breads and cakes are often disappointing, so the family make their own (the gluten-free bread on page 292 is the recipe they use). Louise likes to test her authors' recipes, especially those she can feed her family, and she has a stock of favourites picked up from books, magazines and by word of mouth. This kind of information-gathering is essential for her – a vital need most others can do without.

Bake

Often we don't bake because the industry gives us an excuse not to. Recipes do not get passed on from person to person, because there is no necessity with whole sections of supermarkets devoted to selling crumpets, pancakes and pies which taste good enough – though rarely great. It may seem a terribly obvious thing to point out, but if there is no verbal tradition of food, the blame must be laid at the door of the food industry, happy to destroy it for us and profit considerably. I talk to Louise about recipes for hours. I pass on what I hear to others. It is like a live frequency. Imagine if you were listening to the radio one day and every channel went dead. How disturbing would that be? That is how I imagine life without cooking conversations, like an Orwellian world with no shared thought. It hasn't happened – yet.

Tartiflette - baked cheese, bacon and potatoes

This recipe is one of Louise's, a good way to make the classic French tartiflette, a magazine recipe she cut out once. It is a clever recipe because the greater part of it can be done in advance. She is generous with the cheese but since you can buy decent, generic reblochon cheese easily and relatively cheaply, and this is a very filling dish, it is a great way to feed a hungry bunch economically. You will need a large ovenproof dish. I use a shallow enamelled pan because I can use it on top of the hob and in the oven.

SERVES 6

1kg/2lb 4oz waxy new potatoes – charlotte, pink fir and Jersey royal
   are ideal
2 tablespoons olive oil
300g/10½oz smoked bacon, streaky or back, cut into small chunks
2 onions, chopped
6 dessertspoons crème fraiche or Greek yoghurt
1 reblochon cheese, cut in half horizontally, the rind left on

Preheat the oven to 220°C/425°F/Gas 7. Heat a large pan of water
and boil the potatoes until just tender. Drain, allow them to cool a
little then cut in half if small, or slice diagonally. Fry the bacon in the
olive oil with the onion for a minute or two in a large pan, then add
the potatoes. Cook over a medium heat, stirring occasionally, for a
few minutes. Transfer the mixture to the ovenproof dish. Dot the
surface with the crème fraiche or yoghurt. Place the cheese halves,
cut side down, on top and bake for 20–30 minutes until the cheese
has melted and collapsed, oozing and bubbling all over the other,
crisp ingredients. Serve straight away.

Practical pastry

Since we can buy ready-to-use pastry, and good stuff made properly
with butter, too, I hesitate before offering a recipe. Being practical
and adopting the 'life's-too-short' attitude is perfectly fine. But you
may discover that you enjoy making it, and even have a talent for it
(there is truth in the saying that you need cool hands to handle
buttery dough).

My mother loved 'short' buttery homemade pastry, but hated making it. When as a teen I became interested in baking, she was encouraging. 'I like it rolled thinner,' she prompted, watching me work a circle of sweet pastry for a scallop-edged apple tart. She was not one of those mums who stuck your bad paintings on the wall – and she was wary about the good ones. Highly critical and demanding, she expected that if you were going to do something creative, and she saw cooking as an art, it had to be done right. This kind of parenting is very out of style. But it is not cruel. It dents confidence in a child, forcing thought and the question – is this the right way? 'I wouldn't do it that way,' was my mother's subtle line, watching me make something. She had spotted that I was interested in cooking, and was going to see me do better. She would never have bothered to tutor me had I hated to cook. If you do something, do it (very) well, went our unspoken family mantra. There is a case for suggesting that parents who heap praise on their children each time they make wonky fairy cakes have bred a generation of bumptious, overconfident adults who should never be let loose in the kitchen for fear of what might end up on the table.

The logical summary to this preamble is that if you are interested in making pastry, a truly mesmerising area of cookery that gives years of joy, always make it better than the one that can be bought in the shop.

Rich pie pastry

Good pastry depends on adding as much fat as possible to flour, without it becoming impossible to handle. The more fat in the pastry, the less it tastes of flour. This is a combination of a recipe my mother used to use when she first began to make pies, and one in Eliza Acton's 1845 book *Modern Cookery for Private Families*. I am a fan of Acton. She had a much better eye for good food than Isabella Beeton (though she never sold as many books). When you read her book you can sense how much she respected and loved ingredients and what you could make them do. Hence the dangerous (in terms of handling) quantity of butter and lard in her 'very superior suet pastry'. I love this rich pastry because it is as good cold as it is hot.

MAKES ENOUGH PASTRY FOR 2 LARGE PIES
375g/12oz suet
120g/4oz butter
675g/1½lb plain flour
½ teaspoon salt
about 4 tablespoons ice-cold water
1 egg beaten with 1 tablespoon of milk, for glazing

Store both the suet and the butter in the fridge before you begin making the pastry. Put the flour and salt in a bowl. Add the suet, then grate in the butter. Work quickly to a dough using the ice-cold water. Wrap in clingfilm and rest the dough in the fridge for about 30 minutes so it will be easier to roll. Roll out on a floured board to a thickness of 3–5mm/⅛–¼in. To cover a pie, cut a piece about 4cm/1½in larger all round than the pie dish. Brush the lip of the pie

Bake

dish with the beaten egg 'wash'. Use a pie chimney (or upturned ceramic egg cup) to support the pastry. Lay the pastry over the dish, allowing the overlap to hang down the sides. Refrigerate again, for about 30 minutes, then bake at 200°C/400°F/Gas 6, until golden.

Leek and tarragon flamiche

Based on a tart from Picardy, this can be made and loved at almost any time of year. It is filled with leeks, cheese and eggs, which are transformed by the aroma in the tarragon leaves. Add a little smoked ham to the mix, if you wish, to make it more meaty. It's worth doubling up and making two tarts when you have a lot of people to feed.

MAKES ONE 30 X 25CM (12 X 10IN) TART (SERVES 6)
3 young fresh leeks, split lengthways and sliced
30g/1oz butter
120g/4oz Wensleydale cheese, crumbled into small pieces
100g/3½oz cooked smoked ham, cut into small dice (optional)
3 egg yolks
300ml/½ pint single cream
pinch of grated nutmeg
leaves from 5 sprigs (40g/1½oz) fresh tarragon, chopped
salt and black pepper

FOR THE PASTRY:
375g/13oz plain flour
pinch of salt
250g/9oz chilled unsalted butter or lard, diced
3–4 tablespoons ice-cold water
1 egg, beaten, for glazing

To make the pastry, put the flour and salt in a bowl and rub in the fat lightly but thoroughly with your fingertips until the mixture resembles breadcrumbs. Work in enough cold water to form a dough. (This can all be done in a food processor, if you prefer.) Leave to rest for 30 minutes in the fridge, then roll the pastry out on a floured work surface to about 2mm/⅛in thickness. Use a baking tray of about 30 x 25cm and 2.5 cm deep/12 x 10in, 1in deep. Line the baking tray with pastry, prick all over with a fork, brush the edges with beaten egg, then put back in the fridge to chill.

Preheat the oven to 190°C/375°F/Gas 5.

Meanwhile, cook the leeks in the butter until just soft, about 15 minutes, then allow to cool. Put the cheese, ham if using, egg yolks, cream, nutmeg and tarragon in a bowl and mix well. Add the leeks and season with a little salt and pepper. Pour into the prepared pastry case (you do not need to blind bake the pastry) and bake until puffed and lightly golden on the surface. Cut into squares while still warm and serve.

Bake

Picnic pie

see PLATE 21

Two circles of shortcrust butter pastry (either bought or see page 273), pinched at the sides to make a galette, hiding layers of thin herb omelette, melted cheese and ham. Very easy to make, incredibly pretty when sliced, it is a parcel of favourite flavours. I made several of these pies for the party to celebrate my sister Samantha's wedding to Sam Clarke. When I saw the married couple's former bosses, Rose Gray and Ruth Rogers, helping themselves to more slices, I drowned in delicious pride.

SERVES 4–6
500g/1lb 2oz shortcrust pastry
6 eggs
1 tablespoon each chopped chives, basil, tarragon and parsley (you
  can leave out one or more of these, but the combination is lovely)
pinch of salt
30g/1oz butter
6 large or 9 small slices of ham
350g/12oz grated Gruyère
1 egg, beaten, for glazing

Preheat the oven to 200°C/400°F/Gas 6. Cut the pastry in half and, on a floured board, roll out two rounds of pastry, each about 30cm/12in in diameter, to a thickness of 3–5mm/⅛–¼in. Reserve a small strip of pastry – 1 x 4cm/½ x 1½in – to make a 'chimney'.

Beat the eggs and add the herbs with the pinch of salt. Melt a third of the butter in a 25cm/10in frying pan and pour in a third of the egg mixture. Cook for a minute or two, without stirring, then slide onto a plate. Make two more of these flat omelettes.

Lay one round of the pastry on a baking sheet. Place one of the omelettes in the centre of the round of pastry, then cover with a third of the ham. Grate a third of the cheese over the ham, follow with an omelette. Continue until you have three layers of omelette, ham and cheese.

Brush the edges of the pastry round with egg glaze. Cover the layers on the first round of pastry with the second round. Press the edges together. Brush the whole with more glaze then roll the edges, pinching them to seal. Brush the extra strip of pastry with egg glaze and form into a cylinder to make a chimney. Place on top of the pie. Use a pointed knife to make a hole in the pie, through the chimney. Bake the pie until crisp and golden (about 20–30 minutes). Serve hot or at room temperature.

Kitchen note

Use any remaining pastry to make straws. Roll it out, sprinkle with grated cheese and pinches of smoked paprika, cut into strips and bake until pale gold and crisp.

Puff pastry pie filled with squash and washed-rind cheese

This recipe is one I shared with Laura Hynd, whose photographs illustrate *Kitchenella*. I have worked with Laura since 2007. Sent on an assignment to Italy, we drove through a thunderstorm, arriving late for dinner. I had warned ahead that Laura did not eat meat or fish. 'Pig's liver, OK?' said our host Sarah Sesti, relieved we had finally arrived. 'Um, Laura doesn't . . .' But without blinking Sarah produced a dish Laura could eat. I vaguely remember her making a frittata (vegetable omelette) in minutes, or something similar. What a contrast to the afterthought vegetarian option, often added grudgingly to chef's menus in restaurants where facilities are perfect for a variety of choice. Whenever I work with Laura she unwittingly concentrates my mind on vegetables, and ways to use them that honour both the vegetable, and the person who loves them.

This is a pie to eat hot or at room temperature; the pungency of the cheese counters the sweetness of squash. I like it properly high baked, with dark glistening pastry.

SERVES 4–6
1 medium butternut squash, quartered, the seeds removed
1 tablespoon olive oil
500g/1lb 2oz ready-prepared puff pastry
plain flour for dusting
salt and black pepper
4 egg yolks, beaten
1 whole egg, beaten
100ml/3½fl oz milk
100ml/3½fl oz double cream
200g/7oz slices of semi-soft, washed-rind cheese, e.g. Stinking Bishop,
    Celtic Promise, Munster – or any smelly French cheese
1 egg, beaten, for glazing

You will need a shallow 25cm/10in baking tin.

Preheat the oven to 200°C/400°F/Gas 6. Rub the squash with the
olive oil, place in a roasting tin and bake for about 20 minutes.
Remove and allow to cool a little; cut the flesh from the hard skin and
slice. Set to one side.

Cut the pastry in half, dust the work surface with flour and roll out each
piece into a circle, slightly larger than the baking tin. Roll the pastry as
thinly as possible. Take one piece and line the baking tin with it.

Fill the pastry liner with the squash. Season with salt and pepper. Mix
together the egg yolks, egg, milk and cream and carefully pour over
the squash, but do not overfill. You will probably have some of the
mixture left – it is hard to say. Lay the slices of cheese on top of the
squash. Brush the edges of the pastry liner with the beaten egg and

Bake

place the second circle of pastry on top. Pinch the edges together. Brush the whole surface with the beaten egg and make a cut in the centre of the pie with a knife to allow steam to escape during baking. Bake for 45 minutes then remove from the oven and serve.

A pot of supplies

Like making pastry, it seems that life is too busy to make pâtés and terrines; useful foods to keep in the fridge for instant meals with hot toast, butter and pickles. Walk into a deli, and there are dozens of terrines on counters, sitting nobly behind glass like museum pieces. Lower-grade pâtés, wrapped in blister packs, are stacked in supermarket chiller cabinets, or on shelves in tins. I am suspicious of the vast majority of commercial pâtés because they are an opportunity to dump poor-quality meat that could have come from anywhere. It is only necessary, under EU rules, to show in which country the pâté or terrine was made, and not the country of origin of the meat.

Baked pork terrine with figs

Looking so good, with their layers of meat and wrapping of bacon, does not necessarily mean that terrines are difficult to make. And the reward is wonderful: freshly cooked, the flavours of the meat, marinade, herbs and seasoning come as notes, like a robust song. In the terrine below, one to make at any time of year, figs and hazelnuts hide inside a mix of fresh and cured pork (ask the butcher to prepare the meat for you). In autumn, look out for fresh cobnuts and use them instead of the hazelnuts. This terrine will keep for at least a week, in the fridge.

SERVES 8

375g/13oz fresh pork shoulder meat, chopped

375g/13oz fresh pork belly, minced

225g/8oz ham, diced

black pepper

pinch of dried thyme

100ml/3 ½fl oz white wine

10 Smyrna figs

2 tablespoons butter

2 onions, finely chopped or grated

1 egg, beaten

4 juniper berries

1 bay leaf

8 rashers green (unsmoked) streaky bacon, very thinly cut

2 tablespoons hazelnuts

You will need a 20cm/8in-long ceramic terrine dish, preferably with lid, or a small casserole.

Put the pork shoulder and belly meat into a bowl with the ham, season with pepper and thyme and add the wine and figs. Mix well and leave to marinate for about 1 hour. The meat will absorb much of the wine and become quite fragrant.

Melt half the butter in a pan and sauté the onion until lightly coloured. Allow to cool a little then add to the pork. Add the egg and stir the mixture well.

Preheat the oven to 160°C/325°F/Gas 3. Grease the terrine dish with the remaining butter, scatter the juniper berries over the bottom then lay the bay leaf roughly in the centre. Line the dish with strips of the streaky bacon.

Fill the dish half full with the pork mixture. Scatter the hazelnuts on top in one even layer. Heap the rest of the meat on top and bring any straggling pieces of bacon over that. Cover with foil then put on the lid and put the dish in a roasting pan half full with boiling water. Bake for 1½ hours.

Once cooked, remove from the oven, open the lid and place a couple of cans of beans on top as weights, having covered the terrine first with a layer of clingfilm. Allow to cool, refrigerate, then serve in thick slices with bread or toast. Put some pickles on the table.

MORE TERRINES
Replace the pork shoulder meat, marinade liquor, seasoning, fruit or nuts with the following alternatives (keep the bay leaf and juniper):
* Duck – with brandy, prunes and walnuts.
* Rabbit – with cider and lemon zest.
* Veal – with red wine and thyme.
* Pheasant or partridge – with gin and pistachio nuts.
* Chicken – with vermouth and tarragon.

Baked pork and saffron rice

A baked rice technique taught to me by a special Spanish chef, Maria José San Roman. San Roman is an expert on saffron who campaigns to encourage cooks to use the real thing from La Mancha in place of less powerful alternatives from other Mediterranean countries. She runs a famous tapas and restaurant in the seaside town of Alicante, called la Taberna del Gourmet. I ate a meal there, memorable not only for her unusual saffron-tinted dishes (fried potatoes; meringues), but also for certain freshly sweet species of fish, including my first taste of sea cucumber, a mysterious creature tasting of Dover sole. We also ate quantities of this easy-to-make yet clever pork dish. It is best to have a small paella pan, so you can cook on the hob as well as in the oven.

SERVES 3–4

For the saffron infusion: 8 strands Spanish saffron and 75ml/2½fl oz boiling-hot water

3 tablespoons olive oil

1 pork neck fillet (about 500g/1lb 2oz), cut into small dice

half a sweet red pepper, cut into very small dice

1 small onion, finely chopped

1 garlic clove, crushed to a paste with salt

1 dried nora pepper (available in Spanish shops), soaked in hot water then chopped, or ½ teaspoon smoked paprika

5 tablespoons paella or risotto (arborio/carnaroli) rice

250ml/9fl oz (or more) chicken or meat stock, or water

1 large head of broccoli divided into bite-sized florets, or a handful of green beans cut into bite-sized pieces

large handful of either wild rocket, watercress, landcress or baby chard

1 medium-sized courgette, diced, or 8 asparagus spears, cut into bite-sized pieces

To serve: half a lemon cut into 2 wedges, olive oil, salt and black pepper

Bake

Steep the saffron in the boiling-hot water for at least 30 minutes (or as long as you like).

Preheat the oven to 200°C/400°F/Gas 6. Heat the oil and fry the pork for 5 minutes. Add the sweet pepper, the onion, garlic and nora pepper (or paprika) with the saffron infusion and the rice. Cook for a minute or two, stirring, then cover with the stock or water so it is 1cm/½in deeper than the level of the rice. Bring to the boil, turn down to a simmer and cook for about 8 minutes.

Add the broccoli or beans to the pan, leaving it on top of the rice, and simmer for 2 minutes. Meanwhile, chop the rocket or other green leaves. Put the leaves on top of the broccoli, then the courgette or asparagus on top of the leaves – they will add humidity to the rice – and put it in the oven for a further 10 minutes. There is no need to cover it, it will cook evenly. Bring to the table. Squeeze over the lemon juice and add a few drops of olive oil, and season with salt and pepper. Give it a quick and gentle stir before serving heaped onto plates.

Roast duck legs, stuffed with apple and black pudding

Another humble roast using cheap-to-buy duck legs, glorious with the addition of a little equally modest stuffing under the skin.

SERVES 4

4 duck legs
1 English dessert apple, cored and chopped
200g/7oz black pudding, cut into chunks
4 heaped teaspoons fresh breadcrumbs
1 egg
sea salt

Preheat the oven to 160°C/325°F/Gas 3. Make a cavity between the
duck skin and thigh flesh, using your finger to separate the two. A
small sharp knife will help but do not pierce the skin. Mix the apple,
black pudding, breadcrumbs and egg into a coarse paste and stuff as
much as you can under the skin. Smooth the skin back into place.
Put in a roasting pan (preferably lined with baking paper) and
sprinkle a little salt on top. Roast for 1 hour, rest the dish in a warm
place for 15 minutes and serve.

Baked buttered white cabbage

I only have to smell white cabbage baking in a covered dish in the oven
with butter and I am back in my mother's kitchen, just before Sunday
lunch; roast pork, armoured with auburn crackling, is ready to carve.
The cabbage itself is transformed by baking into something smoky and
sweet. I find it can have an off-putting smell as it cooks, but this is gone
as soon as it is ready.

Bake

SERVES 6–8

3 tablespoons butter, approximately

1 medium white cabbage, leaves shredded, the stalk more finely
   chopped

black pepper

10 cumin seeds

1 bay leaf

Preheat the oven to 180°C/350°F/Gas 4. (A little hotter is fine if you are roasting potatoes at the same time.) Use half the butter to grease an ovenproof dish and put the cabbage into it, layering it with more butter and black pepper. Scatter the cumin seeds over and put the bay leaf on top. Cover with a lid or foil and bake for 45 minutes.

Baking fish

My mother-in-law, who worked for her local National Health Authority, was once asked to investigate why Afro-Caribbean women in particular were losing weight during a stay in hospital. It was not the obvious reason, bad food, but something much deeper. When interviewed, the women explained that the fish served on the ward was uneatable, because it was always served in fillets. As enthusiastic fish eaters, and cooks, they explained that they could not eat fish unless they could inspect the rest of the body: the heads, bones and tail. It is an anecdote that rings true. Restaurants often have trouble selling a whole fish to diners, who like all sign of life to be absent. Baking fish on the bone has added benefit, because the fish is always juicier – I think this may have been the ladies' main grumble. It is also, for new cooks, an easy way to cook fish and get good results.

Baked trout and spring greens

Trout are one of my favourite fish and even organically farmed are an economical buy. Buy a trout weighing 450g/1lb for each person. Ask the fishmonger to gut it for you. Season with salt and pepper inside. Insert a few thin slices of lemon or fresh fennel (or both) into the cavity, then rub the outside with olive oil. Wrap in baking paper or foil, securing it like a cracker at each end.

Preheat the oven to 200°C/400°F/Gas 6. Bake the trout for 15 minutes or until it feels firm to the touch and a pressed finger does not leave an imprint. This test is always the most reliable when baking fish. Remove the trout from the paper. Eat with a little melted butter, boiled new potatoes and some sautéed spring greens or chicory. Lift away the skin if you prefer not to eat it.

Brown trout stuffed with mushrooms

Mushrooms feature in virtually every traditional French bourgeois fish dish, especially with freshwater fish, yet the combination is unfashionable in Britain. But it is one to discover, not just because mushrooms do go well with fish but because a few chopped, ordinary mushrooms make one fish go a very long way.

SERVES 4
4 medium-sized farmed brown trout, gutted and left whole
1 tablespoon butter
4 small shallots, chopped
1 garlic clove, chopped
500g/1lb 2oz field mushrooms, finely chopped
1 tablespoon breadcrumbs, fresh or dry
salt and black pepper
softened butter or olive oil, for baking

FOR THE SAUCE:
2 tablespoons cider
1 small shallot, chopped
120g/4oz unsalted butter, melted
salt

Preheat the oven to 200°C/400°F/Gas 6. First remove the central bone from the trout (once you have tried this, you will find it easy). Turn the fish so the belly cavity faces you. Run a small sharp knife between the thin layer of 'rib' bones lining each side of the cavity and the flesh. Open out the fish as much as you can, then use the point of the knife to dig out the spinal bone and the smaller bones attached to it. Snip the spinal bone near the head end, and also down by the tail, then pull the whole central skeleton carefully out of the fish.

To make the stuffing, melt the butter and add the shallots, garlic and mushrooms. Fry over a medium heat until soft. Add the breadcrumbs, which should absorb any juice seeping from the fungi, then season to taste. Spoon some stuffing into each fish, place them on a greased baking sheet and bake them for about 15 minutes or until the flesh feels firm to the touch. Make a sauce about 10 minutes before serving. Put the cider in a pan with the shallot, bring to a simmer then whisk in the butter. Season with a little salt. Serve the sauce spooned around the fish.

Roasted flatfish with parsley mayonnaise

Lemon soles, dabs, brill or plaice benefit greatly from being roasted on the bone. They keep their juices and it is less easy to overcook the flesh, which can easily become mushy. Ask the fishmonger to gut the fish, but leave it whole.

To cook one fish, even though sizes vary, preheat the oven to 200°C/400°F/Gas 6. Put the flatfish (white skin/underside down) in a roasting pan, lined with foil. Melt 60g/2oz butter in a pan and pour over the fish. Lift and rotate the fish fully once, so that it gets a good coating. Season with salt and pepper, then bake until the fish feels firm: 10 minutes for small fish, up to 20 for a large plaice.

FOR THE PARSLEY MAYONNAISE:
2 egg yolks
150ml/¼ pint groundnut oil
50ml/2fl oz extra virgin olive oil
fresh lemon juice
1 handful of flat-leaf parsley, finely chopped
sea salt and white pepper

Bake

Put the egg yolks in an electric mixer and slowly whisk in the oils,
drip by drip to begin with, then in a slow stream once half the
volume has been added. Add a little lemon juice, to taste; stir in the
parsley and season with the salt and pepper.

Kitchen note
If you have some ordinary orange calendula (marigolds)
in a pot, break up the petals and add them to the parsley
mayonnaise. They will add a slight flavour and vivid colour.

Time to bake
It is asking a bit much, say the feminist academics, for food writers
to demand women give up their important jobs and bake cakes. We
have come too far, they complain, to put aprons back on and assume
the role of a 1950s housewife. When women were fighting hard for
equality in the workplace, cooking was rejected as a symbol of all
that was wrong with being a woman. He tinkered with the car at the
weekend after a long week's work while she baked, among her other
domestic duties. The feminist movement decreed that getting away
from stove and sink was a priority. Ultimately women got the jobs
they should have been getting, but nearly fifty years later there is a
sense that somehow it is still not right.

Have I time to bake, just for the sake of it? Not really, if I am being
truthful. Extraordinary, really, as it is my job to cook. On top of
cooking dinner each evening and putting in a fairly full day writing,
doing admin, looking after children and testing recipes, it is hard to
set aside an hour to make bread or cakes. I have never, never looked

down on it, however, and I yearn to do more. Being a feminist does not mean not being feminine. I was fascinated to read about a group of women in their mid-twenties who have formed the Shoreditch (East London) branch of the Women's Institute. Jazz Mellor, founder and president, enjoys knitting, embroidery and baking, believing these things to be an essential part of female history. 'We need to look at older crafts and reclaim some of those traditionally female pastimes,' she says. She says she is a feminist, but thinks the ladette culture women now adopt in order to be more like men, totally misses the point that the two sexes are, quite simply, different. Such behaviour has damaged women's self-respect, Mellor believes.

Women should be able to do and be what they are good at, and have both political and earning power. Quite when all this gets done is another matter, and the problem is, the job takes precedence. The family get whatever time is left, and cooking has to be quick and convenient. Forget baking. Why do it anyway when there are bakeries everywhere and supermarkets have entire aisles devoted to bread – some of it good, too?

Well, perhaps it is because the ability to do it is there. Baking is a department of cookery that needs recipes. It will go wrong without a set of instructions and scales. Without being flippant, comparing the behaviour of women to men in the kitchen, women will follow a formula if they know it will produce a result in an allotted time. Men like to cook in ways that are spontaneous – and can be abandoned while they go off and do something else. The cliché goes that men like to be seen to be cooking, and admired. OK, this is a stereotype. I do know men who bake, cook and wash up without complaint. And of course professional bakers are often men. But baking for no

Bake

salary, for the sake of love, in small quantities, is something that is in women. It is something we understand, even if that understanding is dormant. If men have it, it is borrowed.

Baking awakening

If baking is to come back into domestic kitchens, and I address this to both busy men and women, it has to be practical and ways need to be found for it to fit into life. Again, like pastry making, this is something to do only if you are interested in it. If you hate it and get bad results, go to a baker. But if your hands touch flour and you like its soft, flock feel, or you gasp with satisfaction at the sight of sponge in a tin, risen to a perfect dome, then you have begun to excavate that deeply buried need to turn some of the simplest, most economic ingredients into pure, scrumptious art.

Bread matters

Talking of archaeologists, few people have worked harder to dig out the baking instinct and bring it to the surface than teacher and professional baker Andrew Whitley. I know, I know, he is a man, but Whitley, a former journalist and self-confessed hippy, was originally motivated by a horror of the additives put into commercial bread and started a commercial organic bakery in Cumbria, one of the UK's first, so that consumers of convenience bread could choose something good. His book *Bread Matters* is one for anyone who wants the forensics on bread, and his bread-making courses in the Pentland Hills south of Edinburgh are among the best in the UK.

Overnight bread

Andrew's recipe for white bread would suit anyone who wants to start with a simple loaf needing very little thought and time. I have adapted it, and call it my overnight loaf because, while I sleep, the dough has a slow rise, developing twice the flavour. Note that the water is weighed – I recommend this for perfect results.

MAKES 2 LOAVES
3g/½ teaspoon dried yeast
600g/1lb 6oz flour (white or a mix of white and wholemeal)
400g/14oz water
5g/1 teaspoon salt
15g/1 tablespoon olive oil

In a large bowl, mix together the yeast, 150g/5½ oz of the flour and 130g/4½ oz of the water, until you have a smooth sticky dough, then leave covered with clingfilm for at least 15 hours at an ambient temperature. This is the 'sponge' (technical term for a yeast starter).

To make the final dough, mix the sponge with the remaining ingredients, then knead for 15 minutes by hand on the worktop or in a tabletop mixer fitted with a dough hook. The dough should be smooth and elastic but with enough moisture to make it slightly sticky when handled. Put in a bowl and allow the dough to rise a second time for 1½ hours. When it has doubled in size, knock the air out of it once more and divide in half. Shape it into two loaves, and place each on a baking sheet or in a small loaf tin to 'prove' for 30 minutes. Bake in an oven preheated to 230°C/450°F/Gas 8 (then

Bake

turned down to 200°C/400°F/Gas 6 after 5 minutes' baking) for approximately 20 minutes, or until the bread sounds hollow when tapped on the base.

MORE OVERNIGHT BREADS

* Pizza dough – use finely milled Italian '00' flour. Extend the leavening time so the dough is ready for the evening. Make the sponge overnight, as per the recipe, then make the dough in the morning. Leave in a cool place, even in the fridge, during the day. Bring to room temperature (this could take 1½ hours) before stretching or rolling into rounds and using.
* Add fruit – raisins, chopped prunes, sultanas; replace the second quantity of water with milk, replace the olive oil with butter.

Gluten-free chestnut, maize and tapioca bread

Among Andrew Whitley's concerns is the growing number of people with intolerance to bread. Intolerance ranges from quite rare serious conditions to a greater number of people who complain that bread makes them feel uncomfortable. Whitley says the reasons for intolerance are at many levels, from the wheat cultivar, to the way in which it is milled, the speed at which the bread is made and what is added in the process. Better bread, made slowly with good flour to a traditional recipe, seems to deal with most people's intolerance, but the group of people who cannot eat gluten deserve good bread and Whitley has come up with one, which I have adapted with the help of a friend who makes it all the time. The combination of four flours and sharpening of cider vinegar makes a flavoursome, nicely chewy crumb. The bread will toast, and is as good with jam as it is with cheese. Make in small batches.

MAKES 1 LOAF
5g/1 teaspoon fresh yeast
250ml/9fl oz water, heated to 30°C (just below hand temperature)
140g/5oz maize flour
60g/2oz chestnut flour (from Italian food/wholefood shops)
30g/1oz chickpea (gram) flour (from Indian food/wholefood shops)
30g/1oz manioc (tapioca) flour (from wholefood shops)
1 tablespoon cider vinegar
1 teaspoon salt
olive oil, to grease the loaf tin and to glaze the loaf
1 tablespoon golden linseed or sunflower seeds (optional)

Preheat the oven to 200°C/400°F/Gas 6. Dissolve the yeast in the water and set to one side. Put the flours into a separate bowl and add the vinegar and the salt. Add the yeast mixture and beat to make a smooth, pourable batter.

Grease a small bread tin and tip in the dough. Cover and leave to prove in a warm draught-free spot for 1½ hours. Do not expect it to rise as much as wheat-based dough – it should double in volume, however.

Brush the top of the loaf gently with olive oil, sprinkle with an even layer of seeds, if using, then bake the bread for about 30 minutes, until it begins to shrink away from the sides of the tin. Cool before slicing.

Bake

Notepaper bread

see PLATE 3

The result of an experiment, carried out with my daughter, who loves baking. Attempting to make the thinnest bread imaginable, to dip into tomato salads, eat with salami or herbed cream cheese, we got out a dusty old pasta roller and cleaned it up. The results, after a lot of fun and quite a bit of mess, drew gasps.

MAKES 10–14

150g/5½oz plain white '00' pasta flour (ordinary plain is OK but will not roll so thinly)
½ teaspoon salt
1½ tablespoons olive oil
75–100ml/2½–3½fl oz ice-cold water

First make the bread dough; it is best to use a tabletop mixer. Put the flour in a bowl and stir in the salt and oil. Slowly add the water while mixing. Do not add all the water unless the dough is dry. Continue to mix or knead for a minute or two until you have a smooth, soft, velvety dough that will not stick to your hands. Put the dough in a plastic bag and rest in the fridge for 1 hour.

Preheat the oven to 200°C/400°F/Gas 6 and brush a couple of baking sheets with olive oil. Cut the dough into walnut-sized lumps; you should end up with 10–14 pieces. It is a good idea to run a damp J-cloth through the pasta machine to remove any dust. Scatter extra flour onto the machine, set to the widest setting and run a piece of dough through it. Set to a narrower setting and run it through again, then once more on an even narrower setting until you have a long, transparent but easy-to-handle strip. Lay it on the baking sheet. Repeat, and then bake for about 10 minutes until pale gold. You will probably need to bake the bread in batches. Cool on a rack. You can prepare them several hours in advance.

Instant soft flatbreads

see PLATE 4

When the shops are shut, or you cannot find good bread, a simple mixture of water, plain white flour and olive oil will give you a dough that can be rolled thin and cooked in minutes, in a pan. Use it to wrap grilled meat, herbs and salad, or just to dip into vegetable purées and soups. Italian '00' flour will make softer breads. These breads can be stored after cooking and reheated. They keep for up to 24 hours.

MAKES 8 ROUND FLATBREADS
300g/10½oz plain white flour or '00' Italian pasta flour
½ teaspoon salt
3 tablespoons olive oil
150ml/¼ pint ice-cold water

Put the flour in a mixing bowl with the salt. Add the olive oil with the water and mix to a soft smooth dough. Take a piece the size of a golf ball and roll out into a circle on a floured surface, the size of a side plate. Heat a large frying pan and cook the bread on both sides until light brown spots appear and the dough loses its translucency. Small bubbles may form, especially if not used immediately.

Lemon tart

A rich lemon curd tart that has a beautiful, rich and translucent filling and is easy to make. I use bought sweet shortcrust pastry to make this tart. You will need a tart tin measuring approximately 25cm/10in.

300g/10½oz sweet shortcrust pastry
zest of 2 lemons, plus the juice of 1
1 large egg
85g/3oz melted butter
140g/5oz caster sugar
To serve: icing sugar, for dusting, and crème fraiche

Preheat the oven to 200°C/400°F/Gas 6. First line the pastry case with the pastry – you will not have to bake this tart 'blind' (i.e. bake the case first before filling). Roll the pastry out on a floured board to about 3mm/⅛in thick. Pick it up, rolling it onto the pin, and lower it into the tart tin. Press the pastry into the corners of the tin and neatly up against the sides. Patch any tears or holes with pastry off-cuts. Prick the base in a few places, using a fork.

Beat the zest of the lemons in a bowl with the egg, butter, caster sugar and the juice of just 1 lemon. Pour into the pastry case and bake for about 25 minutes. The top will brown. Allow to cool to room temperature. Dust with icing sugar and serve with crème fraiche.

Victoria sandwich

I looked to 1950s food writer Constance Spry's famous book for guidance on this summer classic. It is the one my mother still makes and, if you use good butter and eggs, the sponge will be the colour of buttercups. It may not rise to giddy heights, since I refuse to make cakes with margarine, but it will pass a taste test. Fill with raspberry jam.

3 large eggs, plus their weight (in the shell) of the following:
salted butter, at room temperature
caster sugar
white self-raising flour, sifted
For the filling: raspberry jam

Preheat the oven to 170°C/325°F/Gas 3. Butter two 18cm/7in 'sandwich' cake tins, then dust them with plain white flour.

Put the butter in a mixing bowl with the sugar and whisk until it looks like whipped cream. This is easier with an electric beater. Beat in the eggs, one at a time, each with a teaspoon of the sifted flour. Stir in the rest of the flour quickly, so the lightness of the mix is not broken down. Add a dessertspoonful of wholemilk if the mixture seems very stiff.

Divide the mixture between the two cake tins and bake for 20–30 minutes until risen, spongy to the touch and a skewer comes out clean when inserted into the cake. Turn out the cakes from the tins and allow to cool. Sandwich with a generous layer of raspberry jam, and dust the surface with a fine layer of caster sugar.

Bake

Banana and almond cake

see PLATE 22

Perfect food to carry around; a slice of something to kill hunger and give a little energy along with sweetness. The joy for me is that this is made with ground almonds, so it never dries out and has a real cakey texture.

120g/4oz butter, plus extra for greasing
120g/4oz dark muscovado sugar
120g/4oz golden syrup
1 heaped teaspoon cinnamon
3 medium-ripe bananas, roughly mashed
2 eggs
250g/9oz ground almonds

Preheat the oven to 150°C/300°F/Gas 2. Grease a loaf tin, about 20cm/8in long. Boil the butter, sugar and syrup in a pan together for 3 minutes. Cool for about 15 minutes, then stir in the cinnamon and bananas. Beat in the eggs, one at a time, and fold in the almonds. Bake for about 1½–2 hours, or until a skewer inserted into the cake comes out clean. Makes a soggy cake that lasts for about 5 days.

Doing what she does

We reach the end of childhood sceptical of our parents' ways, full of an urge to lead our own lives. We admire our mothers but we want to show we are different. Single identities are formed, in the choice of career, politics, social scene, art, music (especially music), dress and often food. Away from the watchful gaze, freedom to eat roasts without vegetables, freedom to eat only vegetables, indeed freedom to eat better food than was had at home. But then Christmas comes, that first one away from home, and you miss the idiosyncrasies. The brand of chocolates and the Cheese Footballs, the Christmas cake, quarried for days after Christmas, crumbling all over a scratched silver board.

When you get to cook your first Christmas dinner, don't tell me not a single element of home is there. It is like childrearing. I have the same rows with mine over the same topics my mother picked me up on. When I open my mouth to expostulate, I can hear her voice coming out of my mouth, like a teenager in the grip of a possession.

Christmas in our house was a major event. We were together every other year in my mother's house, with four of us children going to my father's on alternate years. My mother used to prepare for Christmas in the same way that others plan major sporting events. She did things the same way, every year, on a grand scale. When I made my first batch of turkey stuffing away from home, I made hers (see page 377). It was an incongruous situation; just my husband and me in a Dorset cottage, facing a bird that would easily feed ten. 'I see you have the family portion-control problem,' he said. Doing what she does, if she does it well, comes around to you in the end. Indelible delicious influence . . .

Bake

Christmas cake

In protest against the Italianisation of British Christmas, the hare and tortoise race between the light and doughy panettone and the heavyweight Dundee cake, here is my take on fruit cake, influenced by one in Phil Vickery's excellent book about puddings, full of fruit and one secret ingredient, to keep it all juicy long after Christmas is over. Make it about three weeks in advance, store wrapped in clingfilm or in a tin. It is very important to insulate the cake tin and to cook it at a low temperature.

500g/1lb 2oz unsalted butter
500g/1lb 2oz soft light brown sugar
400g/14oz plain flour, sifted
100g/3½oz ground almonds
8 eggs
2 teaspoons ground allspice
2 teaspoons ground mixed spice
100g/3½oz grated fresh pumpkin
2 tablespoons black treacle
5 tablespoons whisky (optional)
zest and juice of 1 orange
85g/3oz whole almonds
200g/7oz currants
200g/7oz sun-dried mini banana, chopped (these are the sticky ones, not the dry chips)
200g/7oz Smyrna figs, chopped
300g/10½oz raisins
100g/3½oz dried blueberries
200g/7oz ready-to-eat prunes, chopped
200g/7oz ready-to-eat dried apricots, chopped

FOR THE DECORATION:

candied mandarins, natural undyed glacé cherries or glacé kumquats; orange syrup (see page 235) or warmed sieved marmalade to glaze

alternatively, decorate the traditional way: good-quality natural marzipan and ready-to-roll fondant icing (available from supermarkets); orange syrup (see page 235) or warmed sieved marmalade to glaze the cake first

Butter the inside of a 25cm/10in springform cake tin, then line the bottom with a circle of baking parchment. Cut a long piece of baking paper (at least enough to go around the tin once) that is about 30–35cm/12–14in in width. Fold it in half and secure it inside the tin to form a cylinder of paper. It should adhere to the buttered sides of the tin. Cut a second piece that goes twice around the tin and wrap this around the outside, to the same height as the inner strip, this time securing by tying it with a piece of string. Preheat the oven to 140°C/275°F/Gas 1.

Put the butter and sugar in a large mixing bowl – a tabletop electric mixer will help – and mix until pale. Have ready the flour and ground almonds. With the beater still running, add 8 eggs, one at a time, adding a dessertspoonful of the flour and ground almonds every time 2 eggs have been added. Fold in the rest of the flour and almonds with the allspice and mixed spice.

Stir in the pumpkin, treacle and whisky, if using, then add the orange zest and juice. Finally, add the almonds and stir in all the fruit. Pour into the tin, to about 2.5cm/1in up above the rim. The strong layers of paper will allow you to do this without it

Bake

overflowing. It will rise as it cooks, too, so you will have a tall cake. You will probably have some leftover mix – perhaps make a spare, smaller cake to give away, or some fruity buns to eat immediately (you may have to wait a while before eating the bigger cake).

Bake the cake for about 5–6 hours. (Bake any buns for 30–45 minutes.) Test to see if the cake is done by inserting a skewer. If it comes out clean, it is ready. Cool in the tin for about 45 minutes, then remove and allow to cool completely before wrapping in greaseproof paper and then clingfilm and storing.

To decorate the cake with the glacé or candied fruit, make a little clump of it at the centre and brush repeatedly with the orange syrup. If using marzipan and fondant icing, decorate the top only (not the sides), using a substantial layer of each; brush the cake thoroughly with orange syrup or marmalade before the marzipan goes on.

Christmas stollen

Sybille Wilkinson is a great baker, and this is her Austrian grandmother Maria Vogginger's recipe, blissfully free of the marzipan worm that most commercial stollen has hidden in its middle. Note that you need a day and two nights to make this – not that you will have to work hard: the slowness of the recipe develops the flavour. Sybille recommends making this cake two weeks in advance of eating it.

100g/3 ½oz raisins
100g/3 ½oz sultanas
4 tablespoons rum
15g/½oz dried easy-bake yeast
125ml/4fl oz milk, heated until lukewarm
125g/4½oz caster sugar
500g/1lb 2oz plain flour
175g/6oz softened butter
2 eggs, beaten
pinch of salt
1 teaspoon cinnamon
100g/3 ½oz candied peel (optional)
100g/3 ½oz chopped almonds
zest of 1 lemon
To glaze: 30g/1oz melted butter; icing sugar

Soak the raisins and sultanas in the rum overnight. The following day, mix the yeast with the lukewarm milk and caster sugar. Put the flour into a bowl, make a well in the centre, add the yeast mixture and partially mix. Leave for 30 minutes.

Work in the butter, using a wooden spoon, then stir in the eggs, salt and cinnamon. Beat with a wooden spoon until smooth and bubbly. Drain the raisins and sultanas and add them to the mixture along with the candied peel, chopped almonds and lemon zest. Leave overnight to prove.

Preheat the oven to 170°C/325°F/Gas 3. On a floured work surface, roll the dough into an oblong about 2.5cm/1in thick. Make into a stollen shape with two overlapping folds, one from each side. Place

on a floured baking sheet and brush with melted butter.
Leave to 'prove' for 20 minutes, then bake for 45 minutes to
1 hour 15 minutes – the stollen is ready when an inserted skewer
comes out clean.

Take out of the oven, brush with more melted butter and dust with
icing sugar. Wrap in foil and clingfilm when cool and store.

Sweet chicory lattice tart with old season orchard fruit

The last winter tart, made with fruits that are always in season but which
remind us of summer, and chicory which after long cooking turns toffee
sweet. Eat with vanilla ice cream, instead of Christmas pudding.

4 tablespoons water
4 tablespoons Demerara sugar
3 chicory heads (red if possible), chopped
3 Bramley apples, peeled, cored and chopped
5 dried, pitted red or yellow semi-dried plums, chopped
5 pitted prunes, chopped
zest of 1 lemon, chopped
large pinch of mixed sweet spice (ground cloves, nutmeg and
    cinnamon)
250g/9oz sweet shortcrust pastry
1 egg, beaten, for glazing

You will need an 18–20cm/7–8in tart tin.

Put the water, sugar, chicory, fruit, lemon zest and spice into a pan and stew for about 30 minutes until soft and sweet-flavoured. Roll out the pastry on a well-floured surface to 3–5mm/⅛–¼in thick. Roll it onto the pin to lift it, then let it unroll over the tart tin so it falls into place. Line the tin with the pastry, pushing it into the edges. Run a sharp knife around the top of the tin to trim away the surplus. Refrigerate the prepared tin for about 15 minutes, and in the meantime knead the remaining pastry into a ball and set aside. Preheat the oven to 200°C/400°F/Gas 6.

Take the prepared tart tin out of the fridge and place a sheet of greaseproof paper inside it. Fill with a 1cm/½in-deep layer of dried beans or rice. Bake 'blind' in the oven for about 15 minutes, then remove. Spoon the chicory and fruit mixture into the tart. Roll out the remaining pastry and cut into 1cm/½in strips. Lay them in a lattice pattern on the surface of the tart, then brush with the beaten egg. Bake in the oven for another 20 minutes until the lattice is browned. Serve hot or at room temperature.

Bake

Asparagus with butter

Crepe-wrapped asparagus with grated cheese

Baked sea trout, with hollandaise sauce

Berries and cream

Raspberry clotted-cream fool, with honeycomb

Wild garlic omelette, with chilli, cheese and ham

Sorrel soup

Fried semolina cake with fresh wild greens and chilli

Venison steaks with warm porcini and watercress

Roast haunch of venison

Butter-braised pheasant, and many ways to eat it:

    Cold, with pink chicory, apple and walnuts

    Cold, with coronation sauce

    Warm, with pak choi, sesame and Shaoxing wine

    Warm, with braised pearl barley

    Warm, with ginger and coconut

    Warm, with rice pilaff

Roast saddle of hare

Three meals from one rabbit:

    Roast rabbit saddle, stuffed with liver and kidneys

    Rabbit soup, 'pistou'

    Salad with slow-cooked rabbit, mustard and honey

Grilled oysters with lettuce, cucumber and butter

Pan-fried smoked eel with mustard

Crab and potato salad, mustard and egg dressing

Bowled shrimps

Whole baked cheese, with toast 'spoons' and leafy celery

Figs with goat's cheese and spelt groats

Winter rhubarb with burnt cider cream

Wild blackberry and apple charlotte

A PLATE OF SOME-THING SPECIAL

The doorbell rings and the moment has arrived when those nice people you met through friends and your boss are on the doorstep. For the next few seconds, going to answer it, you nervously wish that tonight's plans had never been made, or that you could eat dinner out. Once inside your home they are going to know a lot more about you than ever before: chiefly your tastes and domestic skills. When they leave, what will they say to each other in the car on the way home? But then you relax. This time you kept it simple, took the seasonal approach and bought something fresh that needed only the lightest touch. Good ingredients shine, special food fascinates. It is perfectly possible to make a supper an event without melodrama. Who knows – it might even be fun.

It is the exposure that is the most off-putting aspect of dinner parties; the fear of letting guests across the threshold, like a swarm of reconnaissance planes. Their sharp eyes will miss nothing, you fret. Your unmatched cutlery and crumpled tablecloth, the less-than-fresh hand towel in the loo. Will you overdo the meat? Or botch the chocolate mousse? With an outbreak of sweat, ten minutes before eight, you vaguely recall that the colleague who is due to arrive any moment, whom you'd very much like to impress, said something about her husband being vegetarian.

It seems everyone is thoroughly wound up by the Come Dine With Me cult, the concept that you do not invite guests but critics into your house. But this has nothing to do with entertaining. It is masochistic, and obliging to bullies who love to humiliate others. Special occasions do not need to be competitions. Attempts to recreate restaurant gastronomy in homes only put fear into giving a dinner party. Sadly, it is yet another example where broadcasters make claims to having revived an interest in food yet succeed only at increasing a terror of cooking. Call me a killjoy, but like bear-baiting, the sport of laughing at others' failures is gruesomely uncivilised.

Of course, all this can be avoided by a strict rule that only people you love or trust may eat in your house. But I see the anxiety others feel about giving dinner parties. In fact, my own social life suffers because of it. 'I don't dare ask you to dinner, because you are a good cook,' they say, meaning that I am going to measure up their performance after and give it points. I reply, desperately, that I love talk, drink and can be relied upon to clean my plate, which makes me a perfect dinner party guest (surely?). It does not always work.

Hostess

Dinner parties are high risk, and ask a lot of the hostess. Having a tidy home is a nice, self-respecting start. Then there is a long list of rituals to get through without which it is not quite an event: the table to prepare, flowers into a vase, candles to secure into their holders, wine to sort, deciding who sits next to whom, not forgetting a tray set with coffee cups. You have not even started cooking yet. The stress can be enormous, leading to the inevitable row with your other half about who did the most. By the time the doorbell rings, you have not been on speaking terms for over an hour.

Hopefully, by the end of the evening you have drunk yourselves into a peace accord, but Emily Post, the twentieth-century American author on etiquette, always warned that if things go wrong, the fault will ultimately lie with the hostess, not the host. Even in our more equal world, she is probably right.

Post would definitely have got the job presenting *Come Dine With Me*. She knew how to put the fear of all the Gods into novice hostesses. In one description of a hypothetical evening of catastrophe, she explains how bad things can get, with a guest 'looking with almost hypnotised fascination – as her attention might be drawn to a street accident, against her will'.

It is only because people try too hard. My only rule, learned the hard way, is Do Less, and I think, or hope, that most people do this now, for their sanity more than anything else.

My mother did this, eventually. I think dinner parties used to frighten her, and she was a stickler. Fear and perfectionism is a cocktail that would put anyone under pressure. I remember helping her prepare a boiled dinner of salt brisket, ox tongue and watercress dumplings (see page 31) for Easter Day one year. I will never forget her insistence that the dumplings should be cooked at the very last minute, so they could be served when still bright green.

Do less

But she later developed a simpler way, relying on lovely ingredients speaking for themselves. It is funny how the best cooks almost have to go through a period of layering on the fuss, before stripping it away again to become great, simple cooks. Like an artist in training. A typical dinner at my mother's home, mid-summer, might well read as follows: asparagus with melted brown butter, a whole baked fish with hollandaise sauce, berries and crème fraiche. Everyone was happy. The food took no time to make – the ingredients, however, were very special.

Asparagus with butter

It is not just the long wait through a slow-to-happen spring that makes English asparagus so special, but the taste. Growers say that our cold winters and delayed growing season (European asparagus arrives up to two months earlier) allow the hardy asparagus in British fields to develop more flavour. Since one of the best asparagus farms I have come across happens to be in Angus, Scotland, this rings true.

Almost always, I serve asparagus boiled, with melted butter. Occasionally I add chopped parsley and grated lemon zest into the hot butter, or sometimes sprinkle a little grated hard ewe's milk cheese over the spears, either a pecorino, Manchego or British-made equivalent. To boil asparagus, lower the stems into boiling salted water and cook for 5 minutes, slightly more if the spears are very large. Do not dump the spears into a colander to drain after cooking. They are very delicate. Lift them out and drain on a towel. Melt some salted butter and pour over the still warm asparagus, once at the table. Hollandaise sauce (see page 313) is the rich and very delicious alternative.

Special

311

Crepe-wrapped asparagus with grated cheese

see PLATE 23

The exception to simple boiled asparagus: an adaptation of a dish made by Jeremy Lee, who cooks at the Blueprint Café in London. Rolled up in thin, rich crepes, a few stalks of asparagus will go a little further – but nothing is taken from their flavour. Use the crepe recipe on page 113.

SERVES 8

1kg/2lb 4oz asparagus

8 crepes, kept warm in a teacloth, piled on a plate

1 tablespoon olive oil

4 tablespoons Berkswell or other hard ewe's milk cheese, grated
(if you cannot find British cheese, use pecorino or Parmesan)

If necessary, cut the pale, dry, woody part of the stalk from the asparagus (some early asparagus is green, tender and juicy from one end to the other). Fill a large shallow pan with water and bring to the boil. Add a large pinch of salt. Drop the asparagus gently into the simmering water and cook for about 5 minutes or until tender when pierced with a knife. Remove with tongs and place on a towel to drain. It is better to handle the spears gently, like this, than to tip them into a colander. Transfer to a plate and shake over the olive oil, mainly on the spear end. Agitate the plate from side to side to spread the oil. To serve, roll three to four spears in a warm crepe, then sprinkle with the grated cheese.

Baked sea trout, with hollandaise sauce

A party classic, the fish is easy, though it is better to work on the principle that undercooking the fish is better than drying it out – so watch the time, and test the fish for doneness assiduously. You can use this recipe for salmon, sea bass, brill and turbot. The hollandaise is the best recipe I have come across, based on one in Nico Ladenis' book, *My Gastronomy. Lighter*, due to the whisking method. I also find it is less at risk of curdling because adding hot butter means it does not need to be on the hob at the crucial moment.

SERVES AT LEAST 4 – DEPENDING ON THE SIZE OF THE FISH
   (HOLLANDAISE RECIPE SERVES 6)
a 1–2kg/2lb 4oz–4lb 8oz wild sea trout – in season from April
   to late summer – cleaned (gutted)
1 small fennel bulb, sliced thinly, or a few fennel fronds
half a lemon, sliced thinly
salt and black pepper
a few fennel seeds
olive oil

FOR THE HOLLANDAISE:
1 pinch ground white pepper
1 teaspoon white wine vinegar
3 tablespoons water
4 egg yolks
200g/7oz unsalted butter
pinch of fine sea salt
juice of half a lemon

Special

313

Preheat the oven to 200°C/400°F/Gas 6. Stuff the inside of the fish with fennel and lemon, then put a little salt and pepper and about 8 fennel seeds into the cavity. Rub the outside of the fish with olive oil and season. Wrap the whole fish in baking paper or foil, but leave the wrapping slightly open, and place in a roasting pan. Bake for about 20–30 minutes – depending on the size of the fish. To test for doneness (which you should do after 15 minutes with a smaller fish), press the fish body with your finger. The fish is cooked if your finger leaves only a small indent, and the fish feels firm under the skin. If it is underdone, a pressed finger will leave a deeper mark.

To make the hollandaise sauce, put the pepper, vinegar and water in a pan and heat to boiling point. Put the seasoned liquid with the egg yolks in a warmed bowl and whisk until foamy and doubled in volume; this is easiest with an electric tabletop mixer with whisk attachment. Meanwhile, melt the butter, allowing it to come to a simmer, just before adding it to the egg mixture. If the butter is not hot enough, the sauce will not thicken. Begin to pour the melted butter into the frothy egg mixture, while whisking, in a slow thin dribble. When all has been added, stir in the salt and lemon juice. To keep the hollandaise warm, set the bowl over a pan of hot (not boiling) water, and stir from time to time. If the sauce seems thin, raise the temperature of the water in the pan beneath the bowl and whisk until thickened.

Serve the fish hot or at room temperature (though if you serve it cold you may want to eat it with mayonnaise; see page 416). Place on a serving dish and lift off the skin with a knife, revealing the pale pink flesh inside. Once you have carved away one fillet, lift off the central bone, which will come away with the head and tail. You can then take the meat that lies under it.

Berries and cream

My mother grew fat, bluish-red raspberries outdoors and served them in a glass bowl, a caster sugar shaker and a bowl of ripe crème fraiche beside. She also grew strawberries and redcurrants in the netted fruit cage, built to deter garden birds. For the pudding we ate at my sister's wedding lunch, she destalked and mixed all three red fruits herself, and came to church with pink fingers.

The berries that can be bought year round in supermarkets vary in quality, but basically the best are those from British farms, from late June through to October. Breeds vary, and there are new varieties that are not just bred for looks, but taste also. Glenample, Tulameen and Octavia are good raspberry breeds; Gariguette, and especially Ava, are strawberry breeds with a traditional 'wild strawberry' flavour. Aside from that, given the time, I am an avid pick-your-own fruit-farm devotee. They are friendly places that welcome children; I used to go more when they were young and saw an afternoon picking (and eating) as entertainment.

Raspberry clotted-cream fool, with honeycomb

see PLATE 24

A radiant pudding, to show off in a big glass bowl, to eat at a big dinner. It can be made hours in advance and stored in the fridge.

SERVES 8–10
1kg/2lb 4oz raspberries
1 tablespoon caster sugar
300ml/½ pint clotted cream, stirred to loosen
8 teaspoons honeycomb

Put the raspberries in a bowl and stir in the sugar and clotted cream. Mix well, folding with a spoon until the raspberries have broken down and the cream is incorporated. It does not matter if some of the cream is visible. Pour into the serving bowl and refrigerate. Dot with honeycomb pieces before serving.

Something special – rare, seasonal and wild

'What is that?' 'Sorrel – the leaves taste very sharp, of lemon.'
I must have had many conversations like these with my mother, walking through her vegetable patch. This was the place where she was always at her most relaxed, and impressive. There was always something new, cowering in cold soil or climbing up a six-foot pole. She has always loved to find the unfamiliar, and it put the art into her simple home cooking. But I was lucky to have that early primal training. Knowing your ingredients opens up great corridors of inspiration and taste. A bigger palette for the palate, you could say.

Rare, seasonal and wild things transform otherwise simple dishes into the kind of extraordinary cooking that leaves you thinking only of the joy of using them, and not the job. And as for those you feed them to, these plates of something special will become the most memorable they ever ate.

Being 'someone who cooks' begins with knowing how to do one or two things well. Then it grows to five. With some it stops there, and that is fine. Others carry on the big explore, trying out more ways with the meat, fish, fruit and vegetables that all shops sell. But there is a bigger world of food. Wander through a farmers' market or into a specialist food shop and you will often find unusual species of vegetable, wild edible leaves, flowers and herbs, unfamiliar seafood, rare-breed meat, strange pulses and grains. It's all very interesting, but having the confidence to buy into this diverse field of ingredients is sometimes another matter.

Imagine that the following pages replicate the kind of tutored forage that primitive families would have undertaken with every generation. 'You can eat that . . . Here, try this – NO! Don't for God's sake eat that berry!' Mothers are there to tell us what to eat, and what not to eat. Not only that, they show us, in the kitchen, how to turn it into something good. That is the ideal. They talk us through survival; at least, some do. There are great factions of mothers, even grandmothers, who have given up being any sort of kitchen tutor altogether, surrendering the choice of ingredient to whoever makes the ready meal. When a couple of generations stop teaching, when you cannot even ask Grandma what something is or what to do with it and it is down to you to widen the range of actual foods you use, there is an awesome amount to find out.

I am still learning about the special, weird and unfamiliar foods I find – and that is in the UK alone. Why one breed of sheep differs from another in texture and flavour, for example; how many different types of prawn live in the Bristol Channel, or being yet again surprised to find that the flower head of a weed I have always loved

Special

to look at, can be put in a salad and enjoyed for its slight flavour. You could be forgiven for asking, why bother? Beef, pork, lamb and chicken fulfil the needs of carnivores, surely? Why eat pheasant, venison or wild boar? I'd offer two reasons. The more diverse our diets, the healthier we are, and these foods are often economical to buy and good for you. Last but not least it is less boring. Or, it is better to say, and less flippant, that the discovery of new foods keeps cooking, which can feel like a relentless chore, creative.

Not that I indulge every day, because some of these special things will cost more. We may eat something unusual for an everyday meal, but often such food is a feature of occasions. Having people to dinner or Sunday lunch is a good excuse. What I like most about using something different is that while it should not be difficult to cook, it adds subtle enchantment to a dish; an unusual leaf, or the petals of an edible flower, can be transformative. Good becomes great.

First kill

The dark green leaves were a little squashed when they came out of the rucksack, and there were just a few. 'Look, Mum, I got you some wild garlic.' Jack was 14 and had been on a trek with his schoolmates. It was a sweet moment. He had spotted it, not had it pointed out to him ('I could smell it'). I could not have been happier if he'd walked in with seven dozen roses. It was my young hunter-gatherer's first kill, I suppose. I made an omelette with the garlic, and began to look forward to the rest of April, when this dark green, punchy leaf would be in season. While it can be picked in woodland (with permission), it also turns up in farmers' markets (check online for your nearest one), farm shops and specialist shops.

Wild garlic omelette, with chilli, cheese and ham

see PLATE 25

The mild aroma of the garlicky leaves, a little salty ham and melted strings of cheese, all tucked into the rich folds of an omelette.

SERVES 2

1 teaspoon butter
6 eggs
2 handfuls of wild garlic leaves, roughly chopped
¼ teaspoon salt
120g/4oz Gruyère cheese
2 slices of smoked ham, chopped

Have ready a warmed serving plate. Melt the butter over a low to medium heat in a frying pan until it begins to foam. Meanwhile, beat the eggs well, stir in the wild garlic and then the salt. Pour the mixture into the pan, allow to cook until the edges begin to firm, then use a table knife to draw the edges into the centre, in several places. Continue to cook for a few moments then sprinkle the cheese and ham over the surface of the omelette. Do not keep the temperature too high or the underside will become too brown. When the cheese has begun to melt but some of the egg is still a little runny, lift one side of the omelette with a spatula and flip it over to make a semi-circle. Slide the omelette onto a plate and serve immediately.

Special

Kitchen note

Transform this into an omelette to serve at room temperature like an Italian frittata, omitting the Gruyère and ham. A non-stick pan is essential. Add a little more salt and some black pepper. Cook the omelette without stirring over a very low heat for about 6–8 minutes. When it is firm but the top quarter still runny, cover the pan with a plate. Invert and then slide the omelette from the plate back into the pan. Cook for a further 2 minutes. Alternatively, if you have a grill, place it under a medium heat for a few minutes, until the runny top has set firm. Slide the omelette onto a serving plate or board, scatter with plenty of grated Parmesan and serve.

In search of special

We have increasing access to food with a rarity value. Supermarkets may not sell wild garlic, yet, but where there is enough supply, they have tapped into foods like cobnuts, English asparagus, Yorkshire rhubarb, exotic mushrooms, wild venison and game birds, and seafood from artisan fisheries. But these few items are hardly representative of all British specialist food. This is an area of food shopping where independent shops, producers and markets have all the advantage. They can take these foods straight from the harvest, fresh to the market, and not via a centralised distribution system. Supermarket chains are wary of buying into a supply insufficient for their millions of customers, and they think traditional breeds, wild and esoteric seasonal ingredients are far too 'niche'.

Richer hunting grounds are to be found in places run by professionals who can discuss what they sell, with you, over the counter. Or explain perhaps how to cook something unusual. Much as I understand the important role supermarkets play in daily life, it is rare that a member of their staff can give advice on cooking or can match the food knowledge typical of people who run independent food shops.

Unique
In 1993 I met Sheila Dillon, then the editor and producer of BBC Radio 4's *Food Programme*, which was presented by the legendary journalist Derek Cooper. For years I had listened to Cooper's gruff broadcasts, drinking in everything the programme taught me about food, good and bad. The programme made awkward listening for that side of the food industry which had been responsible for some of the more disgusting food safety scandals of the 1980s and 1990s. Cooper and Dillon could be stern in their criticism. But when they found something good, no matter how obscure, and a food producer who had integrity, they heaped honour upon them and campaigned for their survival.

I met Sheila on my birthday in 1993. We talked for hours about good food that was either lost or threatened. We debated the tragedy of independent butchers, fishmongers and greengrocers that had closed, but mostly we talked about delicious things. A year passed, and Sheila asked me to report on a butcher's shop doing great trade in the Test Valley. It was my first piece of food journalism, tutored by a master, and the beginning of the life I know now.

Sheila, who is married with one son, has often talked to me about continuing to buy, cook and eat good food, no matter the other

pressures of life and work. Having a job and a family, she of all people could have made the case for convenience food. But she had always seen eating well as a necessary part of each day. When Derek Cooper retired from *The Food Programme*, Sheila became the presenter and continues to inspire, every week.

Sorrel soup

My husband came back from a day in the West Country with Sheila, saying she had made him the most delicious soup, from a handful of sorrel picked in a garden. Make this soup just ahead of eating it, not because the lovely sharp flavour changes, but because sorrel discolours quickly and it will lose its appetising green colour. This is not essential, however, and you can always add a few parsley, chive and chervil leaves to bring back its charm.

SERVES 4

2 tablespoons butter
1 onion, chopped
2 medium-sized potatoes, finely diced
1 litre/1¾ pints water or fresh stock (use half the butter if using stock)
350g/12oz sorrel
4 tablespoons double cream
salt and white pepper

Melt the butter in a saucepan and add the onion. Cook over a medium heat until it softens, then add the potato. Cook for 1 minute, stirring, then add the water or stock. When it boils, turn it down to simmer and cook for 10–15 minutes until the potato is very soft. Add the sorrel, and bring back to the boil. Simmer for 1 minute then add the cream, plus salt and pepper to taste. Liquidise the soup, in batches, until smooth, and serve.

Kitchen note
For a greater treat, a raw Pacific-type oyster (see page 340), taken from its shell and added at the last moment so it part poaches in the hot soup, will be very elegant.

Wild greens
Wild food, including greens, fungi and meat such as venison or pheasant, is often low in fat and carbohydrate (sugars). So it is not a bottomless pit of energy resource, but ounce for ounce more nutritious. Wild foods have higher levels of vitamins, minerals and phytochemicals than food produced by agriculture. These are known to build defences against disease – food as a preventative remedy, if you like. Yet knowledge of nutrition in the UK is generally scanty among those who could be the most influential. Our general practitioners are barely trained in the subject and much of the information in newspapers about 'superfoods' is sensation planted by public relations companies working for big business. Our medical orthodoxy still concentrates on treating symptoms, usually with pharmaceutical drugs, rather than following a preventative policy based on good nutrition. Elsewhere, however, you witness something very different.

Travelling along a main road in the Peloponnese with a slickly dressed Athens business woman, Rea Kartelia, on the way to report on the olive oil harvest in winter, I was thrown forward in my seat when she screeched her gleaming saloon car to a halt. She leapt out, throwing her mobile phone back into the car and grabbing a folding penknife from the glove compartment, then staggered a few yards up the hillside in her heels. 'Radiki,' she exclaimed, hacking away at a clump of spiky, endive-type leaves. She filled an entire carrier bag, to take back to the city. 'We eat this at this time [December] boiled with the new season's extra virgin olive oil. It is very healthy, very very good for you.' When I asked her how she knew this, I already knew what the answer would be. Her mother had told her, who had been told by Rea's grandmother, and so it goes on. Lore, passed down through generations and now taken for granted by this modern woman. Everyone believes it, yet there is science to back up the claim that the diverse Mediterranean diet contributes to good heart health and lower incidences of diabetes than here in Britain, or America. Similar enthusiastic foraging goes on in many countries, all over the world, all in the name of good health – but also for pleasure.

Fried semolina cake with fresh wild greens and chilli

A crisp bread-crumbed shell hides a simple polenta-style 'cake', with lush greens and a small prickle of chilli pepper. Wild garlic, nettle tops or dandelion leaves can be used, but it is fine to add spinach (cooked first and the water squeezed out), rocket, chicory-type leaves or even watercress. This recipe is based on a Neapolitan dish, scagliuozzi, where rapini (sometimes called friarelli), a type of straggly broccoli, was used.

SERVES 6
2 tablespoons olive oil
½ teaspoon dried red chilli flakes
1kg/2lb 4oz friarelli, washed – substitute with spinach or curly kale
2 tablespoons grated pecorino cheese
1 teaspoon freshly ground black pepper
1 litre/1¾ pints water
2 teaspoons sea salt
500g/1lb 2oz semolina (ground durum wheat, from wholefood and
    Italian food shops)
1 egg, beaten
150g/5½oz dried breadcrumbs
olive oil for frying

You will need a 25 x 30cm/10 x 12in baking tray – about 3cm/1¼in deep, brushed with olive oil, then dusted with semolina – and a large whisk.

Heat the olive oil and chillies in a pan and add the friarelli. Cook for about 5 minutes, stirring occasionally, until tender but still bright green. Transfer to a bowl and allow to cool. Roughly chop, then add the pecorino and pepper.

Heat the water to boiling point in a large pan and add the salt. Begin to stir the water with the whisk then pour in the semolina in a steady thin stream, whisking all the time. Keep the mixture moving until it boils, about 5–7 minutes – it will be quite thick and start to come away from the sides of the pan.

Pour half into the prepared baking pan, lift the pan and slam it down on the surface so the mixture fills every corner, then spread the friarelli on top. Pour over the rest of the semolina mixture and leave to cool. It will set firm.

Cut into 5cm/2in squares, then each into 2 small triangles. Dip each in beaten egg, then breadcrumbs. Fry in olive oil, on both sides, until golden.

Kitchen note
You can make this dish using polenta meal, using the method and quantities on page 55.

Wild birds of paradise
On 1 February the British game bird shooting season is over. It begins on 12 August with grouse; partridge shooting starts on 1 September and, from 1 October, no pheasant is safe until the season ends. Pheasant, and to an extent partridges, became a feature of my life in winter, because my husband loves to both shoot them and eat them.

An occasional roast game bird is a feast close to nature and one that almost without fail brings tears of happiness to the eyes of men. But while men mostly have the job of providing game, even now, the skill of game cooking is feminine. It is an area of cookery where the allocation of roles in providing a meal is unchanged from our primitive beginnings and has been likened to a metaphor for sex and reproduction. Men give, women receive and then produce, the suggestion being that game remains a very sexy area in cooking. The only part of this I beg to alter, is that if he is going to bring me his quarry, could it please be oven-ready? My cookery books with the best game recipes are written by women who do things the old way, deft at plucking and dressing (gutting). Through the pages you can feel their disapproval of wimps who pay butchers £3 to do this. Wimps like me. Do I want to sit in the garden on a freezing December day, one hand clasped round a pair of scaly feet, the other grabbing at a handful of down, feathers stuck to my nose? No thanks. Some practices are best left in the past.

There have been a spate of hunter-gatherers on TV, killing, cooking and eating. If this is part of a campaign to encourage game cooking at home, I have doubts about its effectiveness. While the panoramas of the British countryside are always enjoyable, do we really need to confront the kill? We do not need to watch a scene in an abattoir to be talked into buying a pound of sausages. In fact, it's more likely to have the opposite effect. Women are rarely involved in killing for food, and often possess an integral distaste for it. There are nearly twice the number of female vegetarians as men who do not eat meat. If programme-makers genuinely want to introduce female cooks to game, it would be better to march us into a butcher's where there is a £2 rabbit on the counter, or off to Sainsbury's, where you can now buy an oven-ready pheasant, or wild venison.

For the same reason, the clumsy machismo and the assumption that game comes served with a side order of blood and gore, has to be dropped. There is a real case for bringing the naturalness of game to kitchens where factory-farmed chicken rules, but absolutely no reason why it has to arrive looking like it went ten rounds with a flyweight champion. My modern manifesto for the encouragement of game eating says that it has to be appetising – no bruised meat, please – and it must be accessible, meaning we need to dust off the old ways of preparing it. The gentlemen's club style with its bread sauce, gravy and game chips has a place, but I want to eat game dishes that have colour, drama and aroma, made with fresher meat in easy cuts.

Thankfully there are major game suppliers who realise this and who now present game beautifully, offering neatly tied birds or easy-to-use fillets. Supermarkets have actually become good places for game birds and wild venison – just don't ask for cooking advice. Good game is also available online.

Venison steaks with warm porcini and watercress

Quick to prepare, with flavours that conjure the woods and streams of the West Country. Venison steaks are nicest eaten rare, flashed briefly on a hot grill then rested for a few minutes in a warm place. Keep in mind that this is meat with no fat, which can dry out if overcooked. Any venison breed, red, roe, sika or fallow, is suitable for this dish. Eat with any of the following: braised puy lentils (page 53), boiled new potatoes, parsnips sautéed with butter or roasted slices of squash or pumpkin.

SERVES 4

100g/3½oz dried porcini mushrooms, soaked in a cup of boiling
  water or stock
3 tablespoons butter
1 garlic clove, finely chopped
2 tablespoons sherry
1 teaspoon honey
butter for grilling
4 boneless venison leg or loin steaks or medallions, weighing
  150–250g/5½–9oz, cut to about 2cm/¾in thick
salt and black pepper
1 large bunch of watercress, chopped

Have ready some warm plates: venison cools very quickly once sliced.

Drain the porcini, reserving the liquid, then chop finely. Melt the
butter in a pan and add the garlic and porcini. Fry over a low
temperature until glossy and fragrant, then add 100ml/3½fl oz of the
soaking liquid, the sherry and honey. Cook, simmering, for about
3 minutes, then turn off the heat and set to one side.

Shortly before serving, heat a grill pan and melt a little butter in it.
Season the venison steaks with salt and pepper, then cook them for
approximately 1–2 minutes either side or until you can see little red
droplets rise to the surface of the meat (indicating rare/medium-rare).
Remove from the pan and allow to rest, covered in foil, for about
10 minutes. Meanwhile, heat the sauce until it bubbles, and add the
watercress. Cook for about 2 minutes.

Serve each steak with the sauce beside it.

Roast haunch of venison

All breeds of venison (roe, sika, fallow and red) have fine-grained meat with absolutely no fat marbling and a haunch cannot be roasted at a high temperature like a leg of lamb. There is a good chance it will dry out. Added to this, it is hard to be certain of the age of the animal, and unless it has been hung for long enough, it may never be tender. I do not agree that either marinating or larding (threading with strips of lard) whole pieces of meat helps.

Simply rub the whole joint with a lot of butter, season it then roast at 150°C/300°F/Gas 2 for approximately 1½–2 hours or until the meat inside reaches about 55°C/130°F. Use a thermometer probe to check, or keep an eye on the meat. You can also use the test on page 248. When you see the juices are bubbling under the thick but transparent membrane that covers venison, take it out of the oven, cover with two layers of foil and rest it for 1 hour. Essentially, you have brought the meat 'to the boil' and switched it off. As it rests, the juices will gradually settle back into the meat fibre. When you carve, the meat inside should be evenly pink throughout, like medium rare, and very juicy. Always serve on warm plates. And put a large jar of orchard fruit or rowanberry jelly on the table. Make a gravy by pouring off half the fat in the pan, then placing over a higher heat and sautéing a rasher of smoked bacon and 2 shallots in it. Add a large splash of wine, simmer, then add 300ml/½ pint meat stock and a spoonful of rowan, redcurrant or other orchard fruit jelly. Continue to simmer, then season to taste.

Butter-braised pheasant, and many ways to eat it

Stumped for an idea to feed a lot of people, and under pressure to use a surplus of pheasant meat that was clogging the freezer, I looked for an easy way out. I cut the breast meat off each bird, muttering that I'd worry about what to do with the legs later (see the confit recipe on page 417 and the potted pork recipe on page 221). Concerned over the dryness problem – like all game, pheasant has no fat marbling in its meat – I decided not to fry or roast the breasts but to simmer them in spiced butter. Success – the end game was tender, juicy meat, ready to add to other things.

SERVES 4
250g/9oz butter
½ teaspoon ground allspice
8 pheasant breasts

Melt the butter in a pan, add the allspice, then the pheasant breasts. Cook the pheasant breasts over a very low heat for about 20 minutes. Lift out and serve either hot or cold, following one of the suggestions below.

MORE WAYS TO EAT BUTTER-BRAISED PHEASANT

Recipes using 8 pheasant breasts, serving 4 generously:

* Cold, thinly sliced, with pink chicory, thinly sliced apple, toasted walnuts and a dressing made from 2 teaspoons cider vinegar, 3 tablespoons groundnut or walnut oil, 1 heaped teaspoon Dijon mustard (or to taste), a pinch of sugar, salt and white pepper.

* Cold, with the coronation sauce on page 156.

* Warm and sliced with steamed pak choi and a sauce made from 2 tablespoons Shaoxing wine, 1 tablespoon light soy sauce, juice of 1 lime, 1 garlic clove (finely chopped), 1 teaspoon sesame oil, 1 tablespoon sesame seeds (toasted in a dry pan) and 1 red chilli, finely chopped. Scatter coriander over.

* Warm with braised pearl barley and apple or quince jelly. To cook the barley, melt 1 tablespoon butter and add 1 chopped shallot. Cook for 1 minute then add 200g/7oz pearl barley. Add stock to cover, or water, then cook for 20 minutes until the barley is just tender. Add chopped parsley before serving. Apple and other orchard fruit jellies are widely available from delis.

* Warm, with a spiced sauce made with ginger and coconut. Heat 2 tablespoons oil, fry 1 chopped onion, 2 chopped garlic cloves, 1 x 2cm/¾in piece of ginger, grated, and add 1 tablespoon medium curry powder and ½ teaspoon salt. Cook for a minute or two without burning, then add half a block of coconut cream, 4 chopped tomatoes and a glass of water. Simmer until thick-textured and aromatic, then serve spooned over the pheasant with coriander leaves scattered on top.

* Warm, sliced and added to the rice pilaff on page 68 (omit the chicken). Add pomegranate pips, toasted almonds, chopped flat-leaf parsley, yellow sultanas – and serve with Greek yoghurt.

Roast saddle of hare

It is better to roast a saddle (loin joint) of hare on the bone, then carve it off and slice it. This way the meat will keep its lovely juices. Again, keep it very simple, and serve it a little rare. Hares are in season from 1 August to 28 February.

SERVES 2–4 (DEPENDING ON THE SIZE OF THE HARE)
1 saddle of hare
1 tablespoon butter
salt and black pepper
To serve: thin slices of bread, spread with butter and baked in the oven with the hare until crisp, then spread with the piquant chicken liver on page 166, and apple or other orchard fruit jelly, available from delis

Preheat the oven to 220°C/425°F/Gas 7. Rub the joint with butter, then season it. Place a roasting pan over the hob and heat. Brown the joint on the meaty side then put in the oven for 10–15 minutes (the longer time for a larger joint). Test for doneness, pressing with a finger. The outer side of the meat should feel firm but there should be some softness or 'give' inside, showing it is still rare. Remove from the oven, then cover with foil and rest in a warm place for 10 minutes.

To serve, have warm plates ready. Put the joint on a wooden board and use a knife to fillet the meat away from the rib bones. Slice, not too thinly, and serve with the toasts and a spoonful of jelly. If there are any juices in the pan, pour them over the top.

Special

Three meals from one rabbit

Anthony Demetre is the most instinctive cook and one of the kindest chefs I know. He senses exactly what it is we feel like eating on a particular day. At his London restaurants, Wild Honey and Arbutus, soups and braises often come to the table in lidded copper pots. I have talked much about the mères of France in this book, exemplary cooks who design their menus around possibilities, and who are stylishly under-ambitious. It is as if he asks himself what is practical, within his capabilities (small kitchen, just a few staff), but does not stint on creativity. It is not a bad philosophy to adopt at home.

This is Anthony Demetre's way with rabbit, or close to it. He stretches one recipe into three. It might seem ambitious, but done once, it makes perfect common sense. He uses farmed rabbit, but his recipe can be adapted to wild rabbits, too. They are much smaller, so you will need to make more to serve four. If jointing the rabbit is too much to cope with, ask the butcher to do it for you. Rabbits have no closed season, and are available all year round.

Roast rabbit saddle, stuffed with liver and kidneys

see PLATE 26

The first recipe, to eat with crushed, boiled, buttered new potatoes, and young broad beans or peas, with a little mint or the herb summer savory, if available. If you ask in advance, the butcher might take the bone out of the rabbit for you, saving about 20 minutes' preparation time.

SERVES 3–4

1 whole large tame rabbit (or 2 fat, very fresh wild rabbits), including
    liver and kidneys
salt and black pepper
1 tablespoon roughly chopped tarragon
4 slices of Parma ham
2 large pieces pig's caul (ask the butcher for this) – to wrap, or some
    fine string

Butcher the rabbit by removing the front and back legs, then remove
the head and split in half. Remove the liver and kidneys and set
aside. Remove the ribcage and backbone from the saddle, using the
point of a sharp knife, without piercing the skin. You should be left
with two loins, still attached together. Season with salt and pepper.
Put the offal down the centre between the loins of meat with the
tarragon, roll the saddle encasing the offal, wrap in the Parma ham
and pig's caul and tie. If you have no pig's caul, tie with string in
about 4–5 places, to secure. It should resemble a sausage shape. If
you had 2 rabbits, and therefore have 4 loins in 2 pairs, then either
make 2 smaller sausages or wrap them together into one.

Season the saddle with salt and pepper, colour lightly in a pan
and roast in a preheated oven at 180°C/350°F/Gas 4 for about
8–10 minutes. Leave to rest, covered, in a warm place, for about
10 minutes. Slice, then serve.

TO PREPARE THE REST OF THE RABBIT FOR THE NEXT TWO RECIPES
salt and black pepper
all the remaining rabbit pieces, including the head and backbone
2 walnut-sized pieces of butter
2 tablespoons olive oil
1 large carrot, sliced
1 celery stick, chopped
1 onion, roughly chopped
4 garlic cloves, peeled and split in half
100ml/3½fl oz white wine vinegar
1 wineglass white wine
2 litres/3 pints water or chicken stock
6 tomatoes, deseeded and roughly chopped
1 bay leaf
1 sprig rosemary

Season the rabbit pieces. Take a thick-bottomed pan and colour the rabbit until golden in a walnut-sized lump of butter and a tablespoon of olive oil. Lift out and set aside. Now add the second piece of butter and tablespoon of olive oil, and colour the vegetables and garlic. Put back the rabbit, add the vinegar, boil for 1 minute to reduce, then add the wine and reduce by two-thirds. Add the water or chicken stock, tomatoes, bay leaf and rosemary, bring to the boil and skim, gently simmer for about 1 hour or until the meat is tender.

Lift the shoulders and rabbit legs out and set aside for the next two recipes. Strain the stock (this will be used for the soup, so set to one side or store). Pull the meat from the bones, keeping the legs and shoulder meat separate.

Rabbit soup, 'pistou'

The second recipe, a very fragrant, uplifting soup, made with the meat picked from the braised rabbit shoulders in the recipe opposite.

SERVES 3–4
2 tablespoons olive oil
100g/3½oz each of onion, carrot, leek and squash or pumpkin,
    cut into 1cm/½in dice
3 small/medium new potatoes, cut into 1cm/½in dice
½ courgette, cut into 1cm/½in dice
1 litre/1¾ pints rabbit stock (from recipe opposite)
1 bay leaf and 1 sprig each parsley and thyme
100g/3½oz fresh peas or broad beans, podded
100g/3½oz cooked-weight short-cut macaroni (boiled until just tender)
100g/3½oz cannellini beans, from a can, drained (use rest in a salad
    with olive oil, shallots and herbs)
4 tomatoes, skinned (nick skin with a knife then plunge in boiling-hot
    water for 1 minute and the skins should come away easily),
    deseeded and finely chopped
all the meat from the rabbit shoulders
salt and black pepper

FOR THE PISTOU SAUCE:
3 garlic cloves, peeled
leaves from 4 sprigs basil
50g/1¾oz Parmesan, grated, plus extra to serve
4 tablespoons olive oil, plus extra to serve
salt and black pepper

Special

Heat the olive oil in a pan and add the onion, carrot, leek and squash/pumpkin. Cook until soft but not coloured. Add the potatoes and courgette, sweat a little further, cover with the rabbit stock, add the bouquet garni of bay, parsley and thyme, cover and cook gently until all the vegetables are tender. Add the peas or broad beans, the macaroni, cannellini beans and tomatoes, followed by the rabbit shoulder meat, torn into small pieces. Allow to warm through, then season the soup to taste.

Chop or liquidise the sauce ingredients until you have a paste. Ladle the soup into 4 bowls and add the pistou sauce at the last minute along with a little more oil and grated Parmesan.

Salad with slow-cooked rabbit, mustard and honey

The third recipe: a rich little salad to eat as a starter or light supper dish with a new potato salad.

SERVES 3–4

200g/7oz young assorted beetroot, roasted in oil until just tender and peeled

200g/7oz young turnips, roasted in oil until just tender then peeled

12 baby plum tomatoes

4 sprigs flat-leaf parsley

all the meat from the rabbit legs

2 handfuls of assorted young salad shoots

FOR THE VINAIGRETTE:
1 egg yolk
2 tablespoons red wine vinegar
1 tablespoon liquid honey
5 tablespoons groundnut oil
1 tablespoon olive oil
1 tablespoon double cream
salt and black pepper

First make the vinaigrette, whisking together all the ingredients until you have a smooth emulsion.

Arrange the beetroot, turnips, tomatoes and flat-leaf parsley on a plate with the seasoned rabbit meat. Spoon vinaigrette over. Lightly dress the salad shoots and arrange alongside.

Fish specials

Seafood cookery needs a little courage. How many times have I looked at something unusual on the fishmonger's counter, nearly asked for it, then thought: perhaps another time . . . The dark mystery of eels, oysters with rocky fortified shells, the slow-motion movements of a live lobster's eye or the fiddly legs on a tiny brown shrimp. 'Haven't time,' I decide, wriggling out of adventure. On an ordinary day I will go the safe route that promises success, a piece of smoked haddock with butter and a poached egg, or bread-crumbed sole fillet for the children. Easy fish, nothing bad about them, but nothing special either. I am not alone, I know. We love our white fish, preferably skinned, and will tolerate the pale pink of salmon or the ruby of tuna. Prawns are fine, and smoked fish very acceptable.

Dealing with the new is something for a relaxed moment: on a weekend, attracted by something exotic on a market stall, or on holiday near the sea, encouraged by the sight of fishermen landing a catch in its freshest state. This is when fish cookery becomes irresistible, a journey into the unknown. And do you know, the secret is – it is never as difficult as it first seems.

Grilled oysters with lettuce, cucumber and butter

Not least because they appear to lock themselves away from the outside world, oysters seem better off in the hands of professionals, behind the counter of an oyster bar. But, having learned how to open them, they are one of the easiest fish to deal with. First I need to allay some fears. The production of oysters in the UK is very strictly governed. Unless they are harvested from the very cleanest grade 'A' waters, they are purified before sale, meaning they spend a few days in a bath of clean running water. Your nose is the best tool – if an opened oyster does not smell of good clean sea water, don't eat it. Always buy oysters from a reputable supplier.

Eat raw oysters with lemon juice, or as they are served in oyster bars, with either Tabasco sauce or a shallot and wine vinegar relish. Choose between the more expensive round-shaped natives, which have a more resonant flavour, and the elongated Pacific rocks, which are cheaper and the most widely farmed.

And yet, since this is your kitchen, playing with them is irresistible. Pacific farmed ('Gigas') oysters, flashed under the grill so they are semi-cooked, are delicious with a little buttery, lemony sauce.

SERVES 4
16–24 oysters
table salt – to make a 'bed' to balance the oysters on
2 cos or butterhead (floppy type) lettuce hearts
½ cucumber
150g/5½oz butter
salt and black pepper
1 tablespoon gin
pinch of paprika

Preheat the oven to 230°C/450°F/Gas 8, or heat the grill. To open the oysters, hold each one, curved side down, with a cloth, and insert an oyster knife into the hinge and twist. Discard the flat shell; sever the oyster flesh from the curved shell. Flip the oyster over in its shell.

Fill two roasting trays with a layer of salt about 1cm/½in deep, then balance each open oyster in the salt. Shred the lettuce hearts; peel the cucumber, cut lengthways in quarters, deseed using a teaspoon, then slice thinly. Melt the butter in a pan, pour it into a bowl leaving behind the white sediment that sinks to the bottom, and add the salad vegetables. Season with salt and pepper and add the gin and paprika. Put 1–2 teaspoons on each oyster and bake or grill for 5 minutes. Eat immediately.

Pan-fried smoked eel with mustard

Fresh eel has a strong cartilage which only breaks down and becomes tender after a long simmer. It is a lovely fish, however, and I like it simmered in a stew with shallots, garlic, olive oil, wine, tomato, Pernod and saffron, just as for bouillabaisse. But smoked eel is also a revelation, because the long time in the smoker will also break down any toughness.

Rich, delicate and tender, the fillets are elegant eaten cold as a starter with horseradish cream and a watercress salad, or this way, as a main course, sautéed in a pan – a dish I ate at the Severn and Wye Smokery, in Gloucestershire, cooked by chef Tania Steytler. Serve with mashed potato and watercress.

SERVES 4
4 slices of speck (air-dried ham) or thinly cut smoked streaky bacon
1 tablespoon olive oil
walnut-sized lump of butter
4 large smoked eel fillets
2 wineglasses white wine or cider
2 tablespoons Dijon seed mustard (moutarde de Meaux)
4 tablespoons single cream
salt and black pepper

Have ready 4 warmed plates. Fry the ham in half the oil until it is crisp, place on a towel to drain and set aside. Wipe out the pan and reheat, adding the butter. Fry the eel fillets on both sides for 1 minute then put each on a plate. Quickly add the wine to the pan and boil to reduce by one-third. Add the mustard and cream, bring to the boil then season. Pour some over the eel fillets on each plate, and serve with a slice of crisp ham.

Crab and potato salad, mustard and egg dressing

Buying 'dressed crab' takes all the work out of this salad, which uses both the brown and white meat from the shell. The brown adds rich creaminess, the white meat delicate luxury. Both can take the mild kick of mustard, however, and young waxy potatoes will add bulk without diluting the flavour.

SERVES 4
FOR THE DRESSING:
2 egg yolks
1 heaped tablespoon Dijon mustard
200ml/7fl oz groundnut oil (or 50ml/2fl oz olive oil, 150ml/5fl oz
    groundnut oil, to make a tarter-flavoured sauce)
juice of half a lemon: about 1 tablespoon
salt and white pepper
large pinch of cayenne pepper

the brown and white meat from 2 medium-sized dressed crabs
24 small new potatoes, boiled until just tender, cut into 4 pieces
1 romaine (cos) lettuce, washed and sliced into ribbons

Put the egg yolks in a bowl, add the mustard and gradually whisk in the oil (or oils). This will take less time than it takes to make mayonnaise because the mustard prevents curdling. Add the lemon juice, then season to taste with salt and pepper. Finish by stirring in the cayenne pepper.

Put the brown meat of the crab, the potatoes and the lettuce ribbons into a bowl and add the sauce. Mix gently, so everything is covered in dressing but not broken down. Add the white meat, then stir again carefully and serve.

Bowled shrimps

Little plastic pots of shrimps remind me of my father, who always sloshed Tabasco onto them, claiming it did not spoil them at all. Ready-made potted shrimps are still a good buy, made in Morecambe Bay, Lancashire, but my love for them was eclipsed by a magnificent bowlful made by Clara Weatherall. Clara is married to Percy Weatherall, who with his brother Ben runs an online game and rare-breed meat business, and the shrimps appeared on the table at a dinner to celebrate their first decade. Fishmongers should be able to source the ready-peeled, cooked shrimps. You can make this dish a day or two in advance.

SERVES 6–8
500g/1lb 2oz ready-peeled, cooked shrimps
200g/7oz unsalted butter, melted
2 pinches of ground mace
2 pinches of paprika
2 pinches of mixed spice
juice of half a lemon
a few drops of anchovy essence
plenty of wholemeal bread, to serve

Put the shrimps in the bowl you want to serve them in. Pour over three-quarters of the butter, leaving behind the white sediment in the pan, add the spices, lemon juice and anchovy essence and mix. Taste and add more of any of the spices if desired. Pat the mixture down then pour over the remaining butter and place in the fridge until set. Toast plenty of sliced wholemeal bread and wrap in cloth napkins to keep it warm, then eat with the shrimps.

Special cheese

There is cheese, and there is cheese. The cheese we eat every day, the block Cheddars, inexpensive mozzarella and simple cream cheeses, are not to be sneered at. Yet they have some very special cousins: hand-made cheeses made from flavour-giving raw milk that can command a high price. A piece of Cheddar, hand-worked on the same farm where the milk for it is produced, has rarity value, as do over 100 good artisan traditional and new-style cheeses now made in the UK. Just a few parings of a hard, perfectly matured cheese in a well-dressed salad with apple and chicory, or a slice of soft cheese melted over hot bread, its rind exuding strong aroma, is an

exhilarating supper. Occasionally, I make the world's easiest fondue using a whole, soft cheese with a bloomy rind or a sticky, smelly washed-rind cheese, and scoop up the runny interior with slices of thin sourdough toast or leafy celery stalks. Best to do it for when there are plenty of people to finish it up, so none is wasted.

Whole baked cheese, with toast 'spoons' and leafy celery

The size of the cheese will determine how many this serves. But a small washed-rind cheese will serve 6 at least. Choose any cheese with a bloomy rind; good British cheeses that are suitable include Tunworth, Penyston, a heart-shaped cheese from Daylesford Organic, Finn, Waterloo and Milleens (from Ireland). Soft French cheeses are also right for this, such as Camembert, Pont L'Evêque, reblochon, Livarot.

1 whole cheese, preferably in its moulded wooden box to hold it
    during cooking (or wrap in baking paper)
1 sprig rosemary and/or thyme
To serve: thin toasts made from an open-textured sourdough or ciabatta-
    type bread; the leafy, inner stalks of celery, a dish of pickled walnuts

Preheat the oven to 200°C/400°F/Gas 6. Place the cheese, in its box, or in a casing of baking paper, on a baking tray. Stick the herb sprig(s) into the centre of its surface, through the rind. Bake for 15 minutes or until the insides feel very soft when pressed with a finger. To serve, cut a 'door' in the surface, peel it back and eat

346

immediately. If the cheese sets, it can be returned to the oven to soften again.

Figs with goat's cheese and spelt groats

Irresistibly pretty and light, a dish that not only shows a top-quality goat's cheese to its best but figs, too. I have a fig tree, a present from my sister that I never dreamed would fruit, but it does. This salad is the way I celebrate their arrival. Whole spelt groats are often sold as 'faro' in Italian delis. If you cannot find spelt, use pearl barley or whole durum wheat (sometimes sold as Ebly).

SERVES 4
2 tablespoons extra virgin olive oil, plus more for dressing
1 medium red onion, very finely chopped
200g/7oz spelt groats
about 1 litre/1 ¾ pints water or chicken stock
salt and black pepper
300g/10½oz soft fresh goat's cheese (these are sometimes sold in
    little 'cakes' – buy 4 of them)
4 fresh ripe figs, cut into quarters
pips from 1 small pomegranate
2 handfuls of small salad leaves

First prepare the spelt. Heat the olive oil in a saucepan and add the onion. Cook for 1 minute, then add the spelt grains. Cover with water

or stock to about 2cm/¾in depth and bring to the boil. Turn down to a simmer and cook for about 20 minutes until the spelt is tender but not too soft. Add more liquid during cooking if necessary. Put in a bowl, add a little extra olive oil, season to taste, stir and leave to cool.

Onto each plate put 2 tablespoons spelt, some cheese, 4 fig quarters, some pomegranate pips and a few salad leaves. Dress with a little more olive oil.

Rare fruit

Women understand gluts. Gluts are like the July sales, an opportunity to stock up on quality and put something away for future occasions. Like pulling out a dress you bought as a bargain, unsure when you might have the opportunity to wear it. You open a jar of blackberry jelly from the cupboard, stored just like a carrier bag of hasty buys under the bed, and turn a dish of roast duck into a unique event. Its beauty makes your original splurge a forgivable one.

Gluts of fruit, flowers and nuts, both farmed and wild, divide the year like a calendar. In spring there are elderflowers, then red berries, apples, damsons and quince. In autumn I hope for blackberries, sloes, blueberries, cranberries and rowan berries, not forgetting walnuts and cobnuts, and get my preserving book off the shelf. I'd like to be a disciplined forager, but the opportunity is not always there. Still, there is always shopping. I think we can manage that.

Winter rhubarb with burnt cider cream

The first glut of the year: tall, Schiaparelli-pink 'forced' rhubarb, from Yorkshire. Grown in the dark, winter rhubarb is tender-textured, more so than the green variety grown outdoors in summer, and has a pronounced floral flavour. One of the last three growers, Janet Oldroyd will send this rhubarb by post, wrapped appealingly in blue tissue in long cardboard boxes. When I have a glut, I make unsweetened compote to eat for breakfast, or bake it, cover with a sweet froth and burn it for a rich Sunday lunch pudding.

SERVES 6–8
500g/1lb 2oz summer rhubarb
caster sugar

FOR THE CIDER CREAM:
100ml/3½fl oz dry English cider
6 egg yolks
100g/3½oz caster sugar
1 tablespoon double cream, lightly whipped

Preheat the oven to 180°C/350°F/Gas 4 and put the rhubarb in an ovenproof dish. Sprinkle with a little caster sugar and bake until tender – about 15–20 minutes. Divide among 4 small gratin dishes (or put all into one dish).

To make the cider cream, put the cider, egg yolks and sugar in a bowl and place it over a pan of slowly simmering water. Whisk the mixture until it is thick, much bigger in volume and pale-coloured.

Special

Remove from the heat and whisk until completely cold. Fold in the whipped cream then pour over the cooked rhubarb. Heat the grill and glaze – it will brown quickly so watch it carefully. Alternatively, use a blowtorch (available from hardware shops, and much less trouble than you might imagine) to do the same job, holding the flame at an angle, 20cm/8in from the pudding.

Wild blackberry and apple charlotte

How striking that a blackberry, once the symbol of a lazy afternoon's forage along the hedgerows, is now synonymous with high technology and a lifestyle where your time is no longer your own. For anyone who feels this way, a remedy is there in the scent of stewing blackberries. Make just one panful and it will stay in your sensory memory for ever. The picking season in late August will be an unmissable event and the pudding made afterwards a reminder that, in the end, there is more genius in nature than in a street full of phone shops.

SERVES 4
500g/1lb 2oz blackberries, rinsed
300g/10½oz dessert apples, peeled, cored and sliced
caster sugar
200g/7oz butter
8 thin slices of slightly stale white bread, each cut into
    4 squares/triangles
2 pinches of cinnamon
2 dessertspoons caster sugar, to dust
custard or thick double or clotted cream, to serve

Preheat the oven to 200°C/400°F/Gas 6. Put the blackberries in a pan with the apples and stew until softened but not too pulpy. Add sugar to taste and transfer to an ovenproof dish. Melt the butter in a pan and dip the bread slices into it quickly, so they get an even coating. Lay the pieces on the surface of the blackberry mixture, arranging them in an overlapping pattern, like roof tiles. Stir the cinnamon into the sugar, then scatter over the charlotte. Bake until the surface of the charlotte is crisp. Serve with the custard or cream.

Beef, sesame and spring greens in
soy broth
Cottage pie
Beef ragu
Potato, beef and parsley hash
Lamb rice, with golden onions
More rice dishes using leftover
roast meat:
Spiced chicken rice with mint
Duck rice with black grapes and
parsley
Pheasant rice with juniper
Spiced cashew chicken slaw
Cardamom and lemongrass
kedgeree
More kichri:
Green lentils and salmon
Split peas with haddock and
prawns
Salmon, rocket and horseradish
Refried new potatoes with fresh
goat's cheese and pesto

More ways with new potatoes and
fresh cheese:
Refried potatoes with chorizo
Refried potatoes with turmeric
and lamb
Refried potatoes with chilli and
preserved tomatoes
Refried potatoes with black
pudding and radicchio
Carrot, parsnip and chickpea
glazed hash
Bread salads:
Bread salad with olive oil,
leaves, tomatoes and basil
Bread with spinach, bacon and
semi-soft-boiled eggs
Stuffing:
Garlic breadcrumb stuffing
Ricotta and watercress stuffing
Festive stuffing
Pasta with garlic breadcrumbs
Toffee bread pudding

A CLEVER REHASH

'It cost how much?' Unwrapping a piece of beef, I explain my lavish buy. It was grass-fed, slow-grown beef, something I buy on principle – but never a bargain. We eat it on Saturday, at dinner with some friends. Roasted and rare, it is utterly good, and everyone raves. But that is not the end of the story. There are slices of cold, pink meat to eat over the next few days, plus enough bits and pieces to mince or chop for a cottage pie. The broth made from the bones has incredible flavour; I use it in soups and rice dishes at least twice. By midweek I am vindicated, my overspend has been justified and nothing is wasted. Best of all, the dishes we ate were exciting, contemporary and colourful, not dismal plates that conjure austerity. Welcome to the glorious rehash, a world where eating the best ingredients, every day, becomes affordable.

Usually the more you spend on something, the more you respect it. Splash out on a better coat or bag, and it will be worn to death. It will be loved until it hangs by a thread and still be a cherished memory long after its final outing. It is not just about value for money, but something deeper, triggered by the extravagance. At the other end of the scale, the cheapest items get little love. Shoppers confess that some of their Primark buys are never worn and will be thrown away rather than recycled. You can compare food shopping with this conduct. Low food inflation has bred a cult of waste, with families throwing away up to a third of what they buy.

When more is paid for food, however, there might be a little hesitation before tipping any leftovers into the bin after supper. The scraps of a roasted organic chicken, clinging to a cage of bones, have a future during which a bit more value can be had. Mention this to any group of people and you will often hear 'my grandmother always did that' and occasionally 'my mother used up every scrap'. Recycling food was the pride of women, but leftovers have been in the wilderness for decades now. Cheaper food is not the only reason: memories of nasty rissoles in austere times, fears about 'use by' dates on packaging and lack of cooking skills compound the problem and there are too many, as always, who can say they simply haven't the time for all that . . .

The purpose of the next pages is to bring leftovers up to date and offer a solemn promise not to revive rissoles. The recipes are quick and easy and I have included traditional recipes only if they are relevant. I do not have the best memories of rehashed meals myself, though I will always worship both shepherd's and cottage pie. Not every remnant is ideal for leftovers, and it is time to get away from leaving horrid little dishes containing two soggy carrots in the fridge. The crisis is not that bad. This is the opportunity, too, to persuade on the feel-good factor that comes with paying more for certain items of food. Rehash cooking is tied in with an understanding that good ingredients are precious. Caring about animal welfare and green issues comes hand in hand with spending more on food, so there is a need to know how to make the most of it.

Rehash toolkit
A few basic tools to make saving and cooking leftovers easy:
* Manual mincing machine – these cast-iron machines can be clamped to tables, but are less easy to fix to a worktop. Use them for mincing cold meat. You can also buy mincing attachments for electric tabletop mixers. It is possible to chop meat in a food processor for making cottage and shepherd's pie, but do not

over-process or the braised meat will have a texture like paste.
As a last resort you can chop cooked meat finely by hand.

* Containers – stock up on a number of plastic containers, in
different sizes, with tight-fitting lids. Or save sturdy plastic
yoghurt pots and jars with screw-top lids. You will also need
plastic freezer bags, foil and clingfilm.

* Store-cupboard staples – the following ingredients are always
useful: cans of chickpeas, chopped Italian tomatoes and haricot
beans; tubes of harissa (chilli paste); spice mixes like garam
masala, curry paste and ras al hanout; rice, pine nuts, organic
vegetable stock powder or long-life packs of natural meat stock
(with no additives).

* Windowbox herbs – herbs add drama and transform dull foods
into special dishes. Having a few pots saves buying packs of herbs
that perish easily. Easy to look after are basil (kept in a window
spot, but out of the cold), oregano, thyme, bronze fennel, chives
and parsley.

* Primitive breadcrumb machine – bread that has been dried out in
the oven can be made into breadcrumbs using a rolling pin and
sturdy plastic bag. Put the dried bread in the bag and bash the
contents to a rough powder.

Stock

So many recipes I love contain fresh stock, the natural gift of leftover
bones, brewed in a pot. It has become central to my cooking, for
soups, rice dishes and making stews that will have huge depth of
flavour. But there have been wilderness years, with the stockpot put
away in favour of salty, artificially flavoured stock cubes. While
chefs heroically maintained the tradition of making stock in their

restaurants, home cooks made it a symbol of put-upon housewives. Ridiculous, really, when stock makes itself, happily simmering while you can do other things, and doubly absurd when you calculate its health properties, not least the fact that using flavoursome stock dramatically reduces salt in the diet. Recently, however, the art of brewing stock is going through a small but significant revival, and those pots are bubbling again. Fresh, naturally made stock is also available in supermarkets (but watch the salt levels).

Stock is a store staple, an ingredient that underpins many meals and makes it possible to walk in the door late and quickly whisk up a wholesome supper. For this reason I have put all recipes for stock and ideas for the many ways in which it can be used into Halfway to a Meal (see pages 388–394).

An argument for an extravagant roast

The amount I spend on a joint of beef should bother me, but it doesn't. It may be enough to buy a pair of school shoes, or nearly fill the car with fuel. For the same amount I could buy 28 packets of dried pasta, or more than 120 free-range eggs. But three days after the main meal where eight people feasted on a roast, we are still enjoying the benefit of the beef. For Monday lunch two of us fill sandwiches with slices of rare beef, smearing it with horseradish. On Tuesday we finish up the meat in a cottage pie for four. Wednesday, and there is a pot full of stock and the possibility of a bean, tomato and herb soup, then on Thursday enough left over for a mushroom risotto. Spreading the cost over another eight helpings, the £40 is beginning to look like a healthy bargain.

Beef, sesame and spring greens in soy broth

Imitating the big bowls of food that my children love to eat in noodle bars, using thin slices of beef from the roast; the secret is to lay the beef on top of the soup at the last minute, so it does not stew and turn tough in the hot broth.

SERVES 2
2 nests of Chinese egg noodles
2 tablespoons sesame seeds
600–900ml/1–1½ pints beef or chicken stock (see page 390)
2 tablespoons light soy sauce
1 tablespoon Shaoxing wine or sherry
2 handfuls of finely shredded spring greens or pak choi
2 spring onions, green ends only, sliced into rounds
4 thin slices of cold beef
To serve: coriander leaves, sliced red chilli (optional)

Fill a large pan with water, bring to the boil and cook the egg noodle nests for 3 minutes. Drain, refresh with cold water and set to one side. It does not matter if they seem a little sticky, they will loosen up when added to the broth later.

Dry the pan and toast the sesame seeds over a medium-high heat until golden. Transfer to a plate and set aside. Heat the stock with the soy sauce and wine or sherry to boiling point then add the greens (but not the spring onion). Simmer for about 3 minutes, then add back the noodles. Heat to boiling point again, taste for seasoning (add salt or more soy sauce if necessary) then ladle into two bowls. Scatter the spring onion over, then lay the beef slices on top. Finally, scatter over the toasted sesame seeds, the coriander and chilli (if using) and serve immediately.

Kitchen note
You can make this soup with cold chicken, pork or cooked prawns – or just simply use a good, deep-flavoured stock.

Leftover Mondays

Jutting out of the Kenwood mixer, the mincing attachment was regularly brought out at my parents' home to deal with the leftover roast. The wiggling worms of minced meat, emerging from its steel die, held me in spellbound horror from an early age. But these terrors would be long gone before the first mouthful of cottage or shepherd's pie. The minced meat, onion and carrot were braised until soft, then in went a squirt of tomato purée, and an added splash of Worcestershire sauce – or three, if my father had anything to do with it. As the heartening aromas filled the kitchen, large white potatoes were cooked, mashed then spread across the meat in a pie dish. A fork was used to disturb the mashed potato into a choppy sea, and little cuts of butter scattered over. When the dish came out of the oven, held by frayed string oven gloves, the spiky, buttery gold crust on the pie could barely contain the bubbling springs of hot meat juices underneath. We were, by this time, desperate to eat.

Cottage pie

Not as fast a dish to make as others on these pages, but a very easy one. Roast meat that has been minced cooks to a wonderfully rich sauce with a tender texture. Tasting to get the right seasoning is absolutely essential, although there will always be someone who asks for more Worcestershire sauce, so you may as well put it on the table (along with tomato ketchup and Tabasco).

SERVES 4–6
4 tablespoons dripping or olive oil
3 onions, finely chopped
2 garlic cloves, finely chopped
2 carrots, cut into small dice
1 celery stick, diced
about 10 tablespoons minced or very finely chopped cold beef*
2 tablespoons Worcestershire sauce
1 tablespoon tomato purée
about 600ml/1 pint beef stock (see page 390) or water
salt and black pepper

FOR THE TOPPING:
1kg/2lb 4oz floury potatoes
150ml/¼ pint milk
150g/5½ oz butter
salt and white pepper
1–2 tablespoons butter – for the top of the pie

* If you do not have a mincing machine and use a food processor instead, only lightly process the meat or the finished dish will have a nasty, pasty texture.

Heat the dripping or oil in a large pan or casserole and add the vegetables. Fry over a medium heat for about 5 minutes, then add the meat. Fry for another 2 minutes, then add the Worcestershire sauce and tomato purée. Cover with the stock or water; bring to the boil and then turn down the heat and simmer for 1 hour or until the meat is tender. Taste and adjust the flavour, adding more Worcestershire sauce if necessary, then season with a little salt and pepper. Transfer to an ovenproof dish and preheat the oven to 220°C/425°F/Gas 7.

Meanwhile, peel, boil, then mash the potatoes with the milk and butter. Season with salt and white pepper and spread over the meat base in the baking dish. Use a fork to distress the surface of the pie, then dot with butter. Bake until golden on top and the juices under the pie are bubbling.

Beef ragu

To make a pasta sauce, use the method above, omitting the Worcestershire sauce and substituting with a glass of red wine. Add some chopped smoked bacon or pancetta to the minced beef. To make the ragu extra rich, add 100g/3½oz chopped chicken livers to the pan with the meat.

Potato, beef and parsley hash

see PLATE 27

In her 1950s cookery book Constance Spry devotes several pages to réchauffés. Most of these methods designed for recycling leftover cold meat are probably best left in the mists of time – devilled beef rolls, for instance: horrid parcels of thin sliced meat, tortured with mustard and chutney, then finally murdered in a flour-based sauce. Or there's the equally nasty 'beef in batter', which brings back nightmares of the greasy spam fritters dished up in my old school canteen. But now and again in my mother's kitchen, the book would be open on a page featuring American corned beef hash. I loved the giant patty of potatoes, onions and beef with its crisp edges, and have adapted it to using up leftovers of beef, either roasted or braised fresh beef or boiled salt beef. It can also be made with chunks of ham. The addition of parsley greens up an otherwise decadent fry-up.

SERVES 4
2 tablespoons olive oil
1 onion, chopped
about 600g/1lb 6oz larger new potatoes, boiled and cut into
    2cm/¾in cubes
450g/1lb diced salt beef or ham
large handful of flat-leaf parsley, chopped
12 cornichons, sliced
2 eggs, beaten
salt and black pepper
pickled walnuts or spiced apple chutney, to serve

Heat the oil in a frying pan and add the onion. Fry until soft but not coloured, then scoop out with a spoon, leaving the fat behind. Put in a bowl with the potato, salt beef or ham, parsley and cornichons. Pour in the beaten egg and mix thoroughly but carefully so the potatoes do not break up too much. Season as you go with a little salt and pepper (remember the ham or beef will be salty, so don't overdo the seasoning).

Reheat the pan and add the hash mixture. Pat it down to make a patty using a wooden spoon and cook over a low-medium heat for 10 minutes. Place a large plate over the pan. Invert the pan so the hash is sitting on the plate, then slide it back into the pan and cook for another 10 minutes over the same heat. Both sides should be crisp and golden brown in places. Serve in big slices, with pickled walnuts or a spiced apple chutney.

Bubble and squeak to arancini – leftovers gone global

Bubble and squeak, corned beef hash, toffee bread pudding, or ham and potato rissoles with their steamy, creamy centres . . . These were the creations of the women who ran the households of my childhood, a generation who believed the way to a man's heart was to be a damn good housekeeper and stick to a budget.

I did not know the sweet comfort of Tuscan bread soups (see page 147) or the crisp joy of arancini (fried risotto balls) until later. Encounters with Lebanese bread and herb salads, fragrant fried rice dishes from Asia (see page 92) and the luscious French pudding, pain perdu, taught me that there was a whole globe of efficient cooks out there, being creative with leftovers.

The feminine gift – creativity in a crisis

Crude it may be, but women and men feed off each other, addressing and solving problems with talents unique to gender. Men might be more likely to identify the need to be careful with money, but women have always used their creativity as a practical solution to any shortage. The efforts of men, the 'provider', either to hunter-gather food or pay for it, were rewarded by their women, the 'givers', who transform whatever they have been brought into something good – even beautiful. When food or funds are short, cooks are even more heavily tested, yet the ideas have never stopped coming. The art of the clever rehash is a feminine trait.

Despite the ongoing dispute over equality, there is evenness in the various powers that men and women have – that is, if they assume these traditional roles. But women cast aside cooking and 'home economics' as a symbol of inequality, and kicked out, with this, a millennium of savvy kitchen prowess. While men were relieved of some of the full-time responsibility of being provider. A consequence of all this was that healthy, economic cookery more or less vanished.

In our current society, women are still the main carers of family, yet there are a significant number of 'new men' who either share the job or do it alone. The row about equal opportunity in terms of food and cooking made victims of those who needed caring for. I take the pragmatic view that it is easier to fight for equal pay and other rights when nourishment and the household budget are not so much of a concern. Whether you are a woman or man, feeding yourself, children or others, there is a heap to learn from our forbearing mother cooks about maintaining a state of harmony at table. The essential new development is to make it easier to do.

Lamb rice, with golden onions

A sweet, rich and filling refried lamb and rice dish, and my unparalleled favourite way to rehash cold lamb quickly in a pan. The secret is in making sure all the vegetables are cooked until sweet.

SERVES 2

1 tablespoon beef dripping or butter
1 onion, finely chopped
2 tablespoons golden sultanas
pinch of ground allspice
pinch of ground coriander
2 pinches of ground cumin
about 20 cherry tomatoes, cut in half
2–4 slices of cold lamb, cut into slivers
1 garlic clove, chopped
5 heaped tablespoons cooked basmati or long-grain rice
salt and black pepper
To serve: mint leaves or chopped parsley leaves; 2 tablespoons
    pinenuts, toasted in the pan first with no fat until golden, then set
    aside; pomegranate pips (optional); 4 tablespoons Greek yoghurt

Heat the dripping or butter and add the onion. Cook for about 5 minutes over a medium heat until it turns pale gold and smells fragrant. Add the sultanas and spices and cook for 1 minute more, then add the tomatoes. Cook gently for another 5–7 minutes, until they begin to take on a little colour. Add the lamb and garlic and stir-fry for a minute, then stir in the rice. Cook, stirring from time to time, until well heated through – this is very important with leftover

cooked rice. Season to taste. To serve, scatter the leaves, pinenuts and pomegranate pips over the top and eat with yoghurt.

MORE RICE DISHES USING LEFTOVER ROAST MEAT

* Spiced chicken rice with mint – use ras al hanout (a Moroccan spice mix) in place of the other spices and add chopped mint (or coriander) to the pan. A little cooked cauliflower, cut into small 'florets', can be added with the onion.
* Duck rice with black grapes and parsley – do not add tomatoes; use raisins and/or fresh grapes in place of the sultanas, and parsley instead of mint.
* Pheasant rice with juniper – do not add tomatoes; substitute 3 juniper berries for the cumin, crushing them first using pestle and mortar or coffee grinder.

Kitchen note
You can also make a pilaff with cooked Norwegian prawns.
Add 2 teaspoons mild curry powder or paste in place of
the spices, and coriander as well as the mint. Finish with
a little lemon juice.

Spiced cashew chicken slaw

This salad is cloaked in a dressing made with cashew nut butter and tamarind that has something of an addictive quality. It adds fathoms of flavour to modest ingredients, and leaves you feeling invigorated and energetic, after.

SERVES 2
FOR THE DRESSING:
4 tablespoons cashew nut butter (from wholefood shops)
juice of 1 lime
2 tablespoons tamarind purée or 'water'
2 tablespoons Asian fish sauce (nam pla)
large pinch of smoked paprika
1 red chilli, deseeded and finely chopped (optional)

FOR THE SLAW:
450g/1lb cold roast chicken, torn into shreds
2 spring onions, green ends only, finely sliced
¼ white cabbage, shredded very thinly
leaves from 4 sprigs coriander
¼ cucumber, cut in half lengthways, deseeded and sliced
To serve: coriander leaves; more sliced red chilli; 2 tablespoons
    cashew nuts, toasted in a little oil then crushed to a rough powder

In a large salad bowl, whisk the dressing ingredients together thoroughly. Add the chicken, onion, cabbage, coriander and cucumber, then mix until well coated in the dressing. Serve piled onto plates, the extra herbs, chilli and cashew nuts sprinkled over.

Cardamom and lemongrass kedgeree

Not the stolid ballast served in heaps at buffets but a creamier version of
the Indian dish kichri, made with mild curry spices, with cardamom and
lemongrass for extra fragrance. Use up leftover smoked haddock,
cooked fresh salmon (or other fish), hot smoked salmon or smoked eel in
the classic Anglo-Indian breakfast dish.

SERVES 2
2 tablespoons butter
1 onion, finely chopped
1 garlic clove, chopped
1 teaspoon yellow mustard seed
1 lemongrass stick, finely sliced
seeds from 6 crushed green cardamom pods
1 teaspoon ground turmeric
1 teaspoon ground cumin
300ml/½ pint single cream
2 heaped tablespoons cooked yellow split peas (see page 52;
    optional)
6 heaped tablespoons cooked basmati rice – more if you do not use
    the split peas
4 tablespoons flaked cooked fish
salt and black pepper
2 eggs
leaves from 2 sprigs coriander

Melt the butter in a large non-stick frying pan and add the onion and
garlic. Cook gently for about 5 minutes until fragrant, then add the

mustard seed, lemongrass, cardamom seeds, turmeric and cumin. Fry gently for another minute, then add the cream. When the cream comes to the boil, stir in the split peas, basmati rice and flaked fish. Season with salt and pepper and keep warm.

Poach 2 eggs until the whites are firm but the yolks still soft – I poach eggs in little pouches of oiled clingfilm to stop the whites dashing around the pan – and serve on top of the kedgeree. Scatter the coriander on top.

Kitchen note
You can also serve with semi-soft-boiled eggs: prick 2 eggs with a pin, place in a pan filled with cold water and bring to the boil. Simmer for 4 minutes, then place the pan under the running cold tap for 1 minute. Peel the eggs, which are very fragile, carefully.

MORE KICHRI
* Green lentils and salmon – replace the rice and split peas with 8 tablespoons cooked green lentils (see page 53). Use chopped fresh ginger in place of the lemongrass, and 100g/3½oz melted butter in place of the cream. I prefer this without eggs.
* Split peas with haddock and prawns – make extra split peas and leave out the rice. Omit the lemongrass and add 1 teaspoon garam masala. Add 100g/3½oz defrosted cooked North Atlantic prawns at the same time as the haddock. Scatter black onion seed (nigella) over the finished dish.

Salmon, rocket and horseradish

A quick hash to make in a pan, and serve on toasted bread.

SERVES 2
1 tablespoon butter or olive oil
4 tablespoons flaked cooked salmon
2 handfuls of rocket leaves, roughly chopped
1–2 tablespoons creamed horseradish, or to taste
1 teaspoon English mustard
salt and black pepper

Heat the fat in a pan and add the fish. Warm through then stir in the rocket leaves. Stir in the horseradish and mustard, season with salt and pepper, then serve on toast or grilled bread (see page 134).

Kitchen note
Watercress can be substituted for the rocket leaves.

Squeak

Not every memory of leftover meals brings tears of fond happiness to my eyes. Bubble and squeak was one to tolerate, not enthusiastically anticipate. The refried mishmash of cooked green cabbage and mashed potatoes can be sulphurous stodge. Hunting among the clods with a fork for bits that had crisped up in the hot dripping, was the most to hope for. Nostalgia, as they say, is not what it used to be. Dress it up all you like. Rehash the rehash with glamorous additions of Parma ham crisps or soft-boiled quail's eggs, it is still bubble and squeak under there, like a smelly old sofa.

Better, perhaps, to keep the leftover mash apart from the cabbage. I like to mix a helping of cold mash with a beaten egg, grate in some nutmeg and add a heaped teaspoon of plain flour then fry in butter to make a fat potato cake. These are lovely to eat with bacon, a green salad, or grate some Cheddar cheese over the top.

As for the cabbage, make an elegant supper in a pan: melt a nut of butter over a low heat, add a squeeze of lemon, a few rosemary leaves and some chopped ham, then the cooked cabbage. Warm everything through – do not attempt to brown the cabbage or you will be back in school-corridor territory again, sniffing that overcooked cabbagey smell.

Refried new potatoes with fresh goat's cheese and pesto

This rehash of potatoes is one I love. Soft fresh goat's cheese is one of the most useful ingredients to keep in the fridge. It cooks beautifully and has a sweet, clear flavour that allows other ingredients to shine.

SERVES 2

3 tablespoons olive oil
2 helpings of cooked new potatoes, cut in half
100g/3½oz fresh goat's cheese
sprigs fresh oregano, if available
2 tablespoons basil or other pesto

Heat the olive oil in a pan and add the potatoes. Fry, stirring occasionally, until the potatoes are golden but not too dark, then throw over chunks of the goat's cheese. Scatter over the herbs, spoon a little of the pesto over the top and take the pan straight to the table.

MORE WAYS WITH NEW POTATOES AND FRESH CHEESE

* Refried potatoes with chorizo – refry the potatoes with slices of fresh chorizo, serve scattered with parsley and fresh goat's cheese.
* Refried potatoes with turmeric and lamb – refry the potatoes with turmeric, onion, garlic, Moroccan ras al hanout spice and leftover pieces of cooked lamb. Scatter over the fresh goat's cheese and some mint leaves.

* Refried potatoes with chilli and preserved tomatoes – refry the potatoes with slices of red chilli and 'sunblush' tomatoes. Add the fresh goat's cheese at the end.
* Refried potatoes with black pudding and radicchio – refry the potatoes with black pudding and radicchio. Add fresh goat's cheese and toasted walnuts at the end.

Forgotten ways with vegetables

The Irish cook Darina Allen and her mother-in-law Myrtle Allen of the Ballymaloe cookery school and restaurant in Ireland have been an inspiration to me for two decades. Theirs is a great example of cuisine grandmère, traditional cookery that combines art with pragmatism. Clever ideas combined with whatever is best on the day, made special by adding something gorgeous like the edible blossoms of a herb plant, and rarely extravagant. Darina Allen has been involved in many campaigns to encourage young cooks, and has trained thousands at her school.

In 2009 she launched Grandmother's Day, to celebrate the skills of older generations and encourage younger cooks to learn from them. 'Grandparents are the guardians of inherited wisdom,' she says. 'Years ago, at a time when many families lived in multi-generational groups, the skills were effortlessly passed from generation to generation. This situation is more unusual nowadays.' A granny six times over herself, she has also written a huge book, *The Forgotten Skills of Cooking*, inspired by a student in her school who was about to throw away some over-whipped cream that was turning to butter.

The philosophy that it is always well worth hesitating before throwing out what would normally be classed as waste, is one to carry with you whenever you are cooking. In a short list of vegetable trimmings that might usually be headed for the bin, Darina offers some simple ideas. Mushroom stalks, she writes, taste just as good as the rest of the vegetable; add them to stock or any other fungi dish. The tough green ends of leeks make a brilliant coloured soup, and the outer leaves of lettuce can be shredded thinly and tossed over a high heat with olive oil, herbs and chilli flakes for a dish to 'enjoy immediately'.

Carrot, parsnip and chickpea glazed hash

Nibbling at leftover carrots, parsnips and other vegetables while washing up after a Sunday roast is a secret joy. But when there is too much even for this private, indulgent moment, this little hash in a pan is gorgeous to look at and as sweet as toffee to eat.

SERVES 2
2 tablespoons butter
4 tablespoons cooked carrots, sliced or cut into chunks
4 tablespoons cooked parsnips, turnips, swede or squash
1 sprig thyme
1 tablespoon runny honey
400g/14oz can chickpeas, drained
pinch of smoked paprika

Melt the butter and add the carrots and other vegetables with the thyme and honey. Cook over a medium heat until the honey and butter become syrupy. Turn up the heat and caramelise the vegetables slightly so they take on a little colour. Stir in the chickpeas and cook until the pan is sizzling again. Serve scattered with the paprika.

Leftover bread

It isn't immediately obvious that bread was once a dual-purpose food: something to eat fresh but also as it matures. Most bread we buy is made to stay soft for a week, but before preservatives and enzyme-softening agents – and before cheap white sliced bread – there were hundreds of ways to deal with bread that had lost its freshness.

Good bread, made slowly, does not go 'off' when it is less fresh, it simply ages. Older bread shouldn't be written off and wasted when it can be the base of some wonderful suppers. On other pages in this book you will find tomato and bread soups (see page 147), a smooth soup made with pumpkin and garlic, and many ways to eat bread that has been toasted (see page 21). Breadcrumbs are needed for stuffing and to put on top of gratins. Fried bread is a rich treat to eat with scrambled eggs (see page 174) or to float in a soothing pool of soup.

Making sure that every piece of bread was used was an instinct for home cooks who took the job of balancing the household budget. It was a matter of pride linked to value of food. The symbolic importance of bread, a metaphor for money and another name for it,

too, was never underestimated. The advent of cheaper bread and the decline of home cooking go hand in hand, and with that disrespect for the value of bread. When a loaf costs under £1, it is understandable not to think twice about its future but to chuck it in the bin. And you may as well, because white sliced bread is rotten as a leftover food. It clings to twilight, artificially fresh, then suddenly goes past the point of no return and develops a rash of green spots. You can dry it in the oven and make some powdery breadcrumbs. These are OK for coating a piece of fish, but the great bread salads and puddings are denied. Made with low-grade bread, a bread and butter pudding is a spongy marsh with no real flavour of wheat. But the same pudding made with an open-textured, slow-leavened bread has texture and taste.

BREAD SALADS

* Bread salad with olive oil, leaves, tomatoes and basil – tear leftover bread into strips and toast in a pan with olive oil. Put in a salad bowl with rocket or other small peppery salad leaves, add olive oil, skinned and deseeded tomatoes (blanch in boiling water for 1 minute then peel), and basil leaves. Few things are as easy to do, and so delicious.
* Bread with spinach, bacon and semi-soft-boiled eggs – allow 1 egg per person and bring to the boil in cold water. Boil for 5 minutes then flush under cold water, peel and cut into quarters. Toast the bread in a pan with olive oil until it begins to crisp. Remove from the pan, which can then be used to cook a few lardons or chopped bacon. Add these to the salad with young spinach leaves and dress with a mustard vinaigrette.

STUFFING

Bread is the scaffolding that holds a stuffing together and makes it tender to eat. I have two favourites.

* Garlic breadcrumb stuffing – mash garlic cloves with salt then combine with breadcrumbs, a pinch of ground allspice and dried oregano, and pinenuts. Push under the skin of a chicken in the breast and thigh area, and roast. The garlic in the stuffing will flavour the meat. You can also use this stuffing spooned onto halved tomatoes, which are then baked until golden.

* Ricotta and watercress stuffing – use this stuffing inside pancakes (see page 113). Combine 150g/5½oz ricotta with 2 tablespoons breadcrumbs, 1 tablespoon grated Parmesan, a pinch of nutmeg and a bunch of chopped watercress. Fill 4 pancakes and roll them up. Grate over some cheese and bake for 15 minutes until crisp.

Festive stuffing

This is close to my mother's Christmas turkey stuffing, an inherited recipe which I now use every year. I never stuff the main cavity of the bird because the meat will be dried out in an effort to cook what has been put inside it. So I roast this stuffing in a pan instead. I put a mixture of sausage meat and chestnuts, bolstered with breadcrumbs and an egg, into the turkey's smaller neck cavity.

4 tablespoons pinenuts
3 tablespoons butter or dripping
8 sprigs thyme
10 sage leaves, chopped
4 eating apples, cored and finely chopped
150g/5½oz ready-to-eat pitted prunes, roughly chopped
4 onions, finely chopped
4 celery sticks, finely chopped
2 tablespoons olive oil
6 slices of drying or older sourdough bread, cubed
3 eggs, beaten
sea salt and black pepper

Toast the pinenuts in a large dry frying pan until golden, then scoop them out and put in a large bowl. Melt the butter or dripping in the same pan and add the herbs, apples, prunes, onions and celery and cook gently for 5–7 minutes. Remove and add to the bowl.

Fry the bread in olive oil until golden. Add to the bowl with the apple mixture and leave to cool. Stir in the eggs, mix well and season with salt and pepper. The stuffing is now ready to use. It can be made the day before and stored in the roasting pan.

Pasta with garlic breadcrumbs

A favourite, classic recipe from Italy and a seductive way to feed children leftover greens they might otherwise be sceptical about. Use shell or cup pasta shapes so they capture the breadcrumbs.

SERVES 4

300g/10½oz dried shell pasta
2 garlic cloves, crushed
4 tablespoons fresh or dried breadcrumbs
4 tablespoons olive oil
4 tablespoons cooked cauliflower, calabrese, broccoli, courgettes
   (one or more of these vegetables can be used)
salt and black pepper
freshly grated Parmesan, to serve

Bring a pan of water to the boil and add salt. Cook the pasta for whatever time is recommended on the packet (reputable Italian brands give very accurate cooking instructions).

Just before you serve, fry the garlic and breadcrumbs in the oil until golden, then stir in the vegetables to heat through. Drain the pasta and return to the pasta pan. Stir in the breadcrumb mixture well; season with salt and pepper and serve with grated Parmesan.

BREAD PUDDINGS

Even great French chefs think 'le pudding' is the best thing about British food. Our great rib-stickers – crumbles, steamed sponges and creamed rice – dissolve bad tempers and centrally heat bellies before setting out on walks after Sunday lunch. But many of the best puddings are not just made for the sake of pleasure. There is a large family of recipes devoted to using up ageing bread, bread and butter pudding being the best known, summer pudding and apple charlotte another two. Many steamed pudding recipes also ask for breadcrumbs, including Christmas pudding. The French have just one famous bread pudding, called pain perdu, meaning 'lost bread'. Dipping a piece of drying bread into a mixture of cream, egg yolk and sugar, they then fry it, with the result being a sweet French toast. It isn't a dish for every day, but an occasional treat to cheer up a child, or yourself.

But there is a version of pain perdu I prefer, buried in *The Constance Spry Cookery Book*. My mother used to make it – to loud cheers – and my children beg for it now. It is also cited as one of the greats in a *Vogue* article written by Arabella Boxer. This is the recipe that appeared in *The New English Kitchen*, a book I wrote in 2005 about eating well economically. I cannot resist using the recipe again.

Toffee bread pudding

see PLATE 28

SERVES 4
120g/4oz butter
120g/4oz Demerara sugar
225g/8oz golden syrup
300ml/½ pint milk
4 thick slices of bread, crusts removed, cut into fingers
whipped cream, to serve

Heat the butter, sugar and golden syrup in a small pan and boil for
3 minutes. Remove from the heat and keep warm. In a separate
pan, heat the milk to boiling point. Put the fingers of bread in a dish
and pour the milk over them. Lift them out straight away – if you
leave them to soak they become too soft – and put them into 4
serving bowls. Pour over the sauce; you can dip them in the sauce
instead but you will have to work fast. Serve immediately, with
whipped cream.

Delicately flavoured meat stock
Rich meat stock
Delicate vegetable stock
'In a minute' soups:
  Mushroom broth
  Lemongrass and greens
  Courgette, basil and egg
Risotto
Various risottos:
  Saffron
  Lemon
  Fungi
  Peas/broad beans
  Squash
  Herbs and leaves
  Alternative cheeses
  Prawns
Store-method risotto
Alternative 'stock'
Sweet cooked tomato
Sweet cooked tomato in other
  dishes:
  Simple fish stew
  Tomato vinaigrette
  Braised lamb shoulder
  Meat balls
Aunts' pasta, with sweet cooked
  tomato and anchovy

A store of cooked rice
Pea and potato spiced rice
Fridge dough
Onion tart
More ways with fridge dough:
  Pizza
  Courgette fougasse
  Spiced flatbreads
  Rolls
Béchamel – white sauce
Ways to use white sauce:
  Baked pasta
  Soft green vegetable gratins
  Cauliflower cheese
  Leek and ham gratin
  Fish pie
Mayonnaise
Other ways with mayonnaise:
  Garlic – also called aioli
  Four herbs
  Caper and tarragon
  Dill
  Saffron and red chilli
  Anchovy
Confit

HALFWAY
TO A
MEAL

There are two large containers that sit side by side in my fridge. One filled with sweet, cooked puréed tomato, the other with delicately flavoured meat stock. If I am honest, I use these two easy-to-make ingredients more than any other in my cooking. They are the link between having nothing proper for supper and feeling as if we have eaten well. When cheese on toast does not seem like a meal, but dinner must be made in minutes, a supply of sweet cooked tomato takes me to within fifteen minutes of eating an aromatic saffron- and fennel-scented fish stew. Using the stock, I can have a bowl of soup with courgettes, Parmesan, basil and rich little shreds of egg in five minutes, or risotto with mushrooms in twenty-five. Most importantly, I can relax. With these two jars in my store, I am always halfway to a real, homemade meal.

It is in the psyche of women to prepare for trouble. Carrying a bag filled with all that is needed to get through the day is part of this mindset, but it extends to the home. In every respect women hate to be caught without a plan or tool to tackle a problem. Women bulk-buy enthusiastically, seeking out multi-packs, and tend to collect 'things' that might one day come in useful. There is truth, too, in the old cliché that over-packing for trips away is a feminine trait. Just in case? You bet. The phrase is so apt, it ought to be a luggage brand.

I know very few female minimalists. But step into a kitchen and this is no longer the case. Where a woman would once have squirreled a supply of homemade stocks or sauces, ready to transform into a proper meal, I find virtually empty fridges. The usual stand-in for larder-cooking is a stack of ready meals, or a takeaway menu, pinned by a magnet to the fridge door.

I can't count the number of times I have been told that this is the answer. There is no need to make stock when you can buy stock cubes, say detractors; no need to make a sauce for pasta when supermarkets devote whole aisles of shelves to ready-made. It is true that some processed foods are made with integrity, advertising the provenance and naturalness of the ingredients inside the pack, but most manufacturers take advantage of loose labelling laws that allow vagueness about the raw materials. This is especially so in the case of cheaper ready meals, and this distance from the truth can have dangerous consequences. Ambiguous nutritional information on packaging that disguises high salt levels and meat from an unknown source could put our health at risk. Other ingredients may be produced unethically and have a wider impact. Poor-quality ready-made food is a very short-term solution.

The rift between wanting to cook and cooking can be wide, sometimes endless. Everyone has at least one thing on a wish list that they would like to change about themselves, to make life better. The ambition to cook is popular – and growing. A survey of 5000 Europeans in 2008 found that over 52 per cent of young people wanted to change the way they eat and learn to cook meals from fresh ingredients, but that few did more than go on to cook the odd showpiece meal. The overall trend shows a loss rather than a gain in skills.

Convenience food is not always a dirty phrase, though. This chapter is all about convenience food, but it won't tell you to open a can of ready-cooked mince or use Aunt Bessie's frozen mashed potato. For the time it takes to go out and find all those specific items you can make a couple of sauces from ingredients that can be bought

anywhere, and brew a pot of meat stock. With these good things in store, you are 'halfway to a meal'. It can take just minutes to make a dish of something real and properly cooked.

Busy people who want to cook deserve special attention. Because what they are trying to do is heroic. The way our lives are structured now is extraordinarily stressful and exhausting. There is not only working life and home life but the expectation, spread by celebrity culture, to do it in style. The messages we receive are intimidating. There is an expectation that our kitchens should be Ikea-ed to the nines, and every meal served on carefully selected, colour-coordinated plates. One peep inside the covers of a lifestyle magazine and we know we are not getting it right. Consumerism has – bizarrely – been bad for the advancement of home cooking.

The gentle art
The more I understand about feminine food, the more I am struck by the creativity. When a cook is confident, it becomes easier to improvise. Good home cooks are not rigid; they do not rely on prescriptive recipes and menus like restaurants but constantly adapt to suit season, weather, economy, availability of time and ingredients. Ultimately we face a battle not to become bored of cooking, not to see it as a dreary chore. When the basics are in place, it is time for the art of cooking. There are hundreds of ways to use stock, a dozen different exciting things to fill or top flatbreads, and sweet cooked tomato has many diverse uses. Hilda Leyel, an early-twentieth-century food writer and herbalist, called cooking 'the gentle art'. This short phrase sums it up more beautifully than any other.

Time investment

There is a price to pay, and that is to give a little time to preparing your halfway-to-a-meal basics. An hour waiting for poultry stock to simmer in a pan; twenty minutes to make a supply of béchamel; even less to make bread dough and just a few moments to give a basil plant a drink of water. Investing this time buys back a great deal more as the week unfolds. In a hurry on, say, a Thursday, you will thank yourself for making that sweet cooked tomato as you stir it into big bowls of pasta before scattering over some healthy, just picked herbs.

In the store cupboard

My fridge stores of stock and other halfway-to-a-meal staples go nowhere without having a few handy 'dry' store-cupboard foods in the kitchen, plus a handful of fresh ones that have a long shelf life. The shopping list that follows is one I have carried with me for years.

Dry

* Grains – rice (arborio and basmati), couscous, bulgur wheat, pearl barley and other whole grains such as oats and spelt.
* Dried pulses – green lentils, including Puy, and red lentils.
* Pasta – both long and short durum-wheat pasta, and nests of noodles made with egg.
* Cans – tomatoes, coconut milk, artichokes in brine, beans (cannellini, haricot, flageolet, butter beans) and chickpeas. Canned tuna and anchovies are also essentials.
* English mustard powder.
* Jars – French mustard, capers and gherkins, curry powder and other spices.

387

* Packets – flours: strong white and wholemeal, plain and self-raising, plus some alternatives such as gram and potato flour.
* Nuts, seeds, dried fruit – sesame and pumpkin seeds; figs, prunes, sultanas; pinenuts, almonds, walnuts, peanuts and pistachios.
* Oils – extra virgin olive oil and sunflower oil, coconut cream (sold as blocks in packs).

Fresh
* Butter, dripping or duck fat.
* Lemons.
* Smoked bacon.
* Garlic.
* Onions/shallots.
* Parmesan.

Homemade stock
I try to persuade every person I meet to use leftover bones or ask the butcher for free bones the shop would otherwise dispose of. I brown them in a pan then simmer them with water to make a litre or two of rich stock. It can then be the base of swiftly thrown together soups and rice dishes like risotto. Stock divides people. It is often cited – by 'busy' people – as a step too far. We cannot be expected to make stock on top of everything else. Why? The work involved takes minutes and one time investment results in more than one economic, healthy, delicious supper. Stock has its origins in medieval cookery, is still routinely made all over the world in the home, yet in Britain and America, the two 'fattest' countries, making stock went out of fashion with no good reason. Bought stocks vary in quality but the

goodness of all of them is ruined by a high salt content. The whole culture of homemade stock is intelligent, yet serious-minded people claim to be above making it. These same people often pride themselves on their ability to think ahead, to save for the future.

Arguing for stock: it makes itself while we pay attention to other matters. It should not mean huge smelly pans bubbling for hours, steaming up the windows. A home where stock is regularly made is one that has a welcoming atmosphere, and a faint scent of good things happening in the kitchen. I am fond of saying that a store of stock is halfway to a meal, but it is more than that. It builds notes of flavour in food while stock cubes give dishes a tinny finish. It makes use of bones, making the cost of meat go further – justification for meat in the diet is easier when every last bit is used. Vegetable stock makes use of scraps you would never eat like onion skins or the rough end of carrots and celery. It honours food, making sure nothing is wasted. Stock is virtually free of charge. And it reduces the need for salt. I have been able to persuade girlfriends to make stock on the single basis that it brings down water retention – or puffiness – in the ankles.

Uses for stock

I use stock to make soup (but not all soups – see below), for braising, in gravy, in 'jelly' terrines, and often in rice, bean and some pasta dishes. Sometimes I heat a cupful of richly flavoured stock to boiling point, add a little dry sherry and freshly ground black pepper, then sip it – a radiating cocktail for health, wealth and contentment.

Delicately flavoured meat stock

Most butchers will give you chicken carcasses, lamb or pork bones but charge a nominal sum for beef marrow bones, because of the value of the marrow itself. Smaller bones are easier to handle. When I ask the butcher for chicken carcasses, I am usually only given the ribcage section (he will have sold the legs whole, along with the filleted breast meat) – these 'cages' are a perfect size for the pan. Also it has been my experience that the 'classier' the butcher, the more he gives away. One that I visit will often chuck in the wings which he cannot sell to his chicken fillet-addicted customers, but which I roast with paprika and feed to very eager children.

2 tablespoons olive oil or 2 walnut-sized chunks of butter or dripping
poultry or meat bones (approximately 1kg/2lb or half a large
    casserole pan full), either leftover or fresh bones from the butcher
approximately 2.5 litres/4½ pints water, to cover

Heat the oil, butter or dripping in a large pan, and brown the bones for a few minutes, a process that will add extra flavour to the stock. Cover with water, to about a 2cm/¾ in submersion depth. Bring to the boil. As soon as the water boils, turn the heat down so it slowly simmers. Poultry stock can be made in under an hour, meat stock will be ready in 1½–2 hours. To test if it is done, taste the stock, looking for a delicate yet clear savour of the ingredients in the pot. Even if stock has a relatively mild flavour, it will add heaps of flavour to the dishes you use it in. You can add a little salt, but I tend to use the stock then season the final dish only at the end of cooking.

When the stock is ready, strain then discard bones.* Store in plastic containers, letting any fat settle on top; it hardens and acts as a protective seal – you can skim it off before using the stock. Meat stock should keep for up to 7 days. Sniff for any sourness that indicates it is going off.

RICH MEAT STOCK

The longer it is cooked, the richer and more concentrated stock becomes, but I am content to use delicately flavoured stock in most cooking, because you will be combining it with further flavours.

* We pick extra pieces of meat and other tissue off carcasses and bones for the dog, yielding a surprising amount.

Delicate vegetable stock

You can use any non-starchy vegetables to make this all-purpose stock, so no potatoes, and no peas or beans – these vegetables can cloud the stock and, if cooked for more than a few minutes, their flavour turns from sweet to musty and slightly sour. You can, however, use pods from fresh young garden peas and broad beans. Avoid any cabbage family plants, because their flavour overpowers other vegetables – but any root or other leaf is fine. This stock can be made from the peelings and waste from any of the mentioned vegetables. Obviously if you have to buy the ingredients it is not a free food, but it is still nevertheless an inexpensive one, especially if you use produce that is past its best. Greengrocers and markets will usually strike deals on vegetables that are no longer picture perfect, and supermarkets should discount them.

More is the pity that supermarkets do not sell much 'knobbly' produce when it is ideal for soup and stock.

MAKES ABOUT 1.5 LITRES/2½ PINTS
2 tablespoons olive oil or 2 walnut-sized chunks of butter or dripping
4 onions, roughly chopped, plus their skins (dirty root end discarded)
4 celery sticks and leaves, roughly chopped
4 carrots, roughly chopped
3 handfuls of mushrooms or their stalks and skins, roughly chopped
1 garlic clove, crushed with the back of a knife and peeled (optional)
at least 2 handfuls of other leafy or root vegetables, roughly chopped
handful of parsley stalks and/or leaves, roughly chopped
1 bay leaf
10 black peppercorns
1 teaspoon dried thyme
1 teaspoon dried oregano
2 litres/3 pints water

Heat the oil, butter or dripping and add all the vegetables, seasonings and herbs; cook over a medium heat until they begin to take on a little colour. Add the water and bring to the boil. Cook for about 30 minutes, no more. Leave to steep for about 1 hour, then put through a sieve, squeezing the vegetable pulp to extract all the liquid.

Store in the fridge, in plastic containers, leaving the fat to settle and harden on top. The fat adds shelf life to the stock, which should keep for up to 7 days. Sniff for any sourness that indicates it is going off.

Kitchen note

You can extend the shelf life of fresh stock for another few days by bringing it back to just below boiling point and keeping it there for 5 minutes. Only do this when the stock still has a fresh, slightly sweet scent – you cannot revive stock that smells sour, having gone off.

'IN A MINUTE' SOUPS

* Mushroom broth – add a splash of sherry, black pepper and some thinly sliced mushrooms and simmer with rich stock for 1 minute.
* Lemongrass and greens – bash a piece of lemongrass and slice a red chilli. Add to rich stock with some bean sprouts and pak choi and simmer for 1 minute.
* Courgette, basil and egg – boil the stock and add some very small dice of courgette; beat an egg and whisk into the boiling stock with a few torn basil leaves. Serve with Parmesan (this recipe is one taught to me by the brilliant Italian cook Carla Tomasi). See plate 29.
* Beef with sesame and spring greens in soy broth (see page 358).

BIG BROTHS

Soups that can be eaten as a main course, with chopped vegetables, salt pork (bacon), beans or pulses. Try the following recipes:
* Summer vegetable broth (page 27).
* Autumn vegetable harvest soup with grains (page 29).
* Winter vegetable stew-soup (page 30).
* Leek and potato soup with cream (page 34).
* Green cabbage and pickled duck garbure (page 36).
* Clam, cider and potato chowder (page 39).
* Ribollita (page 234).

Ahead

393

BRAISING WITH STOCK

The slow-cooked recipes on pages 199–228 are homage to stock. You can make all stews using only water, but adding meat stock will take the taste from the equivalent of a lone pretty voice to a rousing chorus. This is not fast food, however, but it is convenient in that you can leave a pot to simmer while busy doing something else.

Rice dishes made with stock

In the short moment of wondering which way to use some stock in the fridge, my mind often turns to rice dishes. Sometimes I cook lightly spiced dishes with Arabic flavours and ingredients (see recipes below), but more often than not it is risotto. The little fat grains of northern Italian rice thirstily drink up the fresh stock which then melts their hard, chalky hearts. This is the true mother of comfort food, seasoned with favourite flavours like saffron or fungi, finished with a slick of butter and the resonant flavours of mature Parmesan. You can make risotto with stock cubes, and lots of Italians now do, but taste the real thing and it is very hard to come back from it. Just over 1 litre/1¾ pints of stock is needed for a risotto for four people, so buying fresh stock can be rather expensive. I now love the almost 'free' aspect of making your own and, if done in advance, it cuts the cooking time down to 30 minutes, or less if you use the store method on page 397.

Risotto

see PLATE 30

This is the basic recipe for a plain risotto. Suggestions how to dress it up follow.

SERVES 4

1 heaped tablespoon butter, plus an extra walnut-sized piece
1 heaped tablespoon finely chopped white onion
400g/14oz risotto rice
90ml/3fl oz white wine
1.2 litres/2 pints or more chicken stock
2 tablespoons freshly grated Parmesan, plus extra to serve
salt and black pepper

Melt the tablespoon of butter in a pan, add the onion and cook gently until soft. Add the rice and cook, stirring (preferably with a wooden fork), for a minute or so, then add the wine and simmer until absorbed. Over a medium heat, stir in the stock a ladleful at a time, allowing the simmering rice to absorb it before you add more. Continue until the rice has absorbed enough liquid and the rice is just tender but not mushy. Stir in the Parmesan. Stop further cooking with the addition of a piece of butter. Season to taste and take straight to the table. The whole process should take about 35 minutes.

VARIOUS RISOTTOS

* Saffron – steep a pinch of saffron strands in some warmed stock, then strain to remove the threads of the spice, if you wish. Add

Ahead

the infused stock in the last 5 minutes of risotto making. This is the classic risotto to eat with meat or fish, or before, as a starter.

* Lemon – add a celery stick, finely chopped, at the onion stage. Grate in the zest of a lemon halfway through adding the stock. Use cream to finish, adding an egg yolk mixed with the lemon juice. Serve with more Parmesan and some chopped sage that has been lightly fried in butter. This is a highly simplified version of Anna del Conte's original and delicious recipe.

* Dried or fresh fungi – steep dried mushrooms in hot stock for about 15 minutes, until soft, then drain. Add to the risotto at the beginning of cooking (the soaking liquid can be added to the risotto with the stock). Fresh mushrooms should be sautéed with the onion at the beginning of cooking.

* Peas and/or broad beans – simmer peas and broad beans in a little stock, pop the beans from their thin skins and add at the last minute. You can use frozen peas and broad beans with great success but pop the frozen beans out of their outer skin with your fingers before adding.

* Squash – peel, deseed and dice one butternut (or other type of) squash and add with the onion. The dice should be no more than 1cm/less than ½in, or it will not cook fully.

* Herbs and leaves – make use of windowsill herbs, such as parsley, basil, chives or chervil, adding them chopped, at the end of cooking. You can also add leaves like rocket, watercress, baby chard or young beetroot leaves.

* Alternative cheeses – try different cheeses, either pecorino or hard English ewe's milk cheeses (Lord of the Hundreds, Berkswell, Somerset Rambler, Sharpham). Alternatively, continental cheeses such as Gorgonzola can be good, or try fresh cheese such as mascarpone, ricotta or chèvre (fresh goat's cheese). Add a little

Parmesan, too, if you are using fresh cheese, to season.

✻ North Atlantic prawns – add at the end of cooking, after defrosting the prawns and draining them on kitchen paper to remove excess salty water. If you buy shell-on prawns, make a broth with their shells first, toasting them in a pan with a little oil then adding 1 litre/1¾ pints water. You can use a light chicken stock, however. Do not eat this risotto with cheese of any sort.

✻ Tomato – see sweet cooked tomato on page 400.

Store-method risotto

A method sometimes used by restaurants, which enables you to make risotto in about 10 minutes. Carnaroli rice is better for this risotto because it always holds its shape.

SERVES 4
1 tablespoon butter
1 onion, finely chopped
300g/10½oz short-grain Carnaroli rice
1 wineglass white wine (optional)
1–1.5 litres/1¾–2½ pints chicken, vegetable or beef stock

Melt the butter in a large pan, add the onion and cook until soft. Add the rice and cook, stirring (being careful not to mash the rice), for 1 minute. Stir in the glass of wine, if using. When it has been absorbed, begin to add the stock, one ladleful at a time, stirring constantly over a medium heat. After 10–12 minutes, taste the rice – it should be half cooked, with a white, opaque centre. Strain it,

reserving any cooking liquor. Cool the cooking liquor, add it to the remaining stock and store in the fridge, clearly marked. Spread the rice out on a plastic tray, no more than 2cm/¾in deep. Allow to cool, cover with clingfilm and store in the fridge. It will keep for 2–3 days.

To finish the risotto, spoon the required quantity of rice from the tray – as much as you need – and put it in a pan. Cover with just enough of the cooking liquor to make it sloppy when stirred. Bring to the boil, then turn down the heat and cook gently for a few minutes, until the rice is tender but firm to the bite – al dente. Stir in the butter, then the Parmesan. If adding other ingredients that need more than 5 minutes' cooking (such as mushrooms or prawns), part-cook them in a pan with a little oil and stock beforehand.

Alternative 'stock'

When you have no stock but want a full-flavoured soup or braise, the following are very effective.
* Dry cider – for soups and braises with pork or poultry.
* Apple juice – for soups and braises with onion and garlic, pork and poultry. Sharp-flavoured apple juices are best.
* Thyme, rosemary and sage 'tea' – for soups with tomato or courgettes; meat and poultry (add juniper and star anise for game).
* Coconut water – make a brew with 250g/9oz desiccated coconut and 1 litre/1¾ pints boiling water. Leave to steep for 10 minutes then strain. Use with fish and chicken, adding lemongrass, chilli and galangal root.

* Celery, cucumber and mint – juiced, for iced soups. If you find the flavour too intense, dilute the vegetable juice-stock with water.
* Juniper and bay broth – simmer 3 bay leaves with 10 juniper berries and a cinnamon stick in 600ml/1 pint water to make a broth for simmering lamb (see page 94) or for soups and stews with game.

Serious about tomatoes

Beside the bottles of fresh stock in my fridge are others filled with an orangey-red sauce. The children call it 'pomodoro' sauce because I went to great lengths to find a recipe that had the true character of the sweet tomato sauces eaten on Italian holidays.

It is very close to the sugo di pomodoro made by mothers and grandmothers in millions of Italian households and served with endless dishes of pasta, rice and gnocchi. It can also be added to fish soups, vegetable broths and meat stews, used in baked dishes of vegetables or pasta or spread on fresh dough to make pizza. I use it even more widely in my English kitchen, in curries and other non-Italian ways, but it is still the best example of the perfect logic of Italian home cooking: taking one essential food, cooking it to preserve its usefulness, then adding it as a core ingredient to umpteen satellite dishes. For any new cook this sauce is an ideal point at which to begin.

Sweet cooked tomato

The secret of this sauce is in adding water. This flies in the face of most recipes for tomato sauce, which insist that the sauce will sweeten after a long boil. All tomatoes, from sun-ripened fresh ones to budget cans, need time to develop sweetness as they cook, but if there is too much evaporation, the sauce will taste burnt. Water acts as an agent; the sauce cooks longer and sweetness has time to grow, resulting in a very fresh-flavoured, orangey-coloured sauce. I admit to always adding a spoonful of sugar anyway, for good measure, because the fresh tomatoes, bought here, need that little bit of extra help.

Note that the sauce is puréed until smooth in a liquidiser or through a food mill after cooking, to take out the 'bits' element that many children loathe. You can make a rougher-textured sauce if you wish.

MAKES APPROXIMATELY 16–20 SERVINGS
150ml/¼ pint extra virgin olive oil
4 x 400g/14oz cans Italian tomatoes, chopped or whole
1kg/2lb 4oz plum, cherry or other fresh tomatoes, roughly chopped
300ml/½ pint water
8 garlic cloves, crushed with the back of a knife then peeled
2 sprigs basil
1–2 heaped dessertspoons sugar

Put all the ingredients in a large heavy-based pan; bring to the boil and stew, bubbling over a medium/low heat for 30–40 minutes. Stir from time to time to prevent the contents sticking to the base of the pan. The tomato mixture will become paler in colour, while the oil will rise to the surface and have a dark appearance. Allow to cool a little, then liquidise until very smooth. Or put through a food mill, sometimes called a mouli legumes (this will not pulverise the sauce but separate out pips and skin, which can then be discarded). Store the sauce in plastic containers – this sauce will keep for up to 10 days in the fridge and freezes well.

Kitchen note
Canned San Marzano tomatoes, from Italian specialist food shops, are the best, but most Italian brands or supermarket own-label Italian tomatoes are fine.

SWEET COOKED TOMATO IN OTHER DISHES

* Family food – see page 64 for seven child-friendly recipes containing sweet cooked tomatoes.
* With warm feta cheese – see page 127.
* Simple fish stew with tomato, saffron, garlic and fennel – for 4 people, sauté 1 onion in 3 tablespoons olive oil with 2 chopped garlic cloves, 1 chopped deseeded green chilli and 1 sliced fennel bulb. Cook for a few minutes until the vegetables are soft then add 1 teaspoon ground coriander, 6 saffron threads, 2 wineglasses white wine and 12 tablespoons sweet cooked tomato. Bring to the boil, season with salt and black pepper to taste, then add approximately 500g/1lb 2oz fresh white fish fillet (haddock, gurnard, ling, monkfish) and 4 handfuls of live mussels or clams. Simmer for 5 minutes or until the shellfish have opened (discard any that don't open), then add a dash of Pernod and serve. Good with boiled waxy Charlotte potatoes, fried or grilled/toasted bread.

* Tomato vinaigrette – eat with rich salad ingredients, for example: fresh cooked crab, avocado, cooked peeled prawns, goat's cheese or grilled yellow-fin tuna. Also very good with canned fish like sardines or skipjack tuna. For 2 people combine 75ml/ 5 tablespoons olive oil with 75ml/5 tablespoons sweet cooked tomato from the fridge. Add red wine vinegar to taste, and shredded basil leaves and perhaps a few slivers of black Niçoise olives. Whisk until emulsified.

* Braised lamb shoulder with tomato and herbs – roast a shoulder of lamb, seasoned with salt and pepper and rubbed with olive oil, for 45 minutes at 175°C/350°F/Gas 4. Add 4 chopped garlic cloves and 1 heaped teaspoon dried oregano to the pan, then 500ml/ 18fl oz sweet cooked tomato with 200ml/7fl oz water. Sprinkle the lamb with 1 teaspoon sweet smoked paprika, then cover with kitchen foil. Lower the oven temperature to 150°C/300°F/Gas 2 and bake the lamb slowly for 1 hour or until the meat becomes tender and falls off the bone. Add a little more water during cooking if there is too much evaporation.

* Meat balls in tomato sauce – for 4 people combine 400g/14oz lean minced beef with 200g/7oz pork mince. Beat in 1 egg, a pinch each of salt and pepper, 1 teaspoon dried oregano and 4 tablespoons breadcrumbs. Form into small walnut-sized balls and fry until lightly browned. Cover with sweet cooked tomato, then simmer until tender. Eat with pasta.

Aunts' pasta, with sweet cooked tomato and anchovy

see PLATE 31

I learned to cook this dish in Naples, home of the best tomatoes, which are grown in the threatening shadow of Mount Vesuvius, an active volcano. It was an unforgettable day. In the morning I went to the cathedral to witness the 'miracle of San Gennaro'. During this extraordinary service, 2000 people, many of them the faithful women of the city or 'aunts of San Gennaro', offer fervent devotion to an ampoule containing the dried blood of the city's patron saint, San Gennaro (Saint Januarius). The 'miracle' is the hoped-for liquification of the blood, a sign that the volcano will not erupt. Past eruptions have made this one of the most fertile places in the world and the balance of nutrients in the Neapolitan volcanic soil is always given as the reason why the area produces the sweetest tomatoes in the world.

The extraordinary productivity is enough for farmers to cultivate crops in an area that could be classed as dangerous as a war zone. No wonder, then, that on that morning the aunts' rosaries were clucking like busy knitting needles as the women swayed, wept and prayed in the cathedral, waiting for the miracle that ensures the food supply and their safety. The miracle came, to loud cheers and applause. Later I visited the chef Alfonso Galotti, who cooks his family dishes in his restaurant La Taverna dell'arte. His mother's beautiful, grand dish of tubular pasta – look for dried paccheri in Italian food shops – anchovies and tomato is my favourite pasta dish of all. Look out also for tins of San Marzano tomatoes to make the sweet cooked tomato, the very best for making sauce and grown by a consortium of farmers on the slopes of Mount Vesuvius.

SERVES 6

salt

500g/1lb 2oz paccheri or other large tubular pasta (choose one
    without a ridged surface)

4–5 tablespoons olive oil

1 garlic clove, crushed

10 capers

15 black olives, pitted

400g/14oz sweet cooked tomato (see page 400 and Kitchen note,
    page 405)

1 tablespoon raisins

black pepper

1 teaspoon dried oregano

8–12 good-quality anchovies, drained of their oil, or fresh (head and
    backbone removed), if you can get them, roughly chopped

2 tablespoons grated pecorino, plus extra to serve

1 handful of chopped flat-leaf parsley

Put a very large pan of water on to boil then add 2 teaspoons salt
and the paccheri and cook for about 18 minutes until al dente (a
little firm when bitten) – note that smaller tubes cook in less time,
about 12–14 minutes.

A few minutes before the pasta is ready, make the sauce. Heat the
oil with the garlic and add the capers and olives. Stir with a wooden
spoon, using it to crush the contents. Add the sweet cooked tomato
and the raisins, a pinch of salt, some freshly ground pepper and the
oregano, plus a tablespoon of water. Cook over a high temperature
for 15 seconds then turn off the heat. Add the anchovies and stir –
you do not want to 'cook' them. Stir in the pasta with the cheese and
serve with the parsley and more cheese on the table.

If you are making the sweet cooked tomato specifically for this recipe, process it for a short time so it has a rougher texture. You can also make the sauce using fillets of fresh, deseeded, skinned plum tomatoes. Remove the skins by first nicking each tomato with a knife, then putting them in boiling-hot water for 1 minute. The skins should slip off quite easily. You can also use very sweet, halved cherry tomatoes.

A store of cooked rice

I cook basmati and Thai fragrant rice, and store safely in the fridge for use in biryani (see page 406) or egg-fried rice (see page 92). Mari Roberts, the very patient copy-editor of this book, suggested I try her 'absorption method' of cooking rice, which she learned when living in the Philippines. I did, and loved its common sense.

TO COOK A LITTLE RICE

Rinse the rice first in a sieve under the cold tap until the water runs nearly clear. Use your middle finger as a measure and add the rice (long grain) to a small pan, up to your first knuckle. Fill the pan with water up to your second knuckle. Heat until boiling then cook for 5 minutes uncovered, 5 minutes covered. Turn off the heat and allow to steam for 5 minutes. To make a larger quantity in a bigger pan, measure the rice in the pan up to your second knuckle, then the water up to your third. Cook as for the smaller amount. Mari does not add salt, as in the Philippines. I do add a little with pure basmati rice, because I find it firms the rice grains very slightly and keeps them separate.

Pea and potato spiced rice

I have visited the northern region of India where basmati is grown. The mothers, wives and daughters tend and harvest the rice in the fields; their husbands take it to the market. The girls, dressed in wildly coloured saris, veils across their faces to protect them from dust, harvest the rice at the crack of dawn in pale light. The northern farming lands are reasonably wealthy, and the women are excellent cooks – even those in professions which would normally furnish them the excuse to give the job to someone else. This recipe is very similar to one given me by Dr Nandini Seshadri, a scientist who made hers in her pretty kitchen in Delhi.

SERVES 4
125ml/4fl oz sunflower oil
4 garlic cloves, crushed
4cm/1½in piece of fresh ginger, grated
4 onions, chopped
6 cardamom pods
3 cloves
1 teaspoon ground turmeric
salt
4 tomatoes, chopped
60g/2oz cream cheese, paneer or Greek yoghurt
2 tablespoons non-sweet desiccated coconut, soaked in 3 tablespoons
    water
8–10 green chillies, cut lengthways into slivers
about 6 tablespoons frozen petits pois, defrosted
2 potatoes, unpeeled, cut into thin sticks
650g/1lb 7oz cooked basmati rice (or 4 approximate servings)

To serve: handful of mint leaves; handful of coriander; chopped; 1
    lime, cut into quarters

Heat half the oil in a wide frying pan, add the garlic, ginger and
onions and fry until golden brown. Add the cardamoms, cloves,
turmeric and ½ teaspoon salt, followed by the chopped tomatoes.
Add the cream cheese and coconut and cook for 10 minutes, then
transfer to a bowl and set to one side.

Heat the remaining oil in a separate pan, add the chillies, peas and
potatoes, and fry until the vegetables begin to soften round the
edges. Season with a pinch of salt. Add the rice to the fried
vegetables and heat through, then carefully stir in the tomato and
cream cheese mixture. Serve with the mint leaves and chopped
coriander scattered over the top, putting a wedge of lime onto
each plate.

Kitchen note
If you are storing cooked rice, allow to cool, cover with a piece
of clingfilm and put in the fridge immediately. Reheat well.

Cooking lessons
My school was old-fashioned enough to still give cooking lessons in
the late 1970s, long after the more academic schools had decided
that girls should be studying the same subjects as boys. Once a
week, for a whole afternoon, we took up our positions in the
cookery classroom. Each workstation had an electric cooker and a
basic battery of equipment, each item marked with a splodge of

different-coloured nail varnish so it would not become separated from its proper place when we shared the washing-up sink with the next-door pair.

It was possible even at that age to divide us by our eating ancestry. The majority of the girls had no knowledge of cooking at all and thought the lessons a great time-wasting joke. When their sponge sank, gales of satisfied giggles rang through the room. Our teacher was near retirement and clearly looking forward to it. Eye on the end game, she held back her frustration – and I was one of her two pets. Secretly I took it all terribly seriously, just as meals were taken seriously in my French-influenced home, where food was never played with.

I remember two lessons clearly, because I adored one and hated the other. An afternoon spent making pickled onions defined cooking in its worst incarnation. From the tear-inducing peeling of fifty small, beastly, tight-skinned onions with my blunt fingers, to the revolting smell of them boiling in malt vinegar, with every second I could hear only one word in my head: why? But a few weeks later, when our teacher shuffled over to her demonstration table with the ingredients to make white bread dough, it was the beginning of two hours and fifteen minutes of unremitting bliss. The unfamiliar scent of fresh yeast, the feel of smooth, stretchy dough in floury hands, the science, rules, magic and wonder at the taste of my very own piece of hot bread, spread with melting butter. This was cooking that mattered. Even the giggling gastronomic orphans in the classroom were silent for a moment, watching their dough puff and rise.

I think you only need one bread lesson – after that it is fine tuning. The basic messages are dramatic. I can still hear my teacher tell me that 'too much heat and salt kill yeast'. We were at the age where we considered our dogs to be the love of our lives, and killing a tiny micro-organism seemed mindlessly cruel. We were told to use 'strong' flour to support the shape of the loaf, and when kneading to slam the dough onto the worktop with a bang, encouraging elasticity in the dough. 'I sometimes make bread dough when I am in a bad mood,' our teacher confided. Favourite of my remembered instructions was being told always to knead bread with one hand, 'in case the telephone rings'. Seeing as talking on the telephone came second in the rank of love after the family dog, this was superb logic. Bread-making had common sense written all over.

Fridge dough

see PLATE 9

This bread is a get-together of the old cookery-lesson dough taught to me at school and a trick learned much later. Yeasts are happiest doing their work in a warm room after being kneaded; if you put raw yeast dough in the fridge, it takes four times as long to double in size. A slow, cool rise adds ripe character to the flavour, and I find the dough more tractable. It is ideal for stretching and shaping into flatbreads which can then be topped with other ingredients. The recipe below is similar to the one for overnight bread, on page 291 – but contains a little milk, as taught me by a Neapolitan baker, to keep the thin breads tender even after being fired. Note that the liquids are weighed.

3g/½ teaspoon dried 'fast action' yeast
600g/1lb 6oz '00' plain white Italian flour, or plain white flour
5g/1 teaspoon salt
30g/1oz olive oil
300g/10½ oz water
100g/3½ oz wholemilk

In a large bowl, mix together the yeast, flour, salt and oil. Pour in the water and milk. Mix with a wooden spoon until the dough becomes too heavy to stir and you need to take over with your hands, taking the dough from the bowl and working on the table. (This can also be done with a dough hook in an electric mixer.)

Knead the dough by hand until smooth and elastic. Pull, stretch and fold the dough. Hold it and bang it down onto the worktop to encourage it to stretch. The dough will become soft, smooth and elastic after about 10 minutes' kneading by hand. It should have a slight stickiness, too. Clean the bowl, return the dough to it, cover with clingfilm and put in the fridge for about 20 hours. I usually make dough in the early evening to use at the same time the following day. You can also make this dough in a hurry, allowing it to rise at room temperature for 1½ hours. It will taste fine, slightly blander, and will not be as malleable.

Onion tart

see PLATE 32

Recipes from the French mother cooks, as impressive and delicious as they are easy to make, once you have a supply of bread dough. This is the speciality of the third-generation Niçoise cook Mère Catarina-Elena Barale, who served the tarts in her restaurant in the Riquier area of the southern French city of Nice, along with other French-Italian frontier specialities that reflected the nearness of the border. Mère Barale cooked her tarts in an enormous clay oven, reportedly fourteen of them at a time.

When I stayed with my grandmother in France and we toured the shops in the local town in the morning, pissaladières like these would be coming out of the ovens in the bakeries with all their appetising smells, shiny olives scattered over their surfaces.

MAKES 2 TARTS
2.25kg/5lb onions
4 garlic cloves, chopped
300ml/½ pint olive oil
1 bay leaf, 1 sprig rosemary – tied together with a piece of string
1 quantity of fridge dough (see page 409)
4 tomatoes, sliced thinly
15 anchovy fillets, rinsed and cut into small slivers
250g/9oz pitted small black olives, cut in half
salt and black pepper

Peel and finely chop the onions – I strongly recommend doing this in a food processor or it can be a tearful job. Put the onions and garlic in a large pan with the oil and bundle of herbs and cook over a medium heat, without colouring them, for half an hour.

Grease two baking sheets with olive oil. Cut the dough in half and roll out thinly on a floured work surface. Pause between rolling, because the dough will contract when over-worked. Roll to the size

of the baking sheet and scatter a little flour over the dough rectangle.
Place the rolling pin at one end, hold the edge of the dough to the
pin and roll it up like paper so it is easy to pick up and then unwind
onto the baking sheet. Do the same with the other piece of dough.
Leave to prove, or rise, for 20 minutes before adding the filling.

Preheat the oven to 220°C/425°F/Gas 7. Spread half the onion
over one piece of the dough and the rest over the other, leaving a
1cm/½in rim at the edge. Arrange the tomato slices over one tart,
side by side in rows, then scatter over half the slivers of anchovy.
Scatter the black olives and remaining anchovies over the other tart.
Season both with salt and pepper and bake for 30 minutes. Serve hot
or cold.

MORE WAYS WITH FRIDGE DOUGH

* Pizza – spread a thin rolled circle of dough with the sweet cooked
  tomato (page 400) and scatter over a few slices of mozzarella.
  Add some basil leaves, or a little dried oregano, then zigzag a little
  olive oil over the top. Season with salt and pepper. Bake at
  220°C/425°F/Gas 7 for 10–15 minutes. Shake over a little more
  olive oil before serving.
* Courgette fougasse – a filled flatbread from France. Divide the
  dough in half and roll into 2 similar oblong shapes. Slice 1 or 2
  courgettes thinly and marinate for a few minutes in a mixture of
  2 tablespoons olive oil, 6 torn basil leaves and 2 chopped garlic
  cloves. Put one piece of dough on a baking sheet and scatter the
  courgettes over the top. Cut slashes in the second piece of dough
  and lay it on top of the first. Pinch the edges together and brush
  with olive oil. Scatter sea salt crystals over the top. Leave to rise
  for 20 minutes, then bake for 25 minutes at 220°C/425°F/Gas 7.

* Spiced flatbreads – divide the dough into 8 pieces and roll into small oblong shapes. Scatter a pinch of ras al hanout onto each and leave to rise. Bake at 220°C/425°F/Gas 7 for 10–15 minutes.
* Rolls – shape into buns, dust with flour and leave to rise for 20 minutes before baking at 220°C/425°F/Gas 7 until the rolls feel hollow when tapped on the underside. If making burger rolls, brush with water after shaping and scatter over some sesame seeds. Bake as before.

Useful sauce

After the sweet cooked tomato, two more base sauces keep me out of trouble – and others in the family happy. One is béchamel, the other mayonnaise. I grew up with béchamel. Both my mother and my stepmother showed me how to make the white, flour-based sauce flavoured with bay and nutmeg. Sauces with flour are right out of fashion in restaurant cooking, but in the real, everyday kitchen, I need this sauce to make instant baked pasta dishes for children who are desperate to eat after school and want something they know and love.

Béchamel – white sauce

Based on the master recipe in Julia Child et al's book, *Mastering the Art of French Cooking*, this is the fundamental white sauce to use in a variety of baked 'gratins', from macaroni to fish pie. Child pointed out that sauces like these are the splendour and glory of French cooking – but she could have said, less grandly, that white sauce makes things

taste nice. She was right to say not to obliterate or disguise food with it, just prolong and complement the flavour of the other ingredients. I am reminded of this every time I taste a ready meal with this sauce in it. Manufacturers see béchamel-based recipes as an excuse to add a lot of cheap-to-make sauce, and a reduced quantity of the more expensive ingredients. Child does not add bay or nutmeg to her sauce, but for the suggestions below it is necessary, so best to make your store sauce ready seasoned.

600ml/1 pint milk
1 bay leaf
a few gratings of nutmeg
1 heaped tablespoon butter
1 heaped tablespoon plain white flour
salt and white pepper

Heat the milk in a pan with the bay leaf and nutmeg until it is just about to boil, then pour into a jug through a strainer. Melt the butter in the same pan and add the flour, stirring to make a roux paste. Cook over a medium heat, stirring with a wooden spoon until the texture of the roux is sandy. Add one-quarter of the milk, stirring fast over a medium heat. The mixture will be thick and you can stir out any lumps. Add about a third of the remaining milk, still stirring quickly, until the sauce boils. It is very important at this stage to keep stirring or the sauce can develop lumps that cannot be smoothed out. Add the milk in two more phases, then bring the sauce finally to the boil. Cook for 1 minute over a slightly lowered heat, allowing the sauce to simmer. The sauce should be smooth and as thick as double cream. Season with salt and pepper. To store the sauce, put in a container and cover the surface with clingfilm or baking paper to prevent a thick skin forming. If there are lumps in the sauce, you can put it through a sieve while still hot and discard them.

WAYS TO USE WHITE SAUCE

* Baked pasta dishes – add grated Parmesan, Gruyère or Cheddar to the sauce and cover cooked macaroni or other tubular pasta shapes with it. Finish with sliced tomatoes or a few spoonfuls of the sweet cooked tomato (see page 400). Grate some cheese over the top and bake until browned and bubbling. For children's macaroni, see page 64.

* Soft green vegetable gratins – spoon a little béchamel over sliced, sautéed courgettes, marrow (see page 263), chard, chicory or spinach. Grate over some Parmesan, Gruyère or Cheddar and bake. Scatter over some breadcrumbs to make an extra crisp surface.

* Cauliflower cheese – add Lancashire cheese to the sauce and spoon over boiled cauliflower. Top with more grated cheese and bake.

* Leek and ham gratin – cook leeks in boiling water until soft. Allow to cool then squeeze out excess water. Roll in slices of ham, cover with sauce and grated cheese and bake.

* Fish pie – cook undyed smoked haddock in a small amount of milk with a walnut-sized lump of butter. Flake the fish into a gratin dish and add some cooked peeled North Atlantic prawns. Add 3 tablespoons of the cooking milk to the sauce with 2 tablespoons double cream. Pour over the fish and refrigerate until cold. Spoon over some mashed potato (see page 45), dot with butter and bake until bubbling and browned on top. Some like grated cheese on their fish pie. Not me! But go ahead if you prefer.

Mayonnaise

I have a tricky-to-decipher, blurry facsimile of *Le Tour De France Des Grandes Dames De La Cuisine,* by Yves Hours, Monique Hours and Monique Veyrun. A celebration of French feminine cookery, its cover speaks of the 'simplicité et sincerité' of this remembered cooking that comes straight from the heart. The mayonnaise recipe is the pure original. Just egg yolk, oil and a tiny 'fil' of vinegar.

2 egg yolks
500ml/18fl oz olive oil (use groundnut if you prefer a lighter
    mayonnaise)
white wine vinegar
salt and white pepper (optional)

Put the egg yolks in a bowl and beat or whisk until smooth. Begin to add the olive oil, just a few drops at a time, beating all the time. If you add the oil too quickly, the sauce can separate or 'split'. Continue to add the oil sparingly until half is used, then add the rest in a slow stream. Add the vinegar once you have begun to add the second half of the oil. Be careful not to add too much vinegar, just a few drops, then taste and add more if you like a slightly sharper mayonnaise. At the end, season with salt and pepper – unless you prefer the mayonnaise in its pure form.

OTHER WAYS WITH MAYONNAISE:
* Garlic – also called aioli, and eaten with raw vegetable crudités or white fish. Crush one or two garlic cloves to a paste with salt and add to the mayonnaise with the egg yolk (or later, to stored sauce).

* Four herbs – add chopped tarragon, basil, chives and parsley with Dijon mustard. Serve with cold roast beef or chicken.
* Caper and tarragon – add chopped fresh tarragon, chopped hard-boiled egg yolk, a few chopped capers and cornichons to the mayonnaise and serve with fish. See plate 14.
* Dill – add chopped fresh dill and 1 tablespoon double cream to mayonnaise and serve with salmon, sea trout, prawns or crab.
* Saffron and red chilli – eat with fish soup or stew (see page 179). Soak 5–10 saffron strands in 1 dessertspoon boiling water. Add to the mayonnaise with 2 teaspoons harissa paste.
* Anchovy – add 2 teaspoons Gentleman's Relish and plenty of fresh parsley to mayonnaise and eat with fish, cold roast pork or hard-boiled eggs.

Confit

I am a recent convert to the traditional method of simmering duck, other poultry or pork in fat. It never appealed to me until I met chef Amanda Lodge, the sous chef at Hartwell House near Aylesbury. The famous local duck is an expensive ingredient and Amanda, under the watch of head chef Daniel Richardson, attacks the situation with pragmatism, using every bit of the bird. The bones are brewed into a rich broth, the breasts roasted and sliced and the humble legs marinated in spices and then cooked very slowly. It was the seasoning that won me over, a unique blend of spices that go so well with the rich flavour of the duck. If you are not keen to simmer the duck in the fat, you can always use this mix to rub the bird's skin with before roasting.

SERVES 4
4 large or 8 small duck legs
1–2 teaspoons Maldon salt
200ml/7fl oz duck fat

FOR THE SPICE MARINADE:
12 peppercorns
6 juniper berries
2 cloves
1 teaspoon coriander seeds
½ teaspoon dried thyme
½ teaspoon dried rosemary
zest of half a lemon
zest of half an orange

Sprinkle the duck leg meat with Maldon salt and leave in a dish for 1 hour. Rub off the salt and pat the duck legs with a paper towel. Blend the marinade ingredients to a powder and rub all over the duck legs. Leave overnight. Poach the legs in duck fat, at 90°C/195°F, overnight or for 8 hours. Store the confit duck in the fridge covered in the fat. It will keep well for weeks.

TO COOK CONFIT DUCK
Wipe the fat from the duck legs. Preheat the oven to 200°C/400°F/ Gas 6, put the duck legs in a roasting pan and cook until crisp. Eat with green salads and fried potatoes.

Kitchen note
You can use pheasant or rabbit in place of duck.

Pots of herbs, edible flowers and tea plants – a note to my mother

I have loved my mother the most when she is in her garden. It is the place where she is her most practical, knowledgeable, curious, determined and creative. She will read this, and probably laugh. She has always been too modest about her talent.

Perhaps to suggest growing food, in addition to the work it involves cooking it, is a tough request. My garden faces the wrong way for growing vegetables. Darkened by the cooler shade of buildings, even runner beans have to climb high to look for light and blossom. My one attempt at a patio garden resulted in a spend of £100 on compost, pots, seeds and plant plugs, and yielded 8 cherry tomatoes. A midsummer hailstorm shredded the leaves of a struggling bean vine to skeletal beauty.

Vegetables, I concluded with disappointment, are cheaper than this in Dubai. But while the patio potager dream is over, and it is clear I possess not one sliver of my mother's talent for growing things, I have learned that just a few aromatic plants will make ordinary ingredients come to life. Where there is a dark back garden there is always a sunny front garden windowsill, and herbs and edible flowers in pots have flourished.

I lazily buy the pots sold in supermarkets that are overly densely planted but burst into strong life if they are thinned, the young leggy shoots used generously, then left for a week and regularly watered. Chives bought from garden centres will always flower in summer and I split up the flower heads and scatter the purple spiky petals on food

419

to great effect. Punchy-flavoured garlic flowers go onto curries; borage onto sweet mustard-dressed cucumber salads.

There is something utterly feminine about decorative leaves and petals. Look for the unusual: bronze fennel; variegated pineapple mint, striped pink, green and white; spearmint, which adds drama to tomato salads and baked aubergines (see page 259). Other edible flowers lend gentle flavour but a rich sense of chintz to fruit or vegetable salads: kitchen marigold petals (calendula), nasturtiums, cornflowers, rocket flower, primrose, violas, rose geranium and busy lizzies are all edible, and have a nourishment value, too. There are also rare and wild varieties to add to cooking. Pick dog roses, elderflower, apple or blackthorn blossom, or contact seed companies for old-fashioned edible flowers such as Livingstone daisy or marsh mallow. Obvious as it may seem, do not be tempted to douse with pesticide the moment you see greenfly on any of these plants. Edible flowers, unusual herbs and cartons of young shoots are available from online suppliers (such as www.firstleaf.co.uk) as well as some shops, market stalls and supermarkets.

I have taken delivery of my first lemon verbena plant, whose pale leaves can be brewed to make a tisane. Herb teas can also be used to gently cook lamb, as they are in Greece, when preparing the slow-cooked stews (see page 213). Fennel foliage, chamomile, rosehip, rosemary, rose petal and elderberry can be used to make tisanes – and used as a stock for poaching.

Occasionally, in a brief outbreak of my former zeal for a back garden larder, I sprout seeds on paper-towel-lined trays – buying bumper bags of coriander seed and whole (not split) lentils from Asian supermarkets. It makes no commercial sense to buy these seeds in those tiny packs sold by garden centres. I also buy microleaf herbs and edible leaf shoots from the same outlets as edible flowers. All these lively things have given drama, aroma and interest to some very humble dinners.

Index